BuiLdiNg SociaL RelatioNSHipS:

A Systematic Approach to Teaching Social Interaction Skills to Children and Adolescents With Autism Spectrum Disorders and Other Social Difficulties

Scott Bellini, Ph.D.

APC

Autism Asperger Publishing Co.
P.O. Box 23173
Shawnee Mission, Kansas 66283-0173
www.asperger.net

© 2006 Autism Asperger Publishing Co.
P.O. Box 23173
Shawnee Mission, Kansas 66283-0173
www.asperger.net

Publisher's Cataloging-in-Publication

Bellini, Scott.
   Building social relationships : a systematic approach to teaching social interaction skills to children and adolescents with autism spectrum disorders and other social difficulties / Scott Bellini. -- 1st ed.– Shawnee Mission, KS : Autism Asperger Pub. Co., 2006.

      p. ; cm.
      ISBN-13: 978-1-931282-94-9
      ISBN-10: 1-931282-94-3
      LCCN: 2006925999
      Includes bibliographical references and index.

      1. Social interaction in children--Study and teaching. 2. Social interaction in adolescence--Study and teaching. 3. Social skills in children--Study and teaching. 4. Social skills--Study and teaching. 5. Communicative disorders in children--Study and teaching. 6. Communicative disorders in adolescence--Study and teaching. I. Title.

RJ506.A9 B45 2006   2006925999
618.92/85882--dc22   0606

Printed in the United States of America.

Dedication

*This book is dedicated to my wife, Kelly,
and sons, Zachary and Addison –
the three loves of my life.*

AcKNoWLedgMeNtS

This book and my work in the field of autism and developmental disabilities are made possible by the support of many wonderful people. In particular, I would like to acknowledge my colleagues at the Indiana Resource Center for Autism for the contribution that they have made to my career. I would especially like to acknowledge and thank two of my mentors and greatest allies, Dr. Cathy Pratt and Dr. David Mank. This book would not be possible without the support and encouragement that they have provided me throughout my career.

I would also like to thank Autism Asperger Publishing Company for transforming this dream into a reality. It has been a pleasure working with such competent professionals, who not only display dedication to their craft, but also to individuals on the autism spectrum and their families.

To my wife, Kelly, who gives so much, yet asks for so little. Everything that I have done, and everything that I will do, is because of you. To my parents, David and Carol, you have provided me with the three greatest gifts: life, love, and education. For that I am eternally grateful.

Finally, I would like to extend a special note of gratitude to the many individuals on the autism spectrum, family members, and professionals who have participated in my clinical practice, workshops, and various research projects over the years. This book is the culmination of what I have learned from each of you. I am proud and honored to share it with you and the wider community.

Dum Spiro, Spero – "While I breathe, I hope"

Table of Contents

Introduction

*"I am not asking for my child to be the life of the party,
or a social butterfly.
I just want her to be happy and have some friends
of her own. She is a wonderful kid,
and I hope some day others can see that."*

Many parents of children with autism spectrum disorders (ASD) echo this sentiment concerning their child's social functioning. They know that their children have many wonderful qualities to offer others, but the nature of their disability, or more precisely, their social skill difficulties, often preclude them from establishing meaningful social relationships. This frustration is amplified when parents know that their children want desperately to have friends, but fail miserably when trying to make friends. Sadly, often their failure is a direct result of the ineffectual programs and inadequate resources typically made available for social skills instruction.

This book addresses the need for social programming for children and adolescents with ASD by providing a comprehensive five-step model. Parents and professionals often ask *how to* teach social skills and *how to* design social skills programs for children with ASD. Many are seeking answers to basic questions such as "where do we start" and "what strategies do we use?"

The five-step model presented in this book will show you where to start and how to implement a social skills program for children with ASD. It will also show you how to organize and make sense of the myriad social skill strategies and resources currently available to parents and professionals. This model is not meant to replace books that you may already have purchased, or strategies that you have learned. Instead, it will use them and, most important, synthesize them into one, comprehensive program. In fact, this is a "guidebook" more so than a cookbook. That is, you will receive a recipe to guide your social programming, but you are strongly encouraged to refine the ingredients to suit the child's unique needs.

The success of a social skills program is dependent upon the cooperation and contribution of both parents (and other family members and caregivers) and professionals (teachers, counselors, speech and language pathologists, social workers, occupational and physical therapists, psychologists, physicians, case managers, or many others). Social skills are best taught across a variety of settings, including home, community, classroom, resource room, playground, and therapeutic clinic. Therefore, I will provide ideas and strategies that are useful and understandable to parents as well as professionals from a variety of disciplines and across a variety of settings.

I also write this book with the understanding that those who read this text have varying levels of experience and knowledge related to social skills programming. Therefore, I have attempted to avoid technical jargon as much as possible without watering down the message. In sections where jargon is either useful or unavoidable, I have provided sufficient context and explanation so that it is understandable to the most inexperienced of readers.

In most instances, I will be presenting information that is applicable to *both* parents and professionals. In some cases, the message might be more applicable to *either* parents *or* professionals. Sometimes, I write directly to a specific discipline (i.e., teachers or therapists). However, since collaboration between parents and professionals is imperative to the success of social skills programming, I have tried to make every word relevant to all who read it. My hope is that this book will be passed back and forth between parents and professionals to promote both understanding and collaboration.

The content of this book reflects my dual role as researcher and practitioner. I recognize that too often researchers examine interventions in tightly controlled settings and laboratories that share no resemblance to the chaos of the real world. This unfortunately can lead to results that have no practical relevance to parents and practitioners, and interventions that are virtually impossible to implement outside the research setting.

This book is different. It is for parents and professionals who operate under real-world circumstances, and who want to teach children with ASD how to be successful in real-world situations. I do not want to waste your time and money on an overhyped, ineffectual program that fails to deliver on its promises. My goal is to provide you with a model that allows you to practice with purpose, and to systematically evaluate and modify your programming on a continual basis. The result is a collection of practical strategies that are provided within the context of a coherent conceptual framework.

Now more than ever, our field and, more important, our children, are in desperate need of effective social skill programs. Not just EASY social skills programs, but EFFECTIVE social skills programs. I write this book with the belief that we have long undervalued social skill instruction in our schools and clinics, and that we have significantly underestimated the social potential of individuals with ASD. It is time for a change.

What Are Social Interaction Skills?

There seems to be much confusion regarding the term *social skills*. To some, social skills refer to skills that assist a child in developing social relationships. To others, social skills refer to any behavior that keeps a child out of trouble! To avoid confusion, it is important to present a working definition of social skills. I am essentially an academic geek. As such, my favorite definition of social skills happens to be quite dry and boring: "Socially acceptable learned behaviors that enable a person to interact with others in ways that elicit positive responses and assist the person in avoiding negative responses" (Elliott, Racine, & Busse, 1995, p. 1009).

For those of you who fell asleep somewhere between "socially acceptable" and "elicit positive responses," let me tease out the important points of the definition. For me, the most important aspect of the definition is the phrase "learned behaviors." Social skills are indeed learned. Whether you are asking a peer to play on the swings, or asking your boss for a raise, you are using social skills that you have learned in the course of your life.

But here is the rub. Most "neurotypical" children acquire basic social skills (e.g., turn taking, initiating conversations) quickly and easily through experience, modeling, and trial and error. The brains of most children are seemingly prewired to learn and perform social behaviors. For children with ASD, the process is much more difficult, however. Whereas many children learn these basic skills simply through exposure to social situations, children with ASD often need to be taught skills explicitly.

The second aspect of the definition that is important is the phrase "... elicit positive responses and assist in avoiding negative responses." That is, when we develop social goals and objectives, we need to continually ask ourselves, will this skill be positively received by peers and will it help the child avoid negative responses from peers? Remember, the purpose of social skill instruction is to facilitate *positive* interactions with *peers*. Sometimes we make the mistake of focusing too much on teaching skills that only adults will appreciate, such as manners and etiquette.

I have a personal confession to make: I am captivated by social behavior! I can't stop myself from watching and eavesdropping on the social interactions of others. To me, no television shows can match the intrigue and drama of real-life social interactions. It is also a wonderful way to learn about social interaction skills.

Much of the conceptualization that I present in this book comes directly from observing people (both children and adults) interact with others. Next time you find yourself at a PTA meeting, fast food joint, faculty gathering, cocktail party, or other social functioning, watch how people interact. Notice what they are doing, acting, feeling. Notice how they move their bodies, modulate the tone of their voices, or express their feelings and interests through nonverbal means. Though I can't predict exactly what you will observe, you are bound to notice great variety in the styles and skill levels of these adult participants.

Now let's move on to school-aged children and the seemingly chaotic social environment that is the school playground. What are the kids doing? Are they standing around chatting about current affairs and other worldly matters? NO! They are doing what kids were meant to do. They are playing, running, spinning, jumping, arguing their points, braiding hair, and chasing each other. Now ask yourself the following questions: What are the characteristics and qualities of the children who are socially successful? What social interaction skills are required for children to be successful in this environment? And, how do we teach these skills? It is the answers to these and similar questions that this book will attempt to answer.

Finally, when I discuss social skills in this book, I am not referring to generic "pro-social" skills such as raising your hand to speak, standing quietly in line, or other behaviors that make adults happy, or our jobs easier. I am referring to "social interaction" skills because the term accentuates the human interactional component of social skills. *Social interaction skills are the building blocks of successful social relationships.*

Why Teach Social Interaction Skills?

Social interaction skills are critical to successful social, emotional, and cognitive development. Effective social skills allow us to elicit positive reactions and evaluations from peers as we perform socially approved behaviors (Ladd & Mize, 1983). Although social skill deficits are a central feature of ASD, few children receive adequate social skills programming (Hume, Bellini, & Pratt, 2005). This is a troubling reality, especially considering that the presence of social impairment may portend the development of more detrimental outcomes, such as social failure and peer rejection, possibly leading to anxiety, depression, substance abuse, and other forms of psychopathology (Bellini, 2004; La Greca & Lopez, 1998; Tantam, 2000). Most important, social skill deficits impede our ability to establish meaningful social relationships, which often leads to withdrawal and a life of social isolation.

Our lives are filled with thousands of social interactions and relationships that make up our social network, or support system. Many of these relationships are rich and meaningful; others are not so fulfilling. Regardless, our social network provides the foundation for later social relationships and career opportunities. In fact, according to Cohen (2004), the presence of a social support system may prevent or even eliminate the stress associated with peer failure by promoting the ability to cope with stress. Cohen has also found that participation in positive social relationships promotes positive psychological states, such as self-worth, self-efficacy, and positive affect (i.e., general happiness).

Finally, Cohen's research has shown that social participation (which he refers to it as social integration) even promotes physical health and reduces susceptibility to certain medical illnesses.

As we develop and establish relationships with more people, our social network expands ... friends beget friends. However, this expansion of the social network, and the benefits that come with it, will only occur if we have the necessary skills.

The Need for EFFECTIVE Social Skills Programming

In our zeal to advocate for social skills programming for children with ASD, we sometimes find ourselves settling for *any* social skills program. But being in a social skills program does not in and of itself guarantee that your child will learn and demonstrate successful social skills. In fact, research has shown that traditional social skills training programs are only minimally effective in teaching social skills to children and adolescents (Quinn, Kavale, Mathur, Rutherford, & Forness, 1999; Gresham, Sugai, & Horner, 2001). This does not mean that social skill programming should not be implemented. Instead, it demonstrates that simply being part of a social skills program does not necessarily equate to social success. The same holds true for children with ASD. I have received hundreds, maybe even thousands, of calls and email messages from parents of children with ASD who are dissatisfied with the social programming that their child is receiving.

We don't need more social skills programs ... we need better social skills programs!

So what are the features of effective social skills training? Quinn et al. (1999) found that social skills programs that targeted specific social skills (turn taking, social initiations, etc.) were more effective than programs that focused on more global social functioning, such as "friendship" skills, cooperation, and so on. These researchers concluded that effective social skill programs must be adapted to fit the needs of the child. Sadly, too often the opposite logic is used. That is, we force children to "fit" into the social skill strategy or strategies that we have selected for them.

After reviewing numerous studies on social skills training, Gresham et al. (2001) recommended that social skills training be implemented more frequently and more intensely than what is typically the case. They concluded that "thirty hours of instruction, spread over 10-12 weeks is not enough" (p. 341) and that the social skill instructional strategies should match the type of skill deficits. Matching instructional strategies to the type of skill deficit exhibited is a key feature of my social skills model, and will be discussed at length in Chapter 6.

Focusing on specific skills also requires us to assess the child's social functioning. Without an assessment component, interventions are poorly conceptualized, lacking in direction and objectivity. Too often professionals and parents begin social skill interventions without conducting a thorough social skills assessment. When asked what they are teaching the child, they may respond "friendship skills" or "social skills." But what exactly does that mean? It would be analogous to a mathematics teacher responding to a similar question with "math skills" or a dance instructor with "dance skills."

We need specificity in our intervention planning. We do not teach "friendship skills;" we teach the specific skills that comprise "friendship skills," such as joining in an activity with peers, asking a peer to join you in an activity, responding to a greeting of others, initiating a greeting, reading and understanding the facial expressions of others, inferring the interests of others, maintaining reciprocal conversations, and so on.

Another reason why many social skills strategies, especially those designed for the general population of children, such as board games, classroom activities, and software packages about friendships and appropriate classroom behavior, are not effective for children with ASD is that they tend to be too subtle, or indirect.

For instance, a school counselor was frustrated with the progress she was making with a student with ASD. She stated that the program was showing positive results with "other kids in the group," but the student with ASD didn't seem to "get it." Indeed, he was not "getting it!" And the reason was quite apparent. The school counselor was attempting to teach the students about the concept of friendship through board games and by showing videos depicting other children singing songs about being a "good friend." This may be acceptable for some children, but for children with ASD it is too subtle a form of instruction. Instead of spending countless hours teaching the child about the concept of friendship, the instruction should have focused on skills that the child could use to make and keep friends.

Plus, the concept of friendship is much easier to understand once you have had a friend or two! For example, I worked with one child who told me that he had two friends at school. When I asked his teachers about this, they informed me that those two "friends" were actually two girls who followed him around calling him names and making fun of him. To him, they were friends simply because they were the only two kids on the playground who paid attention to him!

Finally, not all intervention strategies or modalities are effective for all children. Therefore, it is important to have a large repertoire of clinical tools and strategies to teach social skills. And more important, it is imperative that social skills programs are guided by a conceptual framework that informs our decisions and enlightens our practice.

The social skills model presented in this book addresses the need for effective social programming. The model incorporates the following five steps:

The 5-Step Model

1. Assess Social Functioning

2. Distinguish Between Skill Acquisition and Performance Deficits

3. Select Intervention Strategies
   - Strategies That Promote Skill Acquisition
   - Strategies That Enhance Performance

4. Implement Intervention

5. Evaluate and Monitor Progress

The first step consists of conducting a thorough assessment of the individual's current level of social skills functioning. This book will provide information on how to evaluate social performance and how to identify the specific skills that will be the target of the intervention. After the assessment, the next step is to discern between skill acquisition deficits and performance deficits. Information will be provided on how to distinguish between these two types of skill deficits. This information allows us to focus an intervention on either skill development (skill acquisition deficit) or performance enhancement (performance deficit). Factors that diminish social performance will also be discussed. Based on this information, the selection and implementation of intervention strategies take place. Information will be provided on how to select strategies that provide the greatest opportunity for program success. It is imperative to program success that the strategies are matched to the unique needs of the student, and to the nature of the skill deficits. A wide selection of effective strategies will be covered, including guidelines for implementing them. Finally, the book will present information on how to evaluate progress and modify interventions as needed.

Five Basic Tenets of Social Skills Programming

1

The following tenets reflect both research findings and my clinical experience in teaching social skills to children and adolescents with ASD. They provide the foundation for the social skills program that will be presented. These tenets also illuminate what is missing from many traditional social skill programs. More than anything, they reflect my philosophy and conceptualization of successful social skills programming.

As you read this chapter, I encourage you to think about how these ideas can be incorporated into your current or future programming. They should guide the development and implementation of social skills programming for children and adolescents with ASD.

Tenet #1: Individuals With ASD Want to Establish Meaningful Social Relationships

We need to discard the long-held notion that individuals with ASD lack an interest in establishing social relationships. Many do desire social relationships. However, they typically lack the necessary skills to effectively establish social relationships, or want to establish relationships on their own terms instead of being forced into relationships with people whom they have no interest in interacting with. One young man I worked with illustrates this point quite well.

_____

Zach's Attempts to Make Friends

Prior to my visit, the school staff informed me of Zach's inappropriate behaviors and his apparent lack of interest in interacting with other children. After spending the morning in a self-contained classroom, Zach was given the opportunity to eat lunch with the general school population (a time and place that produced many of his problem behaviors).

As he was eating his lunch, a group of children to his right started to discuss frogs. As soon as the conversation began, Zach immediately took notice. So did I. As he was listening to the other children, he began to remove his shoes, followed by his socks. I remember thinking, "Oh boy, here we go!" As soon as the second sock fell to the floor, Zach flopped his feet on the table, looked up at the group of children and proclaimed, "Look, webbed feet!" Others around him (including myself) stared in amazement.

In this case, Zach was demonstrating a desire to enter and be a part of a social situation, but he was obviously lacking the skills to do so in an appropriate and effective manner. Instead of participating in the conversation about frogs, Zach showed the children his own webbed feet! Sadly, the other children laughed at him.

_____

Despite a desire for meaningful social relationships many persons with ASD have come to dread and fear social situations as a result of years of social failure and peer rejection. Countless parents have shared stories of their children breaking down in tears because of their difficulties making friends. One mother told me that her son's dream was to be invited to a sleep-over at a peer's house … any peer!

I have also received calls from many adults with ASD who are searching for the answers to their chronic social difficulties, and the anxiety and depression that they believe is related to these social difficulties. Some of them have successful careers and families, but are still struggling to establish meaningful social relationships.

Tenet #2: If We Want Children and Adolescents With ASD to Be Successful Socially, We Must Teach Them the Skills to Be Successful

There is a marked difference between teaching social skills and *expecting* somebody to perform them. Too many behavioral and educational plans expect the child to perform socially without providing a framework for actually teaching skills. Such plans typically describe how social skills will be reinforced and encouraged, or how social opportunities will be provided, but rarely do they lay out a plan for directly teaching social skills. For instance, a behavioral plan might outline how successful social interactions will be reinforced, but not taught. Or, the plan might provide the child with an opportunity to interact with peers via a weekly playgroup, but not teach the skills necessary to be successful in that playgroup.

Think about this in a different arena. Imagine you were suddenly told that you would be performing in a dance recital a week from Tuesday. Exciting opportunity, right? But what if you didn't know how to dance? Would a behavioral contract help? What about reinforcement and encouragement? Would they help you avoid failure and embarrassment? NO! What you would need is for someone to TEACH you to dance! Social skills are no different. Again, if we want our children to be successful socially, then we must teach them the skills to be successful socially.

Tenet #3: Successful Social Behaviors Are Not Always "Appropriate" Social Behaviors

Social interaction skills are not always "appropriate" social behaviors! Sometimes behaviors that are most irritating and unacceptable to adults are quite functional and useful with child peers. For instance, passing gas, if you will, is a skill that is both prized and valued by boys all over this country. Although many adults find it disgusting, and it is generally agreed that, at least in our culture, it should be avoided in most contexts and settings, it is a behavior that can put a young man on the fast track to social success!

Perhaps my greatest mistake starting out in my practice was that I was trying to teach proper manners. That is, I was set on trying to train "little gentlemen," instead of teaching functional social skills. In fact, I'm surprised my teachings didn't sometimes get one of my students beat up!

Imagine how the following social initiation would play out on an elementary school playground near you: "Hello, my name is Scotty. How are you today?" I could think of a dozen or so likely responses from peers, and none of them is pretty.

If we want children to be successful socially, we need to throw out "appropriate" and focus on "functional." Social skills are supposed to assist in eliciting positive responses from peers. Let the responses of other children be your gauge. If the other children are noticeably irritated by a behavior, or are laughing at, rather than with, your child, we are probably dealing with a behavior that needs to be addressed through programming. But if other children are enjoying the behavior, and consequently your child's company, even if it is disgusting and irritating to the civilized among us ... consider letting it go!

Tenet #4: Social Success Is Dependent Upon Our Ability to Adapt to Our Environment

The social behaviors that we engage in are dependent upon the setting that we must function in. The environment is a coercive entity that dictates the behavior of those who are in it; at least for most of us. Every setting has an established "standing pattern of behavior" that varies from one setting to another. For instance, the pattern of behavior expected in the library is quite different from that of a sporting event. We are required to modify the volume of our voice, the content of our discussions, and the movements of our bodies based on this established pattern of behavior. For many of us, it is easy to pick up the standing pattern of behavior, even if we have never been in a given setting before. Whether it is a new restaurant, the first day of a workshop, or attending your friend's place of worship, we are able to adapt to the new standing pattern of behavior simply by observing the setting and emulating its participants.

Similarly, the expectations of our interactions vary depending upon the person with whom we are interacting. For instance, more than likely, you act completely differently in interactions with your boss, a police officer, or with your spiritual adviser, than you would with your best friend, spouse, or a family member.

Both of these areas are particularly problematic for children and adolescents with ASD. As a result, they may act no differently at the library than they do at a sporting event, or they may talk with peers in the same way as they do with their teacher or a police officer. The ability to adapt to the environment is critical for successful social interactions and is dependent upon our ability to successfully read and understand nonverbal and contextual cues, and to modify our behavior based on these cues. These skills will be addressed repeatedly by the strategies discussed in this book.

Tenet #5: Social Interaction Skills Are Not the Equivalent of Academic Skills

Interacting with peers is more similar to dropping back to pass and reading a defense in a football game than it is to reading a book or doing a math problem. Therefore, we cannot expect to be able to teach social interaction skills in the same way we do academic skills. Most children with ASD do not learn how to successfully initiate and maintain an interaction simply by listening to a lecture, watching a demonstration, completing a worksheet, or playing a computer or board game.

Social interaction skills are learned and mastered through practice and performance. I discovered this first-hand while working as a school psychologist intern. Desperate to find strategies to teach appropriate behaviors to the students with behavioral difficulties on my caseload, I tried a board game designed to teach appropriate classroom behavior. The game essentially required kids to answer the questions, "what do you do if ...?" For instance, what do you if another kid pushes you? Or, what should you do if you know the answer to a question the teacher asks? I discovered that students who struggled so mightily with their behavior in the classroom were quite adept at this game, and were able to answer the questions with very little trouble. In other words, they could TELL you what appropriate classroom behavior was, but they didn't DO a very good job of demonstrating it in the classroom.

As discussed in the next chapter, worksheets, board games, and computer games can address one aspect of successful social interactions, social-cognitive functioning. But it is not sufficient. Performing socially (or "doing") is what ultimately counts. Think of social interactions skills as a combination of the tango and chess – a combination of strategic planning, analytical thought, movement, adaptability, and perseverance is required to be successful.

If we want our children to be successful socially, we need to address these multifaceted areas in our social programming. And most important, we must give them the opportunity to practice and develop their newly learned skills just as we would a dancer, gymnast, athlete, or a chess champion.

Chapter Summary

The social skills program covered in this book is based on five fundamental tenets of social skills programming. The tenets incorporate both research on social skill programming and clinical experience.

◉ *Tenet #1: Individuals With ASD Want to Establish Meaningful Social Relationships.*

◉ *Tenet #2: If We Want Children and Adolescents With ASD to Be Successful Socially, We Must Teach Them the Skills to Be Successful.*

◉ *Tenet #3: Successful Social Behaviors Are Not Always Appropriate Social Behaviors.*

◉ *Tenet # 4: Social Success Is Dependent Upon Our Ability to Adapt to Our Environment.*

◉ *Tenet # 5: Social Interaction Skills Are Not the Equivalent of Academic Skills.*

The Essence of Social Interaction Skills: Three Integrated Components

As stated in the previous chapter, performance of social interaction skills is much more complicated than the performance of academic skills. Successful social interactions involve the successful integration of three components: *thinking, feeling,* and *doing.* For instance, every social interaction requires that we cognitively process the situation before us. This requires that we understand social rules and customs and read the contextual cues of the environment while examining the nonverbal cues of those with whom we are interacting. This, in turn, allows us to consider and understand another person's perspective, while also monitoring and mediating our own thoughts, feelings, and behaviors.

**Components of
Successful Social
Interactions**

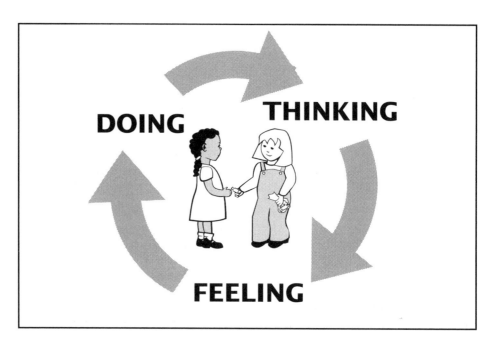

All these processes lead us to ultimately making a behavioral decision. In the course of a two-minute interaction, we typically make dozens of behavioral decisions. But that is not all that goes on during a social interaction.

In addition to cognitive processing, we are also experiencing emotions that positively and negatively impact our thoughts and behaviors. Positive emotions lead to enhanced social engagement and pleasure while negative emotions may lead to physiological stress, self-defeating thoughts, and behavioral avoidance. As such, social interactions require not only successful social-cognitive processing, but also effective regulation of performance-hindering emotions. Sounds complicated already doesn't it? But, wait, there's more!

In addition to effective social-cognitive processing and regulation of emotions, successful social interactions require one additional critical component ... DOING! Social interactions are dynamic performances that require us to make decisions and then execute those decisions. This involves coordinating motor movements and language production, while at the same time maintaining synchronicity with the motor movements and language production of the person with whom we are interacting.

Finally, we cannot forget that each component (thinking, feeling, doing) occurs simultaneously during social interactions. Makes algebra sound simple, doesn't it?

Thinking involves the domain referred to as social cognition. Social cognition involves understanding how we come to understand the thoughts, intentions, motives, and behaviors of ourselves and others (Flavell, Miller, & Miller, 1993). As human beings, we are continually required to make sense of ourselves and others, as well as the world at large. Knowing and understanding social norms, customs, and values is essential to healthy social interactions and is influenced by our social cognition (Resnick, Levine, & Teasley, 1991). Simply put, social cognition involves knowing and thinking about oneself and others as individuals and about the relationships, values, and customs among groups of people.

Within the social-cognitive domain, three processes are particularly important when addressing the social performance of children with ASD: knowledge (know-how), perspective taking, and self-awareness.

Knowledge

Knowledge, or know-how, is an essential component of successful social interactions. Cognitive theorists describe two types of knowledge: declarative and procedural (Pressley & McCormick, 1995).

Declarative knowledge. Declarative knowledge involves knowledge of facts, social rules, definitions, or task sequences. It involves the recollection and expression (often verbal) of information we have been exposed to. Declarative knowledge is an essential cognitive component of social interactions. For instance, if someone compliments you on your new hair style, you "know" that an appropriate response is "thank you." Or, if you want to join in a game with others, declarative knowledge tells you that you need to catch the other person's eye, and then ask, "May I join you?"

Declarative knowledge can be simple or complex, concrete or abstract. For instance, in the latter example, you may also need to "know" that you only ask to join in the activity when there is a pause in the action; that you may need to speak more loudly when the room is filled with a high level of background noise; or that you only ask to join in an activity with Jenna when she is by herself and not with her clique.

Declarative knowledge is responsible for understanding the

often unwritten social rules and customs of society. For example, it is declarative knowledge that tells us that we shouldn't tell a stranger that he is overweight, or that his breath stinks. Declarative knowledge also helps us interpret "figures of speech" or idioms, most of which make no literal sense. It tells us that "raining cats and dogs" means "raining hard."

Although declarative knowledge is essential to successful social interactions, it is not sufficient on its own. While it involves knowing what to do, it does not involve the action of DOING. For instance, I can memorize a dance sequence, and then tell you with little difficulty the steps necessary to perform the dance. However, that does not mean I would know "how to" actually perform the dance. Similarly, in social interactions, children may be able to tell you what they should do in a particular situation, but it does not mean that they can do it. To do so, they need procedural knowledge.

Procedural knowledge. Procedural knowledge involves knowing how to do something, and then doing it. Thus, it goes beyond simply knowing the rules or what to do. Procedural knowledge is acquired through experience and practice, practice – and more practice.

Social skills programs that focus primarily on declarative knowledge are destined for failure. Knowing "what to do" is only half the battle. Actually performing socially with peers is what is ultimately important. This is not meant to diminish the importance of declarative knowledge. On the contrary, well-developed and well-organized declarative knowledge is a prerequisite for acquiring and demonstrating procedural knowledge. In fact, procedural knowledge starts out as declarative knowledge (Neves & Anderson, 1981). That is, when learning a new task, we may first memorize the sequence of steps, perhaps even verbalize them.

As repetitions increase, the procedure becomes more fluent, until finally we reach a level of automaticity, which is the ultimate goal of procedural learning. *Automaticity* refers to the stage of procedural learning where we perform tasks independently, with very little attention or few cognitive resources needed. That is, we no longer have to verbalize, or even think about the task sequence; we just do it.

Due to this freeing up of cognitive energy, individuals who reach a level of automaticity are better able to do multiple tasks simultaneously. Effective social skills programming should address both types of knowledge, and strive to help the child reach a level of automaticity.

Much has been written about theory of mind in the field of ASD. As such it is important to provide some background on the debate surrounding the concept.

Perspective Taking and Theory of Mind

The term *theory of mind* was first coined by Premack and Woodruff (1978) in their work with chimpanzees. According to Premack and Woodruff, theory of mind refers to the ability to understand and explain behavior by making inferences based on the unobservable psychological processes of others, such as feelings, intentions, beliefs, thoughts, perceptions, and desires. Through theory of mind, or "mind reading," we are able to make sense of the world around us to better understand various social situations and predict the behaviors of others. The ability to understand the internal psychological processes of others and to take another person's point of view are both critical to social cognition, and to successful social interaction.

Knowledge of mind is a critical component of successful social interactions (Frith, 1991), as it allows us to continually monitor our own behavior and predict the behavior of those with whom we interact. In children and adults who have an inadequate theory, or knowledge, of mind, such as those with ASD, social functioning is significantly impaired (Baron-Cohen, 1989). Specifically, Baron-Cohen has found that individuals with ASD demonstrate significant deficiencies in the ability to attribute mental states to others and correctly predict the beliefs of others. Consequently, he concludes that individuals with autism have great difficulty taking another person's perspective and understanding that others can have false beliefs. The results of such "mindblindness" (Attwood, 1998) are usually social interactions that lack reciprocity and shared emotion. In addition, empathy, which is defined as the capacity to participate in another person's feelings, or ideas (Woolf et al., 1976), may also be affected by an inability to take another person's perspective.

The following description of a specific perspective task may provide a better understanding of perspective taking.

Example of Perspective Taking

Nelson and her colleagues (1998) developed false belief tests to study children's perspective-taking abilities. In these studies, children are read a scenario where a boy, Maxi, puts some chocolate in a drawer before leaving to go outside. Unknown to Maxi, his mother moves the chocolate to a cupboard before leaving the house. At this point Maxi returns home to find his chocolate. Nelson then asks the children two questions: Where will Maxi look for the chocolate and why will he look there?

In order to answer the question correctly, the children must have sufficient perspective-taking abilities to know that Maxi has different information than they do and, therefore, a different perspective on where the chocolate is located.

Children by about the age of 5 are able to determine that Maxi will look in the drawer because that is where he put the chocolate and that he had no way of knowing that his mom moved it. For children with ASD, this perspective-taking ability may come much later, if at all.

Flavell et al. (1993) highlight three general prerequisites for successful social thinking:

- existence

- need

- inference

These three preconditions must be considered each time we teach children an aspect of social cognition, such as perspective taking. They also have great relevance for the child's understanding of social rules (which will be discussed in Chapter 8).

Existence. Existence refers to a person's knowledge that a particular phenomenon exists. In order for a child to successfully take another person's perspective, she must know that others possess perspectives on life that are different from her own. If a child has no knowledge of the existence of another's unique cognitive perspective, she will not be able to take this person's perspective in social situations.

Need. In order to take another person's perspective, the child must also have the need to do so. That is, a child may have the knowledge that a person possesses a cognitive perspective different from her own, but may have no need to exercise or use this knowledge in social situations. The need to utilize perspective taking is highly influenced by lack of motivation and lack of opportunity.

Inference. The last precondition, inference, involves the ability to successfully carry out a given social cognition. For example, a child may know that another person has a unique cognitive perspective, and may have a need to understand this perspective to interact successfully, but may not be able to do so based on the information provided. This deficiency may be a result of insufficient evidence or due to general inadequacies in understanding social situations, or both.

For instance, the child with ASD might say something that inadvertently hurts another child's feelings. If he does not recognize the body language or facial expressions of others, he would have no idea that the other child is sad because of something that he said. Again, he may know that the other child is capable of thoughts and feelings that are different from his own, and he may truly want to be friends with this child. However, his inability to read non-verbal cues and connect those cues to what he has said to the child (making inferences) significantly derails his ability to make friends with this child.

Most of the children and adolescents with ASD whom I have worked with know that other people have a perspective that is unique, or different from their own (existence). However, they have difficulty identifying and understanding the necessary social cues and contexts (inference), which greatly hinders their ability to successfully take another person's perspective. Alternatively, they simply do not have the desire, or need, to take another person's perspective because they are socially withdrawn and isolated.

Self-Awareness

Whereas perspective taking and theory of mind have received a great deal of attention in the field of autism, self-awareness has not. Self-awareness is the ability to "step outside" oneself to observe and evaluate one's own behavior. Am I talking too loudly? Am I communicating my point clearly? Am I talking too much? Am I boring my listener? Do I have spinach in my teeth? Did I properly wipe my mouth after lunch? Is my zipper down? Did I apply deodorant today?

All these questions are examples of self-awareness. Chances are that since you picked up a copy of this book, you know someone who does not continually ask herself questions like these. Many children with ASD appear as though their behavior is on "automatic pilot," seemingly unaware of what they are doing and why they are doing it. Is this possible? Can a person go through life not reflecting on or monitoring her own behavior? To help answer that question, let me ask you: Have you ever driven to work, parked your car, and then thought to yourself, "Did I stop at any red lights?" Automatic pilot for sure! We do this socially too. For example, have you ever been told by a friend that she saw you somewhere and that she tried to get your attention, but that you ignored her? Automatic pilot!

Successful social interaction requires that we continually monitor our behaviors, thoughts, and feelings during social interactions. By doing this, we are able to modify our actions to ensure that our interactions will be enjoyable and successful. Self-awareness is also inextricably linked to the ability to read nonverbal cues and to perspective taking. Imagine for a moment that you are having a discussion with a colleague. Now imagine that your colleague is desperately trying to look away and hold her breath each time you open your mouth. Perspective taking would tell you that your colleague is experiencing an unpleasant sensory stimulus.

In addition to perspective taking, if you are engaging in self-awareness, you might realize that your colleague's "unpleasant sensory experience" is emanating from your bad breath. Furthermore, self-awareness would allow you to realize that perhaps it was the extra garlic on your pizza lunch that was responsible for your colleague's discomfort.

The point is, self-awareness allows us to monitor how our actions or behaviors impact others. Without proper self-awareness we would engage in one-sided interactions, and perhaps seemingly inappropriate or embarrassing behaviors. Many of the social-cognitive principles discussed under Perspective Taking may be applied to self-awareness (especially Flavell's three preconditions of social cognition: existence, need, and inference). However, it is important to note that successful self-awareness, as is the case with perspective taking, is dependent upon our ability to successfully read and understand nonverbal and contextual cues. Similar to perspective taking, self-awareness can be taught to individuals with ASD.

Feeling

Even after a child has developed sufficient social-cognitive processing to be able to interact successfully with others, her social performance may still be significantly impacted by her feelings or emotions. Too often, the emotional domain is ignored when we implement social programming. This is a critical mistake.

How might our emotions impact social functioning? Anyone who has ever had a bad day at work or school knows the answer. Perhaps after a bad day at the work place you prefer to be left alone to read a good book, watch *Seinfeld*, or simply stare at a blank wall. Or perhaps you prefer to process your day with a trusted friend or family member. In contrast, perhaps there are some days when you feel like going out and being around other people. Either way, our emotions significantly impact both our motivation and our ability to interact socially.

In terms of motivation, individuals who are depressed often prefer to be alone, away from the social spotlight. Mood and motivation are also impacted by our self-efficacy, or our perceptions of our performance. That is, those with low self-efficacy regarding social interactions (children with ASD, for instance) display negative mood and affect, and consequently reduced motivation for interacting with others. (See Chapter 6 for more information on self-efficacy.)

Feelings directly influence our behavior, thoughts, and physiological processing. They influence whether we approach, avoid, or withdraw from social situations. Feelings are also inextricably linked to our thoughts or cognitions. That is, thoughts of self-loathing, inferiority, and excessive worry will lead to feelings of sadness and anxiety, but feelings of sadness and anxiety also lead to negative thoughts. In other words, the relationship is reciprocal.

Feelings also have a reciprocal relationship with physiological responses. For instance, heightened sympathetic responses such as increased heart rate and shaking hands may lead to excessive feelings of anxiety. However, excessive feelings of anxiety also lead to heightened physiological responses. We simply cannot address behavior, thoughts, and physiological responses without also addressing emotions.

Anxiety

Anxiety is a particularly important emotion to address when teaching social skills to children with ASD. A growing body of recent research has demonstrated high levels of anxiety in individuals with ASD (Bellini, 2004; Gillott, Furniss, & Walter, 2001; Green, Gilchrist, Burton, & Cox, 2000; Kim, Szatmari, Bryson, Streiner, & Wilson, 2000).

Individuals with ASD exhibit a broad range of anxious symptoms, including physiological arousal, social anxiety, panic, and separation anxiety. To make matters worse, many children lack effective coping strategies to regulate their heightened physiological arousal and stress (Groden, 1994). According to Biederman et al. (1995), children who are less able to regulate their physiological arousal are more vulnerable to stressful social encounters and more likely to be adversely conditioned by negative social interactions.

Children with lower threshold levels for arousal often experience heightened sympathetic responses, such as increased heart rate in the presence of mild stressors and novel situations (Kagan et al., 1987). For instance, if a child with high levels of physiological arousal is bitten by a dog, she will be more likely to develop a fear of dogs than would a child with low levels of physiological arousal. The same applies to social fears. A child with high levels of physiological arousal is more likely to develop fear of social interactions following an aversive peer experience. Trepagnier (1996) suggests that a maladaptive arousal regulation system in infants with ASD makes them more vulnerable to overstimulation by the social interactions of caregivers. The overstimulation may lead to gaze aversion and ultimately social withdrawal.

The following developmental pathways model (Bellini, 2006) demonstrates how social skill deficits and social anxiety develop in individuals with ASD. Social withdrawal may be the result of an early fearful or insecure temperament that draws the child away from social interaction, thereby impeding the development of social skills by significantly limiting the child's opportunity to interact with others, and preventing the child from acquiring effective interpersonal skills. The presence of social skill deficits increases the likelihood that the child will engage in negative peer interactions, resulting in increased social anxiety, which leads to further social withdrawal and avoidance, beginning the cycle anew.

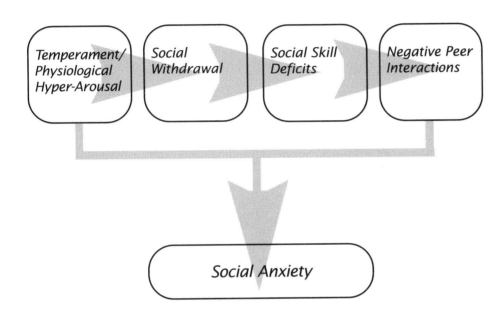

Developmental Pathways Model of Anxiety

This developmental pathways model of anxiety has great implications for social skills programming. Specifically,

1. It is imperative that we assess anxiety in children with ASD to examine how it may be influencing their social performance.

2. Social skill programs should include teaching the child how to regulate her physiological responses to stressful events.

3. Early intervention to decrease social withdrawal is critical to the development of social skills.

4. Peer intervention strategies should be used to facilitate an atmosphere of acceptance and caring to minimize the possibility of negative peer interactions.

Doing

Social interactions require that we plan and select behavioral/social decisions and then execute a motor movement (sometimes referred to as "executive functioning"). For instance, once we make a cognitive decision of when and how to initiate a conversation with a peer, we have to actually do it. As mentioned, it is the *doing* that is often overlooked in social skill programs. In social interactions doing represents more than just moving a pencil, or reciting a correct answer. Doing involves coordinating gross- and fine-motor movements with language production and then integrating these actions with cognitions and emotions (thinking and feeling).

Body movements such as balance, coordination, and motor fluency are part of a connected and integrated neurological system (the nervous system) that is responsible for our thoughts, memories, feelings, motivation, and sensory processing (visual, auditory, etc.). All these processes and components are interdependent and are controlled by the central nervous system (CNS).

Like in any mechanical system, a problem in one area of the CNS can significantly impact the functioning of the system as a whole. A problem in any one area, such as motor coordination, anxiety, sensory processing or limited declarative or procedural knowledge, can significantly derail social interactions. For instance, the child might be willing and able to initiate an interaction with peers, but may struggle with moving his body into the correct position. He may start the initiation too soon (i.e., before getting close to the other person) or wait too long (i.e., after the other person has left the room). What we consider an isolated problem, therefore, is not isolated at all.

Further complicating matters, CNS dysfunction can prevent successful completion of a task even after a sufficient level of mastery, or automaticity, with a particular procedure (see Procedural Knowledge) has been reached. For instance, a professional juggler who suffers a spinal cord injury may no longer be able to juggle, even though she has sufficient procedural knowledge to complete the task. A similar, yet less severe CNS impairment can occur to a gymnast who suffers an ear infection. The gymnast may experience difficulties with equilibrium and suddenly be unable to perform a balance beam routine even though she has mastered the various aspects of the routine. The implications here are that in order to be able to perform a task successfully, we must have sufficient declarative knowledge (knowing what to do), achieve sufficient procedural knowledge (knowing how to do), and have sufficient CNS functioning to execute the movement.

Donnellan and Leary (1995) hypothesize that individuals with ASD experience movement differences that are the result of CNS dysfunction. These movement differences impact the ability to plan and initiate, switch, combine, execute, stop, and continue "movements," which include thoughts, feelings, language, and sensory processing. These differences can negatively impact performance, even after the individual has mastered a particular activity or task. (See Chapter 6 for more information on how movement difference affect performance.)

For most us, the movements associated with social interactions are automatic, the product of years of repetition and "muscle memory." If we had to expend cognitive resources repeatedly thinking about what to do with our body during social interactions, it would significantly diminish our social performances. The presence of motor impairment in individuals with ASD often precludes this muscle memory, or automaticity of movement.

Motor impairment in individuals with ASD has been documented by researchers, who have found impairments in coordination and gross-motor movements (clumsiness), including poor motor-imitation ability and dynamic body movement (Ghaziuddin et al., 1994; Klin et al., 1995; Manjiviona & Prior, 1995).

Persons with ASD often have particular difficulties with proprioception, or awareness of their body in space, which significantly impacts gross-motor skills, and especially coordination. This is problematic, given the emphasis placed on movement activities for school-aged children. Thus, poor motor skills may play a role in the social isolation of children with ASD. Participation in peer play often requires joining in games that require some degree of motor efficiency. For example, most social activities for a 10-year-old involve some form of movement.

The way we move our body, along with our posture, communicates a great deal of the meaning "behind" our words.

Ever noticed your spouse with her arms crossed and a furrowed brow? Body language is the window to the soul.

Some children even have difficulties commanding their body to produce nonverbal gestures when asked to so, such as facial expressions and body language. How we coordinate and position our body is integral to successful social interactions as social interactions are actually a series of social dances. In social interactions motor clumsiness often comes across as awkward body positions, poor timing during initiations, violations of personal space, or perhaps standing too far from the person with whom we are speaking. For example, one young man with ASD whom I know often attempts to initiate an interaction well before he approaches the other person. Sometimes he initiates while he is still in another room! Another common example that I observe in my clinical practice is the act of initiating an interaction while turned away from the person it is directed toward.

Social programming should involve copious amounts of movement-based activities that allow the child to perform the skills that she is being taught. It is no different from other movement-based skills such as dance, athletics, or playing a musical instrument. Could you imagine learning any of these skills without actually performing, or doing them? Could we learn how to hit a baseball or perform a cheer leading routine by listening to a verbal description of the skill, or by playing a board game? Of course not, and we shouldn't expect children with ASD to learn social skills without giving them the opportunity to perform them. I find that most movement-based skill deficits can be addressed through a combination of effective skill instruction, environmental modifications and supports – and practice, practice, practice.

Social interactions involve integrating three components: thinking, feeling, and doing. These components do not work in isolation. Instead they work in concert, each capable of promoting or hindering successful social performance.

- *Thinking* involves knowing what to do (declarative knowledge) and how to do it (procedural knowledge). Thinking also involves taking another person's perspective and self-awareness.

- *Feeling* involves regulating emotions, such as anxiety, that might otherwise hinder successful social performance.

- *Doing* involves the execution (e.g., motor movements) of the social performance.

COMMON SOCIAL SKILL DIFFICULTIES ASSOCIATED WITH ASD

Difficulties with any of the three integrated components described in Chapter 2 (i.e., thinking, feeling, doing) can lead to significant impairment in social functioning as discussed in more detail in this chapter.

The cause of social skill deficits varies, ranging from inherent neurological impairment to lack of opportunity to acquire skills (e.g., social withdrawal). Most important, these social skill deficits make it difficult for the individual to develop, and keep meaningful and fulfilling personal relationships.

In the following, the most common social skill deficits have been divided into six broad categories of social impairment:

- Nonverbal Communication

- Social Initiation

- Reciprocity and Terminating Interactions

- Social Cognition

- Behaviors Associated With Perspective Taking and Self-Awareness

- Social Anxiety and Social Withdrawal

A list of specific skills or behaviors that comprise each category is included. These lists will provide a valuable source of reference as you conduct social skills assessment and subsequent intervention. In other words, they serve as a kind of baseline against which to compare apparent skills deficits.

It is important to understand that specific social skills do not operate in isolation. Every social skill is made up of component or related subskills that are required for successful performance of the skill. For instance, successfully performing the social skill of "joining in a conversation" requires certain prerequisite skills, such as the ability to read nonverbal and contextual cues, knowledge of social rules (i.e., when to join a conversation with two people without interrupting), regulation of emotion, coordination of motor movements, timing, use of eye contact and other nonverbal expression, and effective conversational planning, just to name a few. Similarly, perspective taking requires the ability to read nonverbal cues, such as facial expressions and body language, and the ability to integrate this information with relevant contextual or environmental cues. In addition, every social performance requires the use of numerous social skills, sometimes performed consecutively, sometimes simultaneously, but always coordinated.

It is also imperative to examine skill deficits from a developmental perspective. For instance, it is not developmentally atypical for a 4-year-old child to lack the ability to take another person's perspective, to make inappropriate comments, or to have difficulty maintaining personal hygiene. Therefore, we should consider the sequence and relationship between social skills and components skills, and the developmental level of the child as we assess social functioning and plan and implement the social skill strategies.

Further, the categories are not mutually exclusive. There is overlap between many of them, and most of them influence each other. For example, one must be able to read the nonverbal behaviors of others to effectively take their perspective.

This chapter does not present an all-inclusive list of social skills exhibited by individuals with ASD, nor would you expect to find all of these qualities in any one individual. The purpose of categorizing the social skills is to provide an advanced organizer, or things to consider, as we move on to later steps in the model, including assessment and implementation. More important, these social skills represent many of the skills that we will be directly targeting during the intervention.

Difficulties With Nonverbal Communication

Specific Nonverbal Communication Skills

- *Recognizes the facial expressions of others*
- *Recognizes the nonverbal cues, or body language, of others*
- *Maintains eye contact during conversations*
- *Uses gestures to communicate needs*
- *Has facial expressions that are congruent with emotion*
- *Correctly interprets the emotions of others*
- *Modulates the tone of his/her voice*
- *Demonstrates a wide range of facial expressions*
- *Recognizes the "meaning" behind the tone of another person's voice*

Nonverbal communication is the foundation of successful social interactions. Most, if not all, social interaction skills require the ability to read and understand the nonverbal cues of others. In many ways, our nonverbal communication (body language, facial expressions, etc.) is more meaningful than our verbal communication. Therefore, nonverbal communication is typically the first area that I address in social skill interventions.

Difficulty *reading the body language or nonverbal cues* of others is a common problem for individuals with ASD. Some of them fail to look for nonverbal cues and, therefore, are virtually oblivious to nonverbal communications. Others may look for nonverbal cues, but interpret them incorrectly or fail to understand the intended message. Further, some individuals with ASD exhibit overly selective attention, or attend to irrelevant details of the environment (Happe, 1991; Koning & Magill-Evans, 2001). For example, a child with ASD might attend exclusively to the jewelry the teacher is wearing, and not to more relevant cues such as body language or emotional expressions.

Understanding nonverbal communication requires that we:

1. recognize the body language of others, and

2. infer the meaning of the nonverbal communication.

This is done by integrating all the available nonverbal and contextual cues in the environment. For instance, what would you infer if you saw a little girl walking along the street with a frown on her face, holding a leash and calling out "Woody." That's right, the little girl is sad because she lost her puppy. This scenario, albeit simple for most of us, required that we recognize the girl's emotional expression (i.e., the frown) and then integrate that information with the contextual cues of the leash and her calling out the name Woody. We may have further placed ourselves in her shoes by recalling the time when we lost our own puppy (perspective taking).

One of the reasons why children with ASD have difficulty reading nonverbal cues is that they are not looking for them. They often avert their eyes and look away during interactions, which precludes them from reading facial expression and other salient nonverbal clues. Many describe difficulties integrating auditory and visual information (i.e., looking at another person while at the same time listening to the person).

Much has been debated regarding the appropriateness of insisting that children with ASD *maintain eye contact* during social interactions. Here is an important question: Is eye contact a social necessity or just good social etiquette? To me, it is both. Much of our insistence on eye contact stems from the value placed on it in our society. A person who does not make eye contact is considered aloof, insincere, or untrustworthy. However, too much eye contact is equally troublesome. The comedian Steven Wright said it best when he noted that there is a fine line between eye contact and the piercing stare of a homicidal maniac! When an individual is "trained" to maintain eye contact, it can come across as forced, and even worse, creepy.

Nevertheless, eye contact is a social necessity. In particular, eye contact is integral to successful social initiations. That is, initiating an interaction by first making eye contact communicates to the recipient that what you are about to say is directed towards her. In addition, punctuating or ending a statement or question with eye contact informs the recipient that it is now her turn to talk.

This section did not present an exhaustive list of nonverbal communication skills. Many other nonverbal skills are reflected in the skills listed under social cognition and behaviors associated with perspective taking and self-awareness.

Difficulties With Social Initiation

▪ Joins in activities with peers	▪ Invites peers to join in activities
▪ Asks questions to request information about a person	▪ Joins a conversation with two or more people without interrupting
▪ Requests assistance from others	▪ Initiates greetings with others
▪ Demonstrates proper timing with social initiations	▪ Introduces self to others
▪ Asks questions to request information about a topic	

Specific Social Initiation Skills

Difficulties with initiating interactions are common among individuals with ASD. Many children fall into one of two initiation categories:

1. those who rarely initiate interactions with others, and

2. those who initiate frequently, but inappropriately.

Children in the first category often demonstrate fear, anxiety, or apathy with regard to social interactions. A decade ago, it was believed that the vast majority of children on the autism spectrum fit into this category. In fact, many social skill interventions have been designed with the express goal of increasing social initiations.

Although intense social withdrawal is a problem for many children with ASD, in recent years an increasing number of children fit within the latter category. These children initiate interactions frequently, even excessively, but their initiations are often ill timed and ill conceived. For example, they may interrupt or talk over someone. They may ask repetitive questions or questions that only pertain to their own interests. Or they may talk with others in settings that require silence, such as a library or church. The goal for these children is not to get them to initiate more frequently, but to get them to initiate better!

Social initiations may be divided into separate subcategories such as joining in an activity with others, asking others to play a game, asking questions about a person, asking questions about a topic, requesting assistance, and greeting others, just to name a few. It is important to determine not only how frequently the child is initiating interactions, but also what type of initiations he is demonstrating. For instance, several children in my practice might be considered frequent social initiators if you looked only at the number of times they initiate interactions with others. However, if you looked more closely at the type of social initiations they demonstrate, you would see that they are only asking questions to others regarding their own self-interests (e.g., what type of dinosaur is that? What time is the dinosaur show on? Are there dinosaurs in California?).

- Takes turns during games and activities

- Responds to the greetings of others

- Allows peers to join in activities

- Allows others to assist with tasks

- Ends conversations properly

- Politely asks others to move out of the way

- Maintains the give-and-take of conversations

- Acknowledges the compliments directed at him/her by others

- Responds to the invitations of peers to join in activities

- Responds to questions directed at him/her by others

- Reads cues to terminate conversations

Specific Reciprocal Skills and Behaviors

Social reciprocity refers to the give-and-take of social interactions. Social interactions (at least successful ones) involve a mutual, back-and-forth exchange between two or more persons. If you have ever been on a date where your date would not stop talking about himself, or perhaps you had to do all the talking because your date had little to say, you will understand how problems with social reciprocity can hinder social interactions.

Many children and adolescents with ASD engage in **one-sided interactions** in which they are either doing all the talking or they fail to respond to the social initiations of others and to build on conversations with others. How many times do you find yourself prompting your child/student to respond to the questions posed to her by others, or reminding her to say thank you? Or how often do you have to admonish your child not to "hog" the conversation? In the latter cases, a conversation about current events is often quickly detoured into a monologue about maps or horticulture.

Many individuals with ASD **fail to read the cues that signal the end of a conversation** (see Nonverbal Communication discussed earlier). It seems as though the conversation is not over until our friend, student, or loved one with ASD wants it to be over. The simple cue of looking at your watch to indicate that you are running late may be undetectable to an individual with ASD.

Reading Between the Lines

At a recent event I chatted with a gentleman on the autism spectrum. After introducing himself to me, he proceeded to share with me some of the wonderful work he has been doing in his home state. After 15 minutes of listening, I realized that I was running late and had to terminate the conversation. After looking at my watch, I said, "Well, it sure was nice talking with you; perhaps you could send me an email so we can stay in contact."

You can probably guess what happened next. My attempt to terminate the conversation led my new acquaintance to begin another conversation about his computer at home and his recently installed wireless router. After a few more minutes, I again told him that I had enjoyed chatting with him, but this time I was more direct. I told him that I was late for another meeting and that I had to end our conversation. He gave me a look of "oh, why didn't you just say that to begin with," and we said our good-byes.

There are two things to consider in this interaction. One, I should have known better than to be indirect with my speech. If I had to get going, I should have told him that. And two, this gentleman did not know that I wanted to terminate the conversation because he failed to read the cues that I was sending.

Individuals with ASD also sometimes have difficulties properly ***terminating interactions***. "Good-bye," "nice talking with you," "thanks for your help," or "see you later," are all common methods of appropriately terminating interactions. Many parents I work with seem particularly troubled by what they describe as a hit-and-run method of interaction, whereby their children get what they want from another person and then move on. The termination may not be the first impression, but it often represents a lasting impression. As such, the manner in which we say good-bye is very important to most of us.

- Compromises during disagreements with others

- Understands the jokes or humor of others

- Responds promptly in conversations

- Considers multiple viewpoints

- Talks about topics that other people find interesting

- Correctly interprets the intentions of others

- Avoids being manipulated by peers

- Stays "on-topic" during conversations

- Correctly analyzes social situations

- Uses eye contact or other gestures to direct another person's attention

Specific Social Cognition Skills

Several social skill difficulties exhibited by children and adolescents with ASD may be attributed to the manner in which they process social information, or social cognition (see Chapter 2). This section will detail those social cognition skills that may negatively impact social interaction skills. It is important to note that perspective taking and self-awareness are also considered aspects of social cognition. However, due to the severity and commonality of these deficits in ASD, they are discussed in a separate section.

Here is a common scenario that you may have experienced.

"WHY Did You Do THAT?"

You get a call from your child's school informing you that there was an "incident" in the cafeteria during lunch. The assistant principal tells you that your son told another student that he would "blow him away" if he didn't leave him alone.

When you pick your son up from school, you ask the ever-popular, yet ineffectual question, "WHY did you do THAT?" It is likely that the answer that you will get from your son will be less than satisfactory. The problem is not the answer; the problem is the question.

To correctly answer the question "why did you do that?" requires an adequate level of **social problem solving**, or social reasoning – a level of social problem solving that is typically not present in children with ASD. Often these children do not know why they are engaging in a particular social behavior; they are simply reacting to a situation. So when you ask them afterwards to analyze why they did what they did, you might as well be asking me how the Internet works. I have no idea. I just surf it. Similarly, your child has no idea why he does what he does. He just does it.

Children with ASD also have difficulties **understanding the unwritten rules of social behavior**. Take the following exchange between a child psychologist and his 3-year-old son.

Son: *Daddy why did you call me silly?*

Dad: *Because you were being a silly boy.*

Son: *But, Daddy, you said that we don't call people names.*

Dad: *Well, that's right, son. I did, but some names are good names and some names are bad names. We don't call people bad names.*

Son: *Is silly a good name?*

Dad: *Yes ... I mean, usually ... it depends.*

Son: *Depends on what?*

Dad: *Son, would you like an ice-cream cone?*

The complexity of just that one unwritten social rule (i.e., don't call people names) is astounding. It *is* appropriate sometimes to call people names. So how do we decide when it is appropriate and when it is not? What names are appropriate? In what context is it appropriate to call people names? Whom do we call names?

Unfortunately, there is no adequate social rule book that we can refer to each time a question like this comes up. We learn these unwritten rules through exposure and processing of social situations and social dilemmas, and by watching others experience and process social dilemmas. Perhaps most perplexing for children with ASD is that even after careful consideration and contemplation, we can rarely be certain that our behavioral decision will be the correct one (Myles, Trautman, & Schelvan, 2004).

Many children with ASD see the world through a very narrow conceptual lens, which prevents them from **considering multiple viewpoints**. There is only *one* correct solution or answer to a problem according to these children – and it is typically their solution! Such narrow-mindedness comes across as argumentative and insolent, but it really is just the child defending his reality. He believes that his answer or viewpoint is the only correct answer or viewpoint, just like I believe that the sky is blue. If you try to tell me the sky is a different color, I too would come across as argumentative and insolent. I would be defending my reality!

One young lady with ASD illustrates this point well.

Defending One's Own Reality

Krista never met an argument that she didn't win – at least in her mind. She would argue about anything and everything – not maliciously, but passionately nonetheless. Krista came to my office one day visibly angry. She told me that she read an article on the Internet about how hunters like to shoot baby animals. She told me, "I hate all hunters. I wish that they would all die." I replied that not all hunters shoot baby animals. She quickly dismissed my nonsensical viewpoint, countering that she "read it on the Internet," and that "everything on the Internet is true." How do argue with that?

Joint attention is attending in unison to an object with another person. Translation: If you and I are walking down the street together and I look up to the sky and say "wow," you would likely look up to see what I was looking at. Joint attention allows us to engage another person in a social dance from across a room without even saying a word. It intimately connects two or more people to a beautiful world of their own – a world that few children with ASD experience, because they lack adequate joint attention. Lack of joint attention can negatively impact social development throughout life. Picture the following scenario.

Joint Attention or Lack Thereof

Two 10-year-old children are playing at recess when they notice the assistant principal bending over to pick up some rocks on the pavement. As he bends down, his pants slip down a bit in the back, and the "moon" comes out. Most children would respond in a predictable manner to this lunar event. First they would look at the "moon," then they would look over to the other child (social referencing) to see if he or she had seen it, too. They then would look back at the moon and then quickly look back at each other before laughing hysterically. The child with ASD, on the other hand, might look at the moon and laugh hysterically, but would probably not look back to the other children to see if they too had seen it. That is, he might be laughing, but he would not be "dancing."

Slow processing speed is another common feature of many of the children with ASD that I work with. I am referring here to processing speed during social interactions, not math equations. I know adults with ASD who need over 30 seconds to respond to questions. In our society this presents major problems.

If you asked me a question and I took longer than 5 seconds to answer, you would probably either think that I am ignoring you, or you would rephrase your question, thinking that I had not understood you. Often this happens to individuals with ASD. While they are attempting to process a seemingly simple question, "How was your day today?," they are overwhelmed by a barrage of follow-up questions from the other person who fears that the question was not understood. Well, perhaps the question was understood perfectly, but the social norm was not.

Think about it: *"How was your day today?"* This question, and more important the answer, is not nearly as simple as it appears. If you genuinely tried to answer this question, you too would need time to process it. It is a complicated question! However, most of us know that the customary response to this question is a thoughtless, "Fine, how was yours?"

Social processing speed, or social fluency, comes with understanding social norms and is related to the development of social reasoning and behavioral repetition, or practice. Things that are difficult for us take longer to do. They require more time to perform. As we become more adept, our fluency increases. The same is true for social functioning.

Difficulties Associated With Perspective Taking and Self-Awareness

- *Maintains personal hygiene*

- *Expresses sympathy for others*

- *Talks about or acknowledges the interests of others*

- *Provides compliments to others*

- *Engages in socially appropriate behaviors*

- *Maintains an appropriate distance when interacting with peers*

- *Speaks with an appropriate volume in conversations*

- *Refrains from making inappropriate comments*

- *Offers assistance to others*

Specific Skills Associated With Perspective Taking and Self-Awareness

Perspective taking and self-awareness are essential to successful social interactions (see Chapter 2). Indeed, difficulties with perspective taking and self-awareness are central to the social interaction difficulties of individuals with ASD, and directly impact most of the social qualities listed here.

This section will explore specific social skills and behaviors that I view as directly related to difficulties with perspective taking. In fact, it is my belief that you cannot successfully teach these behaviors without also addressing perspective taking and self-awareness.

In his popular workshop presentations, Tony Attwood uses a phrase to describe the propensity of individuals with ASD to make ***socially inappropriate comments*** – "Self-Appointed Revealers of the Truth." Nothing could be more a propos. Many of the kids that I work with have a knack for saying the wrong thing at the wrong time. For instance, pointing out another person's weight at the grocery store, commenting on the color of another person's skin, or perhaps pointing out that your breath could use some "freshening." These comments are not intended to be hurtful or malicious. They simply represent an expression of fact. Nevertheless, they are hurtful, and represent an impediment to establishing meaningful social relationships. An individual who has difficulties or who is unable to take another person's perspective would not realize that her words were hurtful to others.

Difficulty maintaining personal hygiene is also a source of continual frustration for parents of children with ASD. Refusals to take baths, apply deodorant, comb hair, and wipe their mouth after eating are all common laments that I hear from parents of children and adolescents with ASD. Most of us maintain personal hygiene to avoid a negative response or a negative perception from others – or in the case of body odor, to protect others from our foul emissions. This is an example of perspective taking. We are recognizing how our hygiene might be viewed or perceived by others. Without adequate perspective taking, we too might be less inclined to maintain our personal hygiene.

Another social quality that is common in children with ASD is ***difficulty maintaining personal space***. Personal space, unlike other physical spaces, is not fixed or permanent; it is malleable, and varies from person to person and from situation to situation. For instance, as a person moves her body, her personal space moves. In addition, the amount of personal space we give depends on they type of communication (e.g., a secret vs. a group announcement), our relationship with the person we are speaking to (e.g., a close friend or family member vs. a stranger or acquaintance), and the setting and environment that we are in (sporting event vs. library, or quiet vs. noisy room). Further complicating matters, the amount of personal space that is appropriate for each context is dictated by cultural and societal norms – norms that most of us learn through exposure to social situations. Violation of personal space (standing too close to others or standing too far away) can negatively impact social interactions, and is a common issue for many of the children and adolescents in my practice.

Personal space is intertwined with perspective taking and self-awareness. For instance, how would you know that you are violating another person's personal space or that were standing too far away from someone for them to hear you?

Answer: By reading their reaction and taking their perspective. Perhaps they are noticeably uncomfortable, backing away from you. Or perhaps they are leaning towards you in an effort to better hear you. Successful perspective taking and self-awareness provides us with the necessary information to maintain an appropriate personal space for each interaction.

Many of the children with ASD who come to my practice also *fail to consider the interests of other children*. For example, when I asked one child with ASD, Aaron, to tell me what his friends liked to do, he responded that they liked to collect windshield wipers. My first thought was "Wow, what a coincidence" – since Aaron happens to have the largest collection of windshield wipers in the Midwest. In reality, however, these other children did not have a windshield wiper collection (I checked!), but Aaron never considered that. In fact, like many of the children I have worked with, Aaron never considered the interests of any of his peers. Consequently, he only spoke to other kids about his interests, which frankly wasn't very appealing to the other kids.

Knowing the interests of others also gives us wonderful "openings" for social initiations. For instance, if Aaron knew that James liked dinosaurs, he could very effectively initiate and maintain a conversation by asking James the simple question, "Hey, do you like dinosaurs?" However, if he asked James, "Hey, do you like windshield wipers," the answer would be a simple "No," and the conversation would be over.

Social Anxiety and Avoidance

Specific Behaviors Associated With Social Anxiety and Withdrawal

- Interacts with peers during unstructured activities

- Interacts with peers during structured activities

- Engages in one-on-one social interactions with peers

- Interacts with groups of peers

- Engages in solitary activities in the presence of peers

- Expresses fear that other children will laugh or make fun of him/her

- Experiences positive peer interactions

- Engages in solitary interests and hobbies

- Exhibits or expresses fear or anxiety regarding social interactions

- Experiences negative peer interactions

- Actively avoids social situations

- Exhibits or expresses fear of public performances

The essential feature of social anxiety is an intense fear of social situations or performance situations where embarrassment may occur. It is thought to occur in 3%-13% of the general population (APA, 2000; Stein, Torgrud, & Walker, 2000), but recent research suggests that the rate may be much higher in individuals with ASD (Bellini, 2004).

Within the social anxiety diagnosis, two distinct subtypes have emerged: those who suffer exclusively from performance fears (e.g., speaking in public) and those with a broader syndrome of fears related to both performance and social interaction fears. The latter subtype is common among children with ASD, who display performance fears, fear of negative evaluation, fear of humiliation, and general distress related to social interactions.

Individuals with ASD often describe an anxiety that resembles what many of us feel when we are forced to speak in public (increased heart rate, sweaty palms, noticeable shaking, difficulties concentrating, etc.). Not only is the speaking stressful, but just the thought of it is enough to produce stomach-gnawing butterflies.

Imagine living a life where every social interaction was as anxiety provoking as having to make a speech in front of a large group! The typical coping mechanism for most of us is to reduce the stress and anxiety by avoiding the stressful situation. Similarly, for individuals with ASD, it often results in avoidance of social situations, and subsequently, the development of social skill deficits.

Some children prefer one-on-one social interactions rather than group interactions. Typically, children feel more comfortable in activities that have been set up or structured by adults, as opposed to unstructured activities (recess, for instance). When a child continually avoids social encounters, she denies herself the opportunity to acquire social interaction skills. In some, these social skill deficits lead to negative peer interactions and peer failure. For others, avoidance of social encounters creates a pattern of absorption in solitary activities and hobbies that is often difficult to change.

Chapter Summary

The skills and deficits described in this chapter provide the context for the social skills program to be presented in the following chapters. These are the skills that we will be examining in our assessment and later targeting in our intervention.

The social skill deficits are divided into six broad categories of social impairment. It is important to note that these categories are not mutually exclusive but are interconnected. No single social skill operates in isolation of the others.

◉ **Nonverbal communication skills** are the foundation of successful social interactions. Children with ASD often have difficulties recognizing emotions and inferring the meaning of the nonverbal communication of others.

◉ **Social initiations** involve joining in social activities, greetings, and asking questions, among many others. Children with ASD typically fall into one of two categories of social initiation: those who rarely initiate interactions with others and those who initiate frequently, but inappropriately.

◉ **Reciprocity and terminating interactions** involves the give-and-take of social interactions. Children with ASD often engage in one-sided interactions that lack the mutual, back-and-forth exchange of reciprocal interactions.

◉ **Social cognition** refers to the ability to process social information. Social cognition involves both social problem solving (analyzing social situations) and understanding social rules.

◉ **Perspective taking and self-awareness** pose difficulties for most children with ASD and lead to many of the social behaviors they typically demonstrate. These behaviors include making inappropriate comments, failure to maintain hygiene, violation of personal space, and failing to consider the interests of others.

◉ **Social anxiety and social withdrawal** is common in children with ASD. Social anxiety significantly hinders social performance and may lead to social withdrawal, solitary interests, and isolation.

Five-Step Model For Social Skills Programming

4

The primary purpose of the five-step model is to guide parents and professionals through the process of designing and implementing effective social skills programming for children with ASD. Although practical strategies and tools are presented, this book is more than just a collection of activities.

I have spoken to parents and professionals who have purchased books and resources that were filled with wonderful activities, worksheets, and other strategies to teach social skills to children with ASD. Unfortunately, many never got around to using them, or used them briefly before giving up. The most common complaints that I hear from parents and professionals is that they don't know where to begin the program or how to use the various strategies. Another frustration

I hear from parents is that the particular strategy proposed in a book was not effective for their child. Indeed, not all strategies are effective for every child. As such, it is imperative that we not put all our eggs in one basket, as it were, when it comes to selecting and utilizing intervention strategies.

The model presented here is purposefully flexible enough to allow room for a comprehensive array of strategy options. It provides both a conceptual framework for understanding social functioning and practical tools for assessing and teaching social skills to children with ASD.

5-Step Model of Social Skills Programming	
	1. Assess Social Functioning
	2. Distinguish Between Skill Acquisition and Performance Deficits
	3. Select Intervention Strategies ■ Strategies That Promote Skill Acquisition ■ Strategies That Enhance Performance
	4. Implement Intervention
	5. Evaluate and Monitor Progress

Before implementing social skills strategies, it is important to conduct a thorough assessment of the child's level of social skills functioning. The next step is to discern between skill acquisition deficits and performance deficits. Based on this information, you are ready to select and implement intervention strategies. Once intervention strategies are implemented, it is imperative to evaluate and modify the intervention as needed.

Although I use the term steps, it is important to note that the model is not perfectly linear. That is, in real-life applications social skills instruction does not follow a lock-step sequence from Step 1 to Step 5. For instance, it is not uncommon to identify additional social skill deficits (Step 1) in the middle of the implementation process (Step 4). In addition, it is important to continually assess and modify the intervention as additional information and data are accumulated. We will start by looking at assessment in the next chapter.

ASSeSSiNg SociaL FUNctioNiNg

5-STEP MODEL

1. **Assess Social Functioning**

2. Distinguish Between Skill Acquisition and Performance Deficits

3. Select Intervention Strategies

   - Strategies That Promote Skill Acquisition

   - Strategies That Enhance Performance

4. Implement Intervention

5. Evaluate and Monitor Progress

The first step in any social skills training program should be to conduct a thorough evaluation of the child's current level of social functioning. The purpose of such assessment is to answer one very basic, yet complicated, question: *What is precluding the child from establishing and maintaining social relationships?* For most children, the answer takes the form of specific social skill deficits. For others, the answer takes the form of cruel and rejecting peers. And for yet other children, the answer is both.

Assessment of social functioning is a critical, yet often overlooked component of social skill interventions. But how do you know what to teach, if you have not assessed social functioning? Perhaps you could just assume that the child, like many with ASD, has difficulties with initiating interactions. Fair enough. But what types of initiation difficulties is she having? Is she initiating infrequently? Initiating frequently, but inappropriately? Perhaps she is not initiating play activities with peers, but is initiating interactions by asking questions. If so, are these questions about people, or are they questions about topics? Are these topics of interest to the child with ASD, or are they topics of interest to the other person? You get the idea.

Unfortunately, many social skill programs tend to focus exclusively on intervention strategies, failing to provide information on how to assess social functioning. The result is often ineffectual programming and, ultimately, failure. It is my firm belief that you cannot teach social skills to children until you know precisely what social skills need to be taught! Not all children need the same intervention strategies, and not all children need to be taught the same skills. Too often we begin a social skill intervention without fully evaluating the child's specific needs.

The evaluation is typically conducted by a professionals trained to conduct observations and interviews, such as a psychologist, social worker, counselor, autism consultant, or a speech and language pathologist. The evaluator collects pertinent information from the persons who know the child best, such as parents or classroom teachers.

In this section I am mainly speaking to the professionals conducting the evaluation. However, in some cases, parents and teachers may be involved by observing and recording social behavior. And as with all aspects of social skills programming, the evaluation is a collaborative, team effort between parents and professionals from various disciplines. I highly recommend that parents read this section so that they have a better understanding of what information will be collected during the social skills assessment. The evaluation should detail both the child's strengths and weaknesses related to social functioning. As with all assessment procedures, it should be directly linked to subsequent interventions by developing relevant goals and objectives.

This chapter begins with an overview of methods and procedures for conducting a thorough social skill assessment. It concludes with suggestions for how to establish and write treatment and educational goals and objectives that flow logically from the assessment and provide a bridge to implementation of appropriate intervention strategies.

The purpose of the social skills assessment is to determine exactly what it is that we will be teaching. In addition, it is important to ascertain the child's current level of functioning as that enables us to intervene at the child's level of need.

The assessment should involve a combination of general interview of social functioning (e.g., parents, teachers, other school personnel, and student), problem identification and analysis interview, rating scales (e.g., behavioral check-lists, social skills measures, and affective functioning), and observation (both naturalistic and structured). I have included an assessment flowchart to show the order in which these assessment procedures are typically administered.

Social Skills Assessment

Assessment Flowchart

General Interview of Social Functioning
Parent Interview
Teacher Interview
Child Interview

Rating Scales
Social Skills
Emotional/Affective Functioning
Behavioral Functioning
Self-Concept

Problem Identification and Problem Analysis Interview

Observation
Naturalistic Observation
Structured Observation

Setting Treatment/Educational Goals and Objectives
Select Objectives
Identify Component Skills Necessary to Reach Objectives

General Interviews of Social Functioning

Interviews are a valuable method for obtaining information regarding social functioning in a relatively short time by allowing us to collect and synthesize information from a variety of respondents representing a wide range of settings. The general interviews of social functioning presented in this section are meant to provide an entry point for the social skills program. That is, they allow the evaluator to make decisions regarding the direction and focus of the program. The interviews also allow the evaluator (who may be a professional unfamiliar with the child) to learn about the child's strengths and weaknesses related to social functioning. The interviews are meant to be broad and encompassing, which provides a nice complement to the more focused problem identification and analysis interview discussed later in this chapter.

While respondents can be anyone who has direct knowledge of the child's social functioning, they typically include the parents and the teachers who know the child best. I recommend that an interview also be conducted with an often overlooked source of information regarding the child's social functioning – playground supervisors. Playground supervisors have the opportunity to observe children on a daily basis performing socially in naturalistic settings. They have seen the good, the bad, and the ugly of playground culture and life, and can provide valuable normative information regarding the social behaviors of other children.

The final source of information regarding social skills is the child herself. A wise professor of mine used to say, "When in doubt, ask the kid!" The child can provide valuable information about her social performance and her social interests and motivation. Does the child have friends? Does the child want friends? Do other kids like her? Remember, many of these questions require the child to utilize social problem solving to answer appropriately, so the responses that you get might be incongruent with the responses that you get from parents and teachers. That's O.K. In fact, it's more than O.K. because the child's perceptions reveal a great deal about his social awareness and ability to analyze social situations – information that has great relevance to the selection of intervention strategies.

The child interview is also an opportunity to watch the child interact socially – with you! Do not make too many social accommodations for the child; it is not a "social call;" it is an assessment. That is, don't make the social interaction too easy by doing all of the conversational work for the child. Though you want to avoid agitating or frustrating the child, make the interaction as natural as possible to fully illuminate the child's social interaction skills.

It is also important to realize that *what* the child is saying may be less valuable than *how* he is saying it. For instance, if I asked a child the question "Do you have any friends?" he might reply "I have two friends, Charlie and Michael." Knowing that the child has two friends (or at least believes that he has two friends) is important, but even more valuable is the fact that it took the child 15 seconds to answer the question, and that he exhibited a flat affect, didn't ask questions in return, and looked down at the floor while speaking. Thus, a great deal of information can be collected during the child interview regarding social interaction skills, including eye contact, reciprocity, nonverbal expression, tone of voice, affect, the ability to build on conversations, and much more.

Parent Interview of Social Functioning

Social Functioning

1. How many friends does your child have? If none, does he express an interest in having friends? Has he ever had friends?

   a. How many close friends?

   b. Describe their relationship.

   c. Does he prefer playing with younger children rather than same-age peers?

   d. Does he appear more comfortable interacting with adults rather than peers?

2. How does your child play with other children?

   a. Does he join in games with other children?

   b. Does he ask others to join him?

   c. Does he have trouble taking turns?

3. How does your child typically display his emotions?

   a. Are they appropriate to the situation?

   b. Does your child exhibit fear or distress regarding social interactions?

   c. Does he avoid social situations?

4. Describe his eye contact during social interactions. Does he maintain eye contact? If not, what does he look at?

5. Does your child appear argumentative when disagreeing with others?

6. Does he often say things that are "taken the wrong way" by others?

Social Communication

1. Does your child ask many questions?

   a. To request something (tangible item)?

   b. To request assistance?

c. To request information about a topic?

d. To request information about a person?

2. How would you describe the tone of your child's voice?

a. Different from that of other children?

3. How would you describe your child's ability to engage in conversations?

a. Are they one-sided or do they involve give and take?

b. Does he have difficulty shifting topics in conversations?

c. Does he initiate interactions? What do these initiations look like?

Interests

1. What are your child's interests?

a. How often does he talk about or engage in these interests?

2. Does your child have difficulty transitioning from one activity to another?

a. Difficulty starting a task?

b. Difficulty finishing?

3. Does your child have any play behaviors that are different from those of other children his age? Describe.

4. Does your child have any repetitive behaviors (hand-flapping, rocking, spinning, etc.)?

5. Does your child have any sensory sensitivities that interfere with social interactions (sounds, visual, tactile, smells, taste)?

Other Important Questions

1. What are your child's strengths?

2. What are your goals (short and long term) for your child?

3. What do you see as the biggest obstacle to your child establishing social relationships?

Teacher Interview of Social Functioning

Social Functioning

1. Please describe the student's social relationships with peers.

   a. How many close friends?

   b. Describe their relationship.

   c. What types of children does he prefer to play with?

   d. Does he appear more comfortable interacting with adults than peers?

   e. How do other children treat him?

2. What does the student typically do at recess?

   a. Does he mostly play alone or with other children?

   b. Does he join in games with other children?

   c. Does he ask others to join him?

   d. Does he have trouble taking turns?

3. How does the student typically display his emotions?

   a. Are they appropriate to the situation?

   b. Does the child exhibit fear or distress regarding social interactions?

   c. How would you describe his ability to regulate his emotions?

   d. Does he avoid social situations?

4. Describe his eye contact during social interactions.

   a. Does he maintain eye contact?

   b. If not, what does he look at?

5. Does the student appear argumentative when disagreeing with others?

6. Does he often say things that are "taken the wrong way" by others?

7. Compare the student's social skills to those of students in his class.

Communication

1. Describe the student's language ability compared to that of other children in the class.

a. Does the student ask many questions?

b. To request something (tangible item)?

c. To request assistance?

d. To request information about a topic?

e. To request information about a person?

2. How would you describe the tone of the student's voice?

a. Different from other children?

3. How would you describe his conversational ability?

a. Are the conversations one-sided or do they involve give-and-take?

b. Do the conversations seem planned, or do they appear random and poorly planned?

c. Does he initiate interactions?

d. How would you describe the quality of his initiations?

e. Does the child have difficulty shifting from one topic to another?

Interests

1. What are the student's interests?

a. How often does he talk about or engage in these interests?

2. Does the child have any peculiar play behaviors? Describe.

3. Does the child have any repetitive behaviors (hand-flapping, rocking, spinning, etc.)?

4. Does the child have any sensory sensitivities (sounds, visual, tactile, smells, taste) that may hinder social participation?

Other Important Questions

1. What are your major social concerns for the student?

2. What do you feel is a major obstacle to him establishing social relationships?

3. What are the student's strengths?

4. What are the goals (short and long term) for the student?

Child Interview of Social Functioning

Social

1. How many friends do you have? (If child responds that he/she does not have friends, go to Question 5.)

2. What are their names? What grade/How old are they?

3. Please describe them.

4. What kind of things do you do with your friends? (If the child responds that he/she does not have friends, skip to Question 6.)

5. Would you like to have friends?

6. What is a friend?

7. How are you (or how would you be) a good friend?

8. Do you ever get teased or bullied? Why? What do you do when you are teased/bullied?

9. Do people ever do things that bother you? What?

10. Do you ever do things that bother or upset others? What?

Emotional

1. What kinds of things make you feel happy?

2. What kinds of things make you scared? What makes you nervous? Can you describe what scared feels like? Nervous? (Provide examples if necessary; for instance, "do your hands shake?") What do you do when you feel nervous? Does it help?

3. What kinds of things make you angry? What do you do when you feel angry? Does it help?

4. What kinds of things make you sad? What do you do when you feel sad? Does it help?

5. Do you ever feel lonely? When? What do you when you feel lonely? Does it help?

6. How do you know when someone else is (sad, happy, scared, angry, etc.)?

Interests/Routines and Stereotypical Behaviors

1. What kind of things do you like to do?

2. How much time do you spend on these interests?

3. Does it bother you when you are asked to switch from one activity to another?

4. Do any sounds bother you?

5. Does it bother you to be in a noisy, crowded room? Where do you work best?

6. What makes you different from other people? The same? (If the child engages in any stereotypical behaviors such as hand-flapping, use this answer to assess whether he is aware of the behavior, and if he/she perceives it as problematic.)

Additional Questions

1. What is your best quality? What do you like most about yourself?

2. What is your worst quality? What do you like least about yourself?

3. If you could change one thing about yourself or your life, what would it be?

Problem Identification and Problem Analysis Interview

"Problems I've got ... solutions I need!"

In addition to the general information gathering that takes place during the initial interviews, more structured interviews with primary stakeholders (parents and classroom teachers) are conducted to help direct and guide the intervention process. I hesitate to use the term "problem" when I discuss children's social skills, as I believe that we tend to focus too much of our attention on "problems." However, like it or not, it is problems that we have, and it is problems that motivate parents to seek my clinical services. To date, I have not received a single phone call from a parent saying, "Scott, everything is going great with my son, no problems at all ... can you fit him in for an appointment?" So until I receive this call, I can accept the reality that it is problems that prompt parents to seek my services, and it is solutions that they seek for their child.

My challenge as a professional is to find solutions without dwelling exclusively on the problems and to find strengths with which to leverage. (Please see Reframing Problems Into Teachable Skills on pages 91-92.)

Successful problem solving requires us to answer three basic, yet complicated questions:

1. What is the problem?

2. What is causing or maintaining the problem?

3. How do we solve the problem?

For most of you, the problem has been stated: Your child or client/student is having difficulties building social relationships. It is the reason you picked up this book. Therefore, the next step (and the purpose of this book) is to more systematically identify and describe the problem, understand what is causing it and, most important, develop a plan to solve it.

To answer these three questions, I have modified a general problem-solving interview to address social skill deficits. The interview should include the following problem-solving components:

- Problem Identification

- Problem Definition

- Problem Validation

- Problem Analysis

I recommend that the problem-solving interview be conducted after administration of social skill rating forms because the rating forms will help identify and select skills to target.

Problem identification. The primary purpose of the problem identification phase is to identify specific social skill deficits that are particularly problematic for the child with ASD. Often parents and teachers report dozens of skill deficits that they would like to target. However, it is not realistic (nor is it conducive to our mental health!) to target that many skills at one time.

My recommendation is to select and target three to five skills for intervention at a time by asking the parent or teacher to select social skills that are particularly problematic for the child with ASD and that they would like to address during the course of the intervention. The problem identification phase also provides an opportunity to ask the interviewee what interventions have been tried in the past and how successful they have been. Word of advice: Try to gather as much detail about past interventions as possible. I have found that some interventions have gotten a "bad rap" simply because they have been poorly implemented. It is helpful to know what parents and teachers think about an intervention prior to selecting and recommending it for a given child.

Problem definition. The next step is to ask interviewees to describe in as much detail as possible the social skill deficits that they have selected. The purpose of the problem definition phase is to operationalize (i.e., define) the social skills that we will be targeting. The skills should be clearly operationalized so that all members of the child's team understand exactly what the child is working on. For instance, suppose that the teacher reports that the child has difficulties initiating interactions and that we select the social skill of "initiating interactions" as the target of intervention. This would undoubtedly create confusion because the term *initiating interactions* is too vague and can mean many different things to different people. One child may have difficulties initiating greetings with other children whereas another child may have difficulties initiating play activities.

In intervention planning, precision is imperative. If we select the skill "initiating interactions with peer," make certain that it is clearly defined to all those involved in the child's social skills program. After we have clearly operationalized the social skills that we will be targeting, we can move on to problem validation.

Problem validation. Problem validation is a short, yet important step in the problem-solving interview. It is not uncommon for parents and teachers, or parents and psychologists for that matter, to disagree on what skills to target for intervention. The goal of problem validation is to come to a consensus regarding the need to teach a particular skill.

Experience has shown me that if the parents or teachers do not believe that a skill is important teach, they are less inclined to support the intervention, which is essential to the success of the intervention. (See Chapter 11 for more information on social validity and treatment fidelity.) After we have identified, defined, and validated the social skills that we will be working on, it is time to move on to problem analysis.

Problem analysis. The purpose of the problem analysis phase is to break down the selected social skill deficits into component parts. Here I ask the interviewee to describe the rate, or frequency, and the severity, or intensity, of the problem behavior or desired skill. This takes the form of the question "how often does the child perform the skill?"

I also ask the interviewee to rate how well the child performs the skill relative to other children. In addition, it is important to gather information about the contexts or settings in which the problem behavior or desired skill is most likely and least likely to occur, such as "when is the child most/least likely to perform the skill," or "with whom is the child most/least likely to perform the skill?"

This interview provides an introduction to the process of discerning between a skill acquisition and a performance deficit, which will be discussed more in Step 2 of the model. The final step of the problem analysis phase involves information about the child's strengths and discussing next steps in the social skills program. Make sure that you clearly articulate to the interviewee what will happen next.

Problem Identification and Problem Analysis Interview Form

1. Problem Identification

a. Identify specific social skill deficits.

b. Establish priorities (agree on three to five skills to target for intervention).

c. Discuss and analyze previous attempts to solve the problem (what strategies have been used in the past?).

2. Problem Definition

a. Ask the interviewee to describe the skills in detail.

b. Agree on a behavioral definition of the skill (make sure the definition is clear and measurable).

3. Problem Validation

a. Agree on the social importance (does interviewee think that the skill is important to address?).

4. Problem Analysis

a. Break the social skill into component parts:

- Rate and frequency (how often?)

- Intensity/severity/quality (how well does the child perform the skill?)

- Context and settings (including non-occurrences)

  (Ask the interviewee to provide information about the child's performance of the skill in a variety of settings and with different people)

- Relativistic comparison (how does the skill compare to the skills of other children?)

- Discrimination between a skill acquisition deficit and a performance deficit for each targeted skill

b. Examine strengths of student and setting(s).

c. Discuss next steps (who, what, when, where).

Rating Scales

Rating scales are indirect assessment tools that provide a wealth of information about the child across a variety of functioning areas. These measures range from informal checklists to standardized rating scales and may be administered to parents, teachers, and the child herself. I use rating scales to collect information on social functioning, anxiety, self-concept and self-esteem, and behavioral functioning, and to evaluate progress (or lack thereof). Most of these measures are administered at the beginning of the intervention and at three-month intervals during the course of the social skill program.

The following does not represent an all-inclusive list of available measures. It includes assessment measures that I have found to be of value in my clinical practice and/or research. The following assessment measures will be reviewed: Social Skills Rating System (SSRS), the Multidimensional Anxiety Scale for Children (MASC), the Social Anxiety Scale for Children/Adolescents (SAS-C and SAS-A), the Behavioral Assessment Scale for Children (BASC), the Adaptive Behavior Assessment System-Second Edition (ABAS-II), and the Multidimensional Self-Concept Scale (MSCS).

These measures are well standardized, have demonstrated high reliability and validity in numerous research studies and in clinical practice, and are frequently used as measures of socioemotional functioning by mental health professionals in schools, clinics, and hospitals. Standardized methods of administration (i.e., directions, sample items, etc.) should be followed according to each test manual. The measures were also chosen because of their demonstrated utility as performance monitoring tools (see Chapter 11 for more information on progress monitoring). At the end of this section I will provide a description of two additional measures that have been specifically designed for use with children with ASD.

Social Skills Rating System (SSRS) (Gresham & Elliot, 1990). This questionnaire provides information on the social behavior of children and adolescents ages 3-18. The SSRS has been used in studies examining the social skills of individuals with autism spectrum disorders (Bellini, 2004, 2006; Koning & Magill-Evans, 2001; Ozonoff & Miller, 1995).

The SSRS measures whether the child utilizes various social skills during social interactions. The parent and self-report versions consist of two scales: Social Skills scale and Problem Behaviors scale. The Social Skills scale is most relevant to the social skill model presented here. It consists of five subscales: Cooperation, Assertion, Responsibility, Empathy and Self-Control. The Cooperation subscale includes questions related to helping others, such as "completes household tasks without being reminded," "finishes classroom assignments within time limits." The Assertion subscale measures initiating behaviors such as "initiates conversations with classmates" and "makes friends easily." The Responsibility subscale pertains to behaviors that demonstrate the ability to communicate with adults and includes items such as "asks permission before using another family member's property" and "informs you before going out with friends." The Empathy subscale measures behaviors that show concern and respect for others' feelings and viewpoints. Items include "I feel sorry for others when bad things happen to them" and "I say nice things to others when they have done something well." Finally, the Self-Control subscale measures behaviors in response to conflict and non-conflict situations. Items include "controls temper in conflict with peers" and "responds appropriately when hit or pushed by other children."

Multidimensional Anxiety Scale for Children (MASC)
(March, 1999). This instrument provides an assessment of anxiety symptoms across multiple dimensions, such as Physical Symptoms, Social Anxiety, Harm Avoidance, and Separation/Panic. The Physical Symptoms scale consists of items related to physiological arousal, and includes the subscales of Somatic Symptoms and Tension. The Harm Avoidance scale contains the subscales of Perfectionism (e.g., doing everything exactly right) and Anxious Coping (checking to make sure things are safe). The Social Anxiety scale relates to fear and worry of social interaction and social evaluations and contains two subscales, Humiliation Fears and Performance Fears. The MASC is a 45-item self-report measure for children 8-18 years of age. It has been used in research examining anxiety in children and adolescents with autism spectrum disorders (Bellini, 2004, 2006).

Social Anxiety Scale for Children/Adolescents (SAS-C and SAS-A).
The SAS (La Greca, 1999) is a self-report measure of social anxiety consisting of three factors: Fear of Negative Evaluation, Social Avoidance and Distress in

New Situations, and Social Avoidance and Distress-General. The SAS also provides a total Social Anxiety score. The Fear of Negative Evaluation (FNE) subscale measures fears and worries related to being negatively evaluated by peers. The Social Avoidance and Distress in New Situations (SAD-N) measures distress and discomfort due to new social situations or unfamiliar peers. Finally, the Social Avoidance and Distress-General (SAD-G) measures generalized or pervasive distress or discomfort due to social situations. The SAS-A has been used in previous studies examining anxiety in adolescents with ASD (Bellini, 2004, 2006).

Behavioral Assessment Scale for Children (BASC)

(Reynolds & Kamphaus, 1992). This multidimensional measure of children's behavior contains items assessing anxiety, social skill problems, and other behaviors. The BASC contains five components: Externalizing Problems, Internalizing Problems, School Problems, Adaptive Skills, and a Behavioral Symptoms Index. The Internalizing composite includes the subscales of anxiety, depression, and somatization. The Anxiety subscale contains items pertaining to worry, nervousness, and fear, such as "is fearful," "is nervous," and "worries." The Depression subscale contains items related to affect and mood, such as "cries easily," "is easily upset," and "changes moods quickly." The Somatization subscale pertains to somatic symptoms of distress, such as "complains of chest pain," "has stomach problems," and "has headaches." The BASC is appropriate for use with children and adolescents between the ages of 2 and 18 years of age. It has been used in studies examining externalizing and internalizing behaviors in autism spectrum disorders (Bellini, 2004).

Adaptive Behavior Assessment System-Second Edition

(ABAS-II) (Harrison & Oakland, 2003). This instrument assesses the adaptive skills of individuals ages birth to 89 years old. The ABAS-II may be used to diagnose and classify disorders, identify strengths and weaknesses, and to document and monitor performance over time. The ABAS-II monitors behavior across environments and across multiple informants. The ABAS-II includes norm-referenced scores for children with autism. That is, it allows us to compare the adaptive behavior skills of the child with adaptive behavior of other children with ASD.

Multidimensional Self-Concept Scale (MSCS) (Bracken, 1992). The MSCS is a 150-item self-report scale measuring self-perceptions related to six contextual domains: social competence related to interactions with others; success/failure in attainment of goals; recognition of affective behaviors; academic achievement and competence in other school-related activities; competence related to interactions with family members; and physical attractiveness and prowess. The MSCS may be administered to either individuals or groups of children. The scale has been used in research with general populations of children; however, no documented research studies have examined its efficacy with children and adolescents with ASD.

Social skills rating forms designed specifically for children with ASD. Although social skill difficulties are a central feature of ASD, presently few evidence-based social skill assessment tools have been designed specifically for children and adolescents with ASD.

To address this need, I have developed the Autism Social Skills Profile (ASSP) (Bellini, 2006). The ASSP provides a comprehensive measure of the social functioning of children and adolescents with ASD. The items on the ASSP represent a broad range of social characteristics typically exhibited by individuals with ASD, including initiation skills, reciprocity, perspective taking, and nonverbal communication. The ASSP was designed for use with children and adolescents with ASD between the ages of 6-17.

The purpose of the ASSP is twofold. First, it may be used as an intervention planning tool by identifying the specific social skill deficits of individuals with ASD. These skill deficits may then become a direct and precise target of intervention. In addition, items on the ASSP are phrased in a manner that allows them to be easily adapted for use as social goals and objectives on Individualized Education Programs (IEP). The second purpose of the ASSP is to assist in measuring intervention progress. Thus, it is well suited as a pre- and post-measure of social functioning.

Administering the ASSP prior to conducting the problem identification and problem analysis interview provides a frame of reference for talking with the parents about their child's social functioning. For instance, as the evaluator asks the parent to identify potential social skill deficits, she could refer to their responses on the ASSP; that is, "I noticed that on the ASSP you stated that Johnny rarely joins in activities with peers, would you tell me more about that."

The ASSP may be administered to parents/caregivers and other individuals (e.g., school personnel) who have direct knowledge of the child's social functioning. The ASSP may be administered by professionals (psychologists, psychiatrists, social workers, counselors, and speech and language pathologists) wishing to design and implement social skill interventions.

Autism Social Skills Profile

Scott Bellini

Child's Name:_____
                        FIRST   MIDDLE   LAST

Birthdate: _____ Age: _____ Sex: □Female □Male Today's Date: _____
          MO.   DAY   YEAR   MO.   DAY   YEAR

School: _____ Grade: _____

Your Name: _____
                        FIRST   MIDDLE   LAST

Relationship to Child: □Mother □Father □Guardian □Other _____

Street Address: _____

City: _____ State: _____ Zip: _____

Phone: (_____) _____

The following phrases describe skills or behaviors that your child might exhibit during social interactions or in social situations. Please rate **HOW OFTEN** your child exhibits each skill or behavior independently, **without assistance from others** (i.e., without reminders, cueing and/or prompting). You should base your judgment on your child's behavior over the last **3 months**.

Please use the following guidelines to rate your child's behavior:

Circle **N** if your child **never** or **almost never** exhibits the skill or behavior.

Circle **S** if your child **sometimes** or **occasionally** exhibits the skill or behavior.

Circle **O** if your child **often** or **typically** exhibits the skill or behavior.

Circle **V** if your child **very often** or **always** exhibits the skill or behavior.

Please do not skip any items. If you are unsure of an item, please provide your best estimate. You may use the "Brief Description" section to provide additional information on the particular skill or behavior. For instance, if your child will exhibit a particular skill or behavior more frequently when cueing or prompting is provided, or when interacting with adults rather than peers, please make note of this in the "Brief Description" section.

Autism Social Skills Profile

Never	Sometimes	Often	Very often
N	S	O	V

Skill Area	How Often				Brief Description
Invites Peers to Join Him/Her in Activities	N 1	S 2	O 3	V 4	
Joins in Activities With Peers	N 1	S 2	O 3	V 4	
Takes Turns During Games and Activities	N 1	S 2	O 3	V 4	
Maintains Personal Hygiene	N 1	S 2	O 3	V 4	
Interacts With Peers During Unstructured Activities	N 1	S 2	O 3	V 4	
Interacts With Peers During Structured Activities	N 1	S 2	O 3	V 4	
Asks Questions to Request Information About a Person	N 1	S 2	O 3	V 4	
Asks Questions to Request Information About a Topic	N 1	S 2	O 3	V 4	
Engages in One-On-One Social Interactions With Peers	N 1	S 2	O 3	V 4	
Interacts With Groups of Peers	N 1	S 2	O 3	V 4	
Maintains the "Give-and-Take" of Conversations	N 1	S 2	O 3	V 4	
Expresses Sympathy for Others	N 1	S 2	O 3	V 4	
Talks About or Acknowledges the Interests of Others	N 1	S 2	O 3	V 4	

Autism Social Skills Profile

Never	Sometimes	Often	Very often
N	S	O	V

Skill Area	How Often				Brief Description
Recognizes the Facial Expressions of Others	N 1	S 2	O 3	V 4	
Recognizes the Nonverbal Cues, or "Body Language" of Others	N 1	S 2	O 3	V 4	
Requests Assistance From Others	N 1	S 2	O 3	V 4	
Understands the Jokes or Humor of Others	N 1	S 2	O 3	V 4	
Maintains Eye Contact During Conversations	N 1	S 2	O 3	V 4	
Maintains an Appropriate Distance When Interacting With Peers	N 1	S 2	O 3	V 4	
Speaks With an Appropriate Volume in Conversations	N 1	S 2	O 3	V 4	
Considers Multiple Viewpoints	N 1	S 2	O 3	V 4	
Offers Assistance to Others	N 1	S 2	O 3	V 4	
Verbally Expresses How He/She Is Feeling	N 1	S 2	O 3	V 4	
Responds to the Greetings of Others	N 1	S 2	O 3	V 4	
Joins a Conversation With Two or More People Without Interrupting	N 1	S 2	O 3	V 4	
Initiates Greetings With Others	N 1	S 2	O 3	V 4	

Autism Social Skills Profile

Never	Sometimes	Often	Very often
N	S	O	V

Skill Area	How Often				Brief Description
Provides Compliments to Others	N 1	S 2	O 3	V 4	
Introduces Self to Others	N 1	S 2	O 3	V 4	
Politely Asks Others to Move out of His/Her Way	N 1	S 2	O 3	V 4	
Acknowledges the Compliments Directed at Him/Her by Others	N 1	S 2	O 3	V 4	
Allows Peers to Join Him/Her in Activities	N 1	S 2	O 3	V 4	
Responds to the Invitations of Peers to Join Them in Activities	N 1	S 2	O 3	V 4	
Allows Others to Assist Him/Her With Tasks	N 1	S 2	O 3	V 4	
Responds to Questions Directed at Him/Her by Others	N 1	S 2	O 3	V 4	
Experiences Positive Peer Interactions	N 1	S 2	O 3	V 4	
Compromises During Disagreements With Others	N 1	S 2	O 3	V 4	
Responds Slowly in Conversations	N 1	S 2	O 3	V 4	
Changes the Topic of Conversation to Fit Self-Interests	N 1	S 2	O 3	V 4	
Misinterprets the Intentions of Others	N 1	S 2	O 3	V 4	

Autism Social Skills Profile

Never	Sometimes	Often	Very often
N	S	O	V

Skill Area	How Often				Brief Description
Makes Inappropriate Comments	N 1	S 2	O 3	V 4	
Engages in Solitary Interests and Hobbies	N 1	S 2	O 3	V 4	
Ends Conversations Abruptly	N 1	S 2	O 3	V 4	
Fails to Read Cues to Terminate Conversations	N 1	S 2	O 3	V 4	
Exhibits Fear or Anxiety Regarding Social Interactions	N 1	S 2	O 3	V 4	
Experiences Negative Peer Interactions	N 1	S 2	O 3	V 4	
Engages in Socially Inappropriate Behaviors	N 1	S 2	O 3	V 4	
Exhibits Poor Timing With His/Her Social Initiations	N 1	S 2	O 3	V 4	
Is Manipulated by Peers	N 1	S 2	O 3	V 4	
Engages in Solitary Activities in the Presence of Peers	N 1	S 2	O 3	V 4	

Quill (2000) also provides an excellent social skills checklist for younger children with ASD that can be used by parents and professionals in her book *DO-WATCH-LISTEN-SAY*. This checklist arranges skills in a hierarchy from least advanced to most advanced, which allows the child's team to ascertain current level of functioning and effectively intervene at the child's level of need. Although this checklist has not been standardized, it provides a useful checklist of social skills typically found in young children with and without ASD.

III. SOCIAL SKILLS CHECKLIST

A. Play	Skill Yes/No	Generalized Yes/No	Target three objectives
Solitary play			
1. Functional: Uses one action with one toy	Y N	Y N	
2. Functional: Closed-ended activities	Y N	Y N	
3. Functional: Open-ended activities	Y N	Y N	
4. Symbolic: Routine scripts	Y N	Y N	
5. Symbolic: Creative	Y N	Y N	
6. Plays independently for ____ minutes	Y N	Y N	
Social play			
1. Plays parallel with own set of toys/materials	Y N	Y N	
2. Plays parallel with organized toys/materials	Y N	Y N	
3. Participates in choral/unison group activity	Y N	Y N	
4. Turn-taking with one partner with predictable turns	Y N	Y N	
5. Turn-taking in a group game with predictable turns	Y N	Y N	
6. Shares materials	Y N	Y N	
7. Cooperative play with one partner	Y N	Y N	
8. Cooperative play in structured groups	Y N	Y N	
9. Cooperative play in unstructured groups	Y N	Y N	

III. SOCIAL SKILLS CHECKLIST *(continued)*

B. Group skills	Skill Yes/No	Generalized Yes/No	Target three objectives
Attending			
1. During meals (snack time, lunchtime)	Y N	Y N	
2. During structured projects (art, work)	Y N	Y N	
3. During listening activities (stories, music)	Y N	Y N	
4. During structured games (board games, outdoor games)	Y N	Y N	
5. During play activities (play center, recess)	Y N	Y N	
6. During discussion activities (circle time, meeting)	Y N	Y N	
Waiting			
1. Sits for group activity	Y N	Y N	
2. Raises hand for a turn	Y N	Y N	
3. Stands in line	Y N	Y N	
Turn-taking			
1. During structured activity	Y N	Y N	
2. During unstructured activity	Y N	Y N	
Following group directions			
1. Nonverbal directions (quiet gesture, turn off light)	Y N	Y N	
2. Attention-getting directions ("Everybody _____")	Y N	Y N	
3. Routine verbal directions ("Clean up," "Line up")	Y N	Y N	
4. Verbal directions in familiar contexts	Y N	Y N	
5. Verbal directions in novel contexts	Y N	Y N	

Use of self-reports. There is some debate regarding the appropriateness of administering self-report measures to children with ASD. Those who are against the use of self-report measures for this population caution that individuals with ASD do not have sufficient self-awareness to articulate their emotional, social, and behavioral functioning. This is partly true. For instance, if I asked a child with ASD whether or not she felt "anxious" or "stressed," I would probably not get a very useful response because she may not understand what anxious or stressed means.

Fortunately, most self-report measures pose concrete items, such as "my hands shake" or "I am afraid of other children laughing at me," rather than global "feeling"-type questions. Nevertheless, there are often discrepancies between child self-reports and parent reports, but this is true for all children, not just those with ASD.

My own research and clinical practice suggest that self-report measures are useful for measuring social and emotional functioning in children with ASD. In fact, I have found that adolescents' ratings of their own social skills are better predictors of social anxiety than the social skill ratings of their parents (Bellini, 2004). In other words, the child's perceptions of her social skills may be more important than her actual social functioning. For example, if we have two children with equal social skills, the child who perceives her social skills as weaker is more likely to have greater levels of social anxiety than the child who perceives her social skills as stronger.

Reality is in the mind of the perceiver. Therefore, I recommend including self-report measures of social, emotional, and behavioral functioning whenever reasonable. The following is a list of suggestions for using self-reports with children with ASD.

Suggestions for Using Self-Report Measures

1. Ensure that the measure is appropriate for the cognitive level of the child.

2. Confirm that the child understand the items.

3. Encourage the child to ask questions.

4. Compare the child's ratings with those of parents and teachers.

5. Use responses on individual items as "openings" for further exploration.

It is imperative to consider the child's cognitive and reading level prior to administering self-report measures. The respective test manuals will include information regarding the reading level required to complete the items. It may also be helpful to read the items to children who are very slow readers, or who become easily frustrated with reading tasks. The assessment measures described above have standardized instructions that should be read to the student per the test manual guidelines. In addition, ask questions to ensure that the child understands the items, and modify or restate the instructions or items so that the child understands them fully. It is also helpful to encourage the child to ask questions or ask for assistance when he does not understand an item.

Certain items on each measure may be difficult for some children with ASD to understand (e.g., a question such as "my heart races"). Use these items to gauge whether or not the child is requesting assistance when he needs it. It is also helpful to triangulate, or confirm the child's responses on the self-report, with the responses of parents and teachers. Parents and teachers are sometimes surprised to learn that the child is afraid that other children will make fun of him, because they may view the child as unaware of or unconcerned with his peers' perceptions of him.

Finally, I recommend using the individual items as "openings" for further exploration (but only after the measure has been completed). That is, if a child endorses the item "my hands shake," it is imperative to explore in more depth when his hands shake, where his hands shake, and how severely his hands shake. The child's responses to individual items often become the target of future interventions.

Observation

Observation of social behaviors should follow the interviews and administration of rating scales (please refer to assessment flowchart on page 55). Two traditional methods of observation may be used to assess the social functioning of children with ASD, naturalistic and structured. The purpose of both methods is to observe the child's social performance across settings, persons, and social contexts. By the time the observation is conducted, the evaluator should have a good idea of what social skills she would like to observe, and in what settings she would like to observe them. In particular, the observer should collect data on those skills and social contexts that were identified as primary skill deficits on the rating forms and during the interview.

Naturalistic observation. This type of observation involves observing and recording the child's behavior in real-life social settings, such as the school playground and cafeteria, or in various social settings at or near the child's home. Naturalistic observation is the ideal method of observing social behavior because it involves behavior that is authentic and spontaneous, allowing us to record behavior in settings that the child typically encounters in the course of his daily life.

It also allows us to observe behavior across settings and across persons. This is particularly important in cases where the child might be interacting well in structured settings (i.e., the classroom) but not in unstructured settings (i.e., the playground), or interacting well with certain peers or adults, but not with other children or unfamiliar adults.

Naturalistic observation also allows us to observe and record important aspects of the child's environment, such as physical spaces (noise levels, clutter, and other potential sensory stressors), and the behavior of other children. Observing the behavior of other children is an important component of the observation. It is particularly important to ascertain how other children are reacting to the child with ASD. Are they accommodating and accepting? Or are they rigid and rejecting? This information will be useful in determining whether there is a need for peer awareness or peer mentor training, and, if so, what type of training will be necessary. (See Chapter 9 for additional information on peer training.)

Further, naturalistic observation also allows us to establish a "norm reference" for the child's social behavior. For instance, suppose we are concerned that the child with ASD is not joining in activities with peers. During our one-hour observation we record two instances of "joining-in" behavior. What does this tells us? Is this a low number or a high number? If we also observe and record the "joining-in" behavior of other children in the classroom, we will have a better understanding of how the child with ASD compares with other children in the classroom with regard to "joining in."

Two Ways to Select a "Norm Group"

<table>
<tr><td>

1. Randomly select a small group of children to observe (three children will suffice).

2. Ask the teacher to nominate three children: one who is the most "socially skilled," an average social performer, and the least socially skilled child (other than the child with ASD).

Note. The latter is my preferred method as it provides a representative range of social performance with which to compare the target child.

</td></tr>
</table>

As stated previously, naturalistic observation is the ideal method for recording social behavior. In fact, I prefer to begin social skill assessments with a naturalistic observation to get a sense of the child's social functioning and the social climate of the school setting. However, naturalistic observation has many drawbacks that limit its usefulness and feasibility, particularly for children with ASD.

First, it is time consuming. An observer can spend dozens of hours recording the social behavior of a child with ASD without gathering much useful information. Since we are recording in the naturalistic environment, we may not observe on days that yield the behavior we are looking for. This is especially true for children with ASD, particularly those who are socially withdrawn. In this case, we could spend hours observing the child, but not observe one social interaction with a peer. While this does tell us that the child is socially withdrawn, we probably already knew that prior to the observation. Observing an hour of social isolation also does not tell us much about the child's social skills or social functioning. This is precisely why structured social observations are a highly recommended social skills assessment strategy for children with ASD.

Second, some school systems have adopted policies that limit access to classrooms by outside professionals. In these unfortunate situations, the private therapist may be unable to come to the child's school to observe social behavior.

Structured observations. Structured observations involve observing the child in an environment that has been artificially established for one purpose: to facilitate social interactions between the target child and preselected peers. You can gather significantly more information in a 20-minute structured observation than in a two-hour naturalistic observation. Imagine you were required to observe a child's jumping ability. You could spend hours and days following the child around the playground until you finally observed good examples of the child's jumping ability. Or, you could set up a 10-minute structured activity that required the child to display his leaping ability. Simply put, structured observations give us the most "bang for our buck."

Structured observations involve observing social behavior in a structured playgroup, or structured social group. The child with ASD is grouped with one or two nondisabled peers in a setting that is rich in social opportunities (games, toys, and other age-appropriate play objects). To keep the assessment as authentic as possible, the children are given one specific instruction prior to the observation, "play with each other."

Nondisabled peers may be coached prior to the observation to make sure that they include the child with ASD in their activities. Although this may artificially increase the number of social interactions the child with ASD has with peers, it gives us ample opportunity to observe specific social skills, which is the purpose of the assessment! Peers should be selected who have a positive social history with the child with ASD, and who want to be part of the playgroup. (See Chapter 10 for more information on how to structure playgroups.)

Naturalistic vs. Structured Observations

Type of Observation	Advantage	Disadvantage
Naturalistic	1. Records authentic behavior in "real-world" settings 2. Records behavior across settings and persons 3. Allows observer to record information on environmental stimuli, such as noise levels, clutter, and other sensory stressors 4. Allows observer to record information on the social behaviors of other children	1. Time consuming 2. Child may not exhibit target behaviors during observation 3. Evaluator may not have access to naturalistic settings, such as the school
Structured	1. Less time consuming 2. Allows observer to record larger quantities of information related to the target behavior	1. Behavior observed in structured setting may not transfer to naturalistic setting 2. Does not allow observer to record information related to environmental stimuli 3. Does not allow observer to record information on the social behavior of other children

Recording methods. I recommend two common methods for recording social behaviors in both naturalistic and structured settings: narrative recording and systematic recording.

Narrative recording is a subjective approach to recording the behaviors, characteristics, and social interactions of the target child. In this approach, the observer simply watches the child and makes notes relevant to the child's social functioning. Narrative recording allows the observer to take rich, detailed notes regarding the child's social and physical environment.

The limitation of this method of recording is that the notes generated are anecdotal and tend to be subjective. That is, if you and I were observing the same children on the same playground, the things that we would see, and our perceptions of those things, might be markedly different. This lack of reliability, along with the subjective nature of the notes, makes narrative recording a poor choice for monitoring intervention progress. Nevertheless, narrative recordings do provide valuable information regarding the child's social functioning and environment and provide a nice complement to the more structured, systematic recording.

In **systematic recording,** the observer begins with a set of predetermined behaviors to be observed and recorded. These systematic recordings will provide a detailed measure of the child's present level of social functioning and will also serve as a baseline (or beginning point) for measuring progress throughout the intervention (see Establishing Criteria for Social Objectives on page 90). The behaviors are chosen based on the problem identification interview described earlier. The social behaviors are recorded based on frequency or rate, severity or intensity, duration or latency, and the context of the behavior (i.e., where the behavior occurred and with whom it occurred). Again, it is imperative that the social behaviors are clearly defined or operationalized prior to the observation. This will significantly increase the reliability of the observation, and the ability to detect changes as a result of the intervention.

Narrative and systematic recording complement each other well. I recommend beginning an observation by using narrative recording (for about 10 minutes) and then switching to systematic recording. Narrative notes may continue to be recorded on an as-needed basis to note special circumstances or other events that are not part of the systematic recording. (See Chapter 11 for a more detailed description of types of systematic recording and forms for doing so.)

Setting Goals and Objectives

Nothing has challenged special education teachers more than the writing of IEP goals and objectives. From a parent's point of view, it must seem ridiculous to hear teachers complain about writing goals and objectives. After all, they are getting paid for it, right? Well, writing objectives for one child is not the problem. Writing objectives for 50 or so children – that is the problem! The result too often is generic objectives that lack relevance and individuality. And remember, developing educational objectives is a collaborative process between parents and professionals.

I'm not passing judgment here, but the current system has effectively taken the "individualized" out of the IEP. None-the-less, these dreaded goals and objectives can serve a valuable and integral role in social skill interventions:

- They provide a logical link between assessment and the subsequent implementation of intervention strategies.

- They represent objectivity and accountability.

- They state where we are, and where we would like to go.

- They tell us – most important – when we have arrived.

Love them or hate them, goals and objectives are our reality. The following section will provide suggestions for how to write social goals and objectives, and for making them more useful to social programming. Although the information is geared directly towards parents and school personnel responsible for developing IEP goals and objectives, it is also relevant to practitioners in non-school settings who work with students who have an IEP, or those who are required to develop treatment objectives, such as therapists working in private practice.

Distinguishing Between Goals and Objectives

It is important to first distinguish between a goal and an objective. These terms are often used interchangeably, but they are different, albeit inextricably related. Whereas goals represent long-term behavioral expectations, objectives represent short-term, measurable behaviors. I view it this way: Goals represent our hopes and dreams, and objectives represent reality and accountability. In their book *Teaching Social Competence: Social Skills and Academic Success*, Knapczyk and Rodes (2001) provide excellent information on setting social goals and objectives. Briefly, the authors state that goals should concentrate on building new skills, be realistic, should remain positive, and represent long-term learning.

Building new skills is essential to designing effective social programming. Remember Tenet #2: *If we want children and adolescents with ASD to be successful socially, we must teach them the skills to be successful.* Objectives, according to Knapczyk and Rodes, should be connected to the stated goals, be connected directly to the intervention strategies, describe specific levels of performance, and define short-term, immediate behaviors.

Goals	1. Concentrate on building new skills
	2. Should be realistic
	3. Should remain positive
	4. Represent long-term learning
Objectives	1. Define short-term, immediate behaviors
	2. Should be connected to the stated goals
	3. Should be connected directly to the intervention strategies
	4. Describe specific levels of performance

The Essence of Goals and Objectives

The key is that *objectives must be directly linked to the stated goals.* For instance, I recently read an IEP that stated the social goal as "Student will develop the skills necessary to establish positive peer relationships." As far as social goals go, this is not a bad one. However, the following was listed as an objective below the goal, "Student will complete assignments in class in a timely manner." Now, what does that objective have to do with establishing peer relationships? NOTHING!

In addition, *objectives must be both reasonable and measurable* in order to be useful. One of my favorite bad IEP objectives illustrates this point well, "Student will complete assignments willingly." Perhaps these folks have an assessment tool that specifically measures willingness, but I don't. And furthermore, how many of us would receive a paycheck if our boss required us to "willingly" complete a task?

The following is a short list of social goals and objectives. Notice how the objectives are linked logically to the goals.

Sample Goals and Objectives

> **Social Goal 1:**
> *Scotty will learn the skills necessary to establish and maintain positive social interactions with peers.*
>
> > **Social Objective 1:**
> > *Scotty will join in play activities with peers in a structured playgroup a minimum of 5 times per session.*
> >
> > **Social Objective 2:**
> > *Scotty will respond to the social initiations of peers on the playground with a minimum response ratio of 70%.*
>
> **Social Goal 2:**
> *Scotty will learn the skills necessary to increase pro-social behaviors in the classroom.*
>
> > **Social Objective 1:**
> > *Scotty will raise his hand before answering questions during classroom discussions (90% of questions answered).*

Establishing Criteria for Social Objectives

We are living in the "age of accountability." Educators are being held accountable by state and federal educational agencies. Private practitioners are being held accountable by insurance companies. At times it seems that accountability trumps practice. However, in our effort to determine how best to evaluate learning outcomes, we should not forget to address how best to improve learning outcomes.

Teaching strategies must never take a back seat to evaluation strategies. The goal should be to find a logical median, as both are important.

In educational systems "criteria" provide the mechanism for measuring academic, behavioral, and social objectives. Criteria are defined as "standards on which a decision or judgment can be based." In educational parlance, criteria refer to the mechanisms for judging the success of our educational practices. Therefore, each educational objective must provide a criterion for measuring the child's performance.

The criteria that you select should be directly related the child's "present level of performance." The present level of performance serves as the baseline measure for subsequent progress monitoring. *Criteria should be measurable, meaningful, and realistic.* For instance, if the initial evaluation demonstrated that the child is presently "joining in activities with peers on the playground" 5% of the time, it would be unrealistic to set the criterion for this objective at 90%. Unfortunately, I see this on a frequent basis when I read IEPs. Rarely do I see objective criteria below 75%. Perhaps teachers and other school personnel do not want to be accused of sandbagging (i.e., setting artificially low criteria to ensure success).

In the above example, it would be much more realistic and meaningful to the child, if the criterion was set closer to 25% or 35% rather than 90%. If you increase the social participation of a child with ASD from 5% to 25% in three months, you shouldn't feel bad – you should celebrate! In addition, the present level of performance serves as the baseline measure for subsequent progress monitoring and establishment of criteria. For instance, once the child achieves 25% participation with peers, criteria could be set at 50% participation, and so on. (For more information on measuring social functioning and monitoring progress, see Chapter 11.)

Reframing Problems Into Teachable Skills

Perhaps the most critical aspect of writing treatment objectives is the ability to convert problems into teachable skills. This "reframing" is critical because the primary purpose of social programming is to teach skills. The reduction of problem behavior just happens to be a welcome byproduct of social programming. For instance, although we may start with an identified problem, "has difficulty asking peers to play with him," reframing requires us to state the solution, "will ask peers to play with him." It might sound simple, but the distinction represents the difference between focusing on problems and generating solutions. This distinction is not lost on our children, who tend to be much more receptive to interventions that focus on teaching a new skill as opposed to those targeting their problems.

Occasionally, you will encounter social behaviors that need to be eliminated, and the stated objective will reflect this. For instance, suppose we were working with a child who was repeatedly making sexual comments to classmates. Quite clearly, our express purpose for targeting this behavior would be to eliminate this behavior as it has serious consequences for this child's peer relationships. As such, our stated objective would be to "refrain from making sexual comments to classmates." Although sometimes necessary, as in the above scenario, behavioral reduction techniques should be used sparingly and cautiously in social skills programs.

The following provides an exercise designed to start your brain on the path of reframing problems into teachable skills.

Reframing Problems Into Teachable Skills

Take a few moments and try to reframe each of the problem behaviors into a teachable skill ... you might want to cover-up the right-hand column to make it more challenging!

Identified Problem	Teachable Skill
▪ Blurts out answers in class	▪ Raises hand before answering
▪ Interrupts others in conversations	▪ Waits for others to finish talking before joining in conversations
▪ Is socially withdrawn	▪ Interacts with other children
▪ Does not read nonverbal cues	▪ Recognizes the nonverbal cues of others
▪ Stands too close to others during conversations	▪ Maintains an appropriate distance from others
▪ Has offensive body odor	▪ Applies deodorant on a daily basis

It is easy to become overwhelmed with a deluge of skills and behaviors to work on, especially at the beginning. Select no more than five treatment or educational objectives per three-month period. It is critical to remember that social objectives involve the performance of specific social skills, which are comprised of component skills (i.e., subskills) and related skills. When you select an objective, you may need to teach the child all the component skills necessary to reach the objective (or at least those skills that he currently does not possess). Therefore, when selecting treatment objectives, clearly state the component or related skills that will be required to successfully perform the skill targeted in the treatment objective. Also remember to maintain a developmental perspective when determining what component skills will be required to reach an objective. For instance, the skills required to join in an activity with preschoolers are markedly different from the skills required to join in an activity with adolescents.

Below is an example of how to state the objective and then list the component skills that need to be taught in order for the child to successfully reach the objective. The following was written for a verbal adolescent with ASD.

Linking Social Objectives to Skills to Be Taught

Social Objective:
Scotty will join in interactions with peers during structured playgroup at least 5 times per session.

Skills needed to successfully reach objective (*skills to be taught*):

- Reading nonverbal and contextual cues
- Knowledge of social rules (i.e., when to join a conversation with two people without interrupting)
- Perspective taking
- Regulation of emotion
- Coordination of motor movements
- Timing
- Use of eye contact and other nonverbal expression
- Conversational planning

This structure may be incorporated into treatment plans and educational plans alike. A sample social skills instructional plan is presented on the following pages. The plan provides information on the targeted objectives and criteria, and skills that need to be taught to reach the objective.

Social Skills Instructional Plan (Sample)

Child's Name: ___Tommy___

Child's Age: ___9 years, 6 months___

Date of Services: ___March 1, 2006___ to ___May 31, 2006___

Type of Programming (individual, group, and/or classwide): ___Group___

Social Objective 1: ___Tommy will join in activities with peers at recess in 30% of observed intervals___

Skills needed to successfully reach objective (Skills to be taught):

___Reading Nonverbal Cues___

___Knowledge of Social Rules___

___Personal Space___

___Inferring the Interests of Peers___

___Coordination of Motor Movements___

___Timing of Initiation___

___Conversational Planning___

___Perspective Taking___

(*Note:* These skills will vary based on the needs/skills of the target child)

Social Objective 2: ___Tommy will respond to the social initiations of peers during classroom free-play activity in 50% of observed intervals___

Skills needed to successfully reach objective (Skills to be taught):

  Knowledge of Social Rules

  Timing of Social Response

  Use of Eye-COntact

  Prosody/Tone of Voice

  Reciprocity

(*Note:* Notice that many of these skills are listed under Social Objective 1 and 3 because these are considered foundational, or pivotal skills. That is, they are skills that are necessary for successful completion of many other skills. These are important skills to target.)

Social Objective 3: Tommy will ask one question about other people during conversations in 25% of observed conversations

Skills needed to successfully reach objective (Skills to be taught):

  Inferring the Interest of Others

  Perspective Taking

  Knowledge of Social Rules

  Prosody/Tone of Voice

  Coordination of Motor Movements

  Personal Space

  Use of Eye Contact

  Reciprocity

(A blank form is included in the Appendix.) (See Chapter 8 and Chapter 9 for information on social skill strategies that can be used to teach these skills and many others.)

Final Thoughts on Educational and Treatment Objectives

I realize that not all readers of this book work in educational settings that require them to write IEP objectives. However, best practices dictate that those of us in clinical settings establish clear and measurable treatment objectives that serve as our mechanism for accountability. These objectives also allow us to communicate to parents our goals for the intervention, and to demonstrate to parents (and insurance companies!) intervention progress.

Additional assistance in writing social objectives and reframing identified problems into teachable skills may be found in the items of the Autism Social Skills Profile (ASSP) (see pages 73-77). These items represent a large collection of social skills that could be taught to children with ASD. And even more important, most of the items have already been reframed into teachable skills. If an item has been decided to be particularly problematic, simply select it as a treatment or educational objective, modifying it as necessary to fit the specific needs of the child. In situations where the child has many critical skill deficits, select skills that provide the foundation for other skills, such as nonverbal communication skills and perspective taking.

A thorough social skill assessment allows parents and professionals to identify the critical skills that are hindering the child's social performance. Most important, the assessment helps us identify the skills that the child will need to be successful socially. Identification of targeted skills leads directly to the development of social objectives. That is, the social skills that we will teach to the child as part of the social skills program.

After the social skills assessment is complete, and you have identified the three to five objectives to be targeted, the next step is to determine whether the deficits can be attributed to a skill acquisition deficit or a performance deficit.

- *The social skills assessment consists of the following four components: general interview of social performance, problem identification and analysis interview, observation of social functioning, and rating forms.*

- *Whereas social goals concentrate on building new skills and represent long-term learning, social objectives define short-term behaviors and describe specific levels of performance. Objectives should be connected to the stated goals and linked directly to the intervention strategies selected.*

- *Objective criteria that are realistic and meaningful to the child should be selected. Criteria should be based on the child's present level of performance and should be updated continually based on the child's progress.*

- *In developing social objectives, it is imperative to reframe "problems" into positive, teachable skills.*

- *Three to five social objectives are sufficient per three-month quarter. This will allow parents and professionals to better focus their efforts on critical skill deficits, and to also target the component skills that will needed to successfully reach the social objective.*

DiStiNGuiShiNG BetWeeN SKiLL AcquiSitioN DeFicitS aNd PerForMaNce DeFicitS

6

After a thorough assessment of the child's social functioning and after identifying the skills that we will teach, it is imperative to determine whether the three to five social skill deficits (and component skills) you have targeted (see Chapter 5) are the result of skill acquisition deficits or performance deficits (Elliott & Gresham, 1991). *The success of your social skills program hinges on your ability to distinguish between skill acquisition deficits and performance deficits.* This chapter will explain why.

A ***skill acquisition deficit*** refers to the absence of a particular skill or behavior. For example, a child with ASD may not know how to effectively initiate a conversation with another person; therefore, he/she often fails to initiate conversations. If we want this child to initiate conversations with peers, we need to teach the necessary skills to do so.

A performance deficit refers to a skill or behavior that is present, but not demonstrated or performed. To use the same example, a child may have the skill (or ability) to initiate a conversation but, for some reason, does not initiate conversation with others. In this case, if we want the child to initiate conversations we would not need to teach the child to do so (since she already has the skill). Instead, we would need to address the factor that is impeding performance of the skill, such as motivation, anxiety, sensory sensitivities, etc. (See Factors Affecting Performance on page 107.)

Too often, social skill deficits and inappropriate behaviors are incorrectly conceptualized as performance deficits. That is, we tend to assume that when a child does not perform a behavior, it is the result of refusal or lack of motivation. In other words, we assume that the child who does not initiate interactions with peers has the ability to initiate, but does not want to initiate (performance deficit).

In many cases, this is a faulty assumption. In my experience, the vast majority of social skill deficits in individuals with ASD can be attributed to skill acquisition deficits. That is, children with ASD are not performing socially because they lack the necessary skills to perform socially – not because they do not want to be social or refuse to be social. Therefore, it is essential to focus on skill development when implementing social skills instruction.

A Note of Caution: *When we are dealing with movement-based skills and behaviors (as we are with social interaction skills), being able to say how to perform the skill or behavior does not represent successful skill acquisition. One must be able to do the skill or behavior.*

Let's take learning to drive a car with a stick shift as an example. A person who has never driven a car with a stick shift might be able to recite the necessary steps to successfully manipulate the clutch and stick shift ("depress clutch with left foot, slowly maneuver stick into appropriate gear, slowly release clutch pedal with left foot while gently depressing gas pedal with right foot"). Nothing to it, right? But does this person have the requisite skills to drive a car with a stick shift? Absolutely not. In this case, she will not acquire the skills nec-

essary to drive the car until she actually sits behind the wheel and coordinates the movement of the clutch with the movement of the stick shift and the gas pedal (without repeatedly stalling the engine). The same concept should be applied to social interaction skills. Simply saying how to interact with peers does not represent skill acquisition.

Type of Skill Deficit	Definition
Skill acquisition deficit	Child does not possess skill; therefore, child cannot successfully perform the skill
Performance deficit	Child possesses the skill but does not perform the skill

A Bridge to Intervention Strategies

The ultimate benefit of using a skill acquisition/performance deficit dichotomy is that it guides the selection of intervention strategies. That is, you would not want to deliver an intervention designed to enhance performance, if the child was mainly experiencing a skill acquisition deficit.

For instance, if Tommy has not mastered the skill of hitting a baseball (skill acquisition deficit), all the reinforcement in the world (including pizza) will not help Tommy hit the ball during a game. If we want him to be a skilled hitter, and experience success on the playing field, we need to provide Tommy additional instruction on the mechanics of hitting a baseball. In contrast, if Tommy does have sufficient hitting skills but lacks the motivation to "do his best," then the reward of cheese and pepperoni may be all he needs to excel on the playing field.

The same is true for social skills. If we want a child with skill acquisition deficits to be socially fluent, we need to deliver effective social skills instruction. My early work, and subsequent failure, with one child illustrates this point well.

Performance vs. Acquisition

Todd was an 11-year-old with ASD who frequently engaged in socially inappropriate behavior (inappropriate touching, name calling, etc.). He had no friends, but desperately wanted to develop friendships.

I was asked to observe the child and make programming recommendations. During my observation I conducted a functional behavior assessment. (A functional behavior assessment is commonly used for the purpose of figuring out the function of the problem behavior; that is, why the behavior is occurring.) During the playground observation, Todd ran into the girls' bathroom. As he ran in, about a dozen girls ran out screaming and giggling, followed by Todd who was doing the same. It was a gleeful moment for all involved, save for the two or three playground supervisors, who were horrified at this "despicable" act. Todd was immediately taken to the principal's office.

The observation was over, but I had enough information to conclude that the function of the problem behavior was peer attention. This was also congruent with information from the parent and teacher interviews. That is, Todd was engaging in inappropriate social behaviors to gain peer attention.

As a result, the intervention that I developed focused on providing Todd with ample opportunities to gain peer attention during the course of the day through the use of structured playgroups. Each day, Todd had the opportunity to invite two friends to play games with him for 10-15 minutes. The thought was that if we could give Todd ample opportunity to satisfy his craving for peer attention, he would not have any need to engage in inappropriate behaviors to gain their attention. The intervention also focused on providing frequent reinforcement for appropriate behavior.

Well, guess what happened to my brilliant intervention? It failed miserably! In the structured playgroup, Todd engaged in all the inappropriate behaviors that I mentioned previously, touching, name calling, and many others. But it wasn't Todd's fault; it was mine. I set him up for failure. I provided him with a social opportunity, but didn't teach him the skills to be successful with that opportunity. My intervention was designed to enhance performance, but it should have been focused on teaching skills. If I wanted Todd to be socially appropriate with peers, I should have taught him the skill(s) to act appropriately. It is a mistake that I will not make again.

Type of Skill Deficit	Focus of Intervention
Skill acquisition deficit	Promote acquisition of new skills (teach skills!)
Performance deficit	Enhance performance of existing skills (remove barriers that impede performance)

Skills Deficit vs. Intervention

We often make the mistake of conceptualizing skills as being either present or not present. We can either initiate conversations, or we can't initiate conversations. We can either throw a baseball, or we can't throw a baseball. Unfortunately, this conceptualization is not consistent with what we know about movement-based skills, including social interaction skills. Movement-based skills fall along a continuum from novice to mastery. In other words, our ability to initiate conversations and throw baseballs may range from "novice" to "mastery." Those on the novice end of the continuum will require concentrated skill instruction, whereas those at the mastery end will likely require less instruction, but continued opportunities for performance enhancement.

Skill Acquisition: From Novice to Mastery

I bet you can think of many skills or behaviors that you can do at a basic or novice level, or that you have done in the past, that you wouldn't think of performing in public without additional instruction and practice. Ever learn a new dance? Perhaps you were dragged on the dance floor to take part in a line-dance at a wedding? After you "learned" the sequence of dance steps, it may have taken you some time before you mastered the dance routine well enough to perform the dance fluently and independently (i.e., without looking at the feet of those around you or repeating the dance steps in your head). Perhaps you performed the same dance once or twice at other weddings. Even so, I bet you would need a bit more instruction and practice before appearing on *Dance Fever*!

Novice

Intermediate

Mastery

Social performance is no different. Social skill acquisition cannot be adequately explained by a "present" or "not present" dichotomy. Instead it should be viewed as a continuum progressing from novice to mastery (or automaticity).

As discussed in Chapter 2, the goal of procedural learning (including social interaction skills) is to achieve a level of automaticity. The progression from novice to mastery proceeds through three stages (adapted from Anderson, 1982; Fitts, 1964).

In the first stage, the **Novice Stage**, performers require a great deal of cognitive effort and attention to complete a task. They are attempting to recall rules, task sequences, and other factual information necessary to complete the task. Novice learners are vulnerable to distraction and require additional assistance to complete the task in the form of memory cues and prompts. Novice performers make frequent errors and complete tasks slowly.

In the second stage, the **Intermediate Stage**, the learner becomes more independent with the task, but still needs a great deal of cognitive energy to complete it. The learner may verbalize the sequence to herself or hesitate as she attempts to recall additional steps. Learners at the Intermediate Stage perform inconsistently, although they are making fewer errors than novice learners. Task fluency (time to complete tasks) also improves compared to the novice performer. Both novice and intermediate performers require instant feedback regarding their performance.

During, the third stage, **Mastery Stage**, learners finally achieve automaticity, completing tasks with little or no cognitive energy, requiring very little attention to the task. This allows them to multitask, or perform multiple tasks simultaneously. Further, at this stage learners no longer hesitate during performance of a skill/behavior to remember task sequences and details and, as a result, task fluency improves dramatically. Performances are typically errorless at this stage and external feedback is no longer necessary. In addition, mastery learners are able to perform the skill across various settings and persons. While they may still be affected by external distractions, they are better able than novice and intermediate learners to adapt their performances to specific environmental demands (noisy room, large audience, technical difficulties, etc.). Finally, tasks that required a series of sequences to complete at the novice and intermediate stage become one fluid process at the mastery stage. Once mastery or automaticity of skills is achieved, we can shift our focus from skill instruction (skill acquisition) to performance enhancement. It also provides an opportunity to teach new or more advanced skills, and to facilitate the transfer of skills across other settings and persons.

Stage of Learning	Characteristics of Learner
Novice	1. Exerts a great deal of cognitive effort to complete task 2. Vulnerable to distraction 3. Requires assistance to complete task 4. Makes frequent errors 5. Completes tasks slowly
Intermediate	1. Becomes more independent but still requires a great deal of cognitive effort to complete 2. May hesitate between steps of the task, as she attempts to recall the procedure 3. Performs tasks inconsistently 4. Makes fewer errors than novice learners; fluency is increased 5. Requires instant feedback on task performance
Mastery	1. Completes tasks independently with little cognitive energy 2. Is able to complete multiple tasks at the same time 3. Does not hesitate between steps of a task 4. Fluency is significantly increased 5. Typically performs errorlessly 6. Able to complete tasks across various settings and persons 7. Adapts performances to environmental demands

Stages of Skill Acquisition

Even accomplished performers continue to learn new skills and master previously learned ones. For example, Olympic gymnasts spend countless hours perfecting their craft, developing their skills, and moving from one level of mastery to the next. Skills that are mastered may or may not require additional instruction (skill acquisition) to perform, but they will probably require continual practice (performance enhancement).

Take your swimming skills, for instance. Most of us know "how to" swim – at least well enough to keep from sinking like a bag of cement. But can you swim well? If not, what would you need to be able to swim better? Practice might help, but if your stroke was flawed (that is, if you were a dog paddler!), you would just be practicing a bad technique. Although you might turn into one fast dog paddler, a better intervention would be to pair additional practice with instruction; that is, to teach you better swimming techniques. And if your swimming instructor is competent, she would begin instruction at your level of need. That is, instead of spending a week teaching you about basic water safety or how to float on your back, she would begin with skills that you need the most work on.

Social performance falls on a similar continuum of mastery. A child may possess the basic skills to initiate an interaction with peers, but may do so poorly and awkwardly. Although the child possesses a basic component of social initiation, she does not possess this social skill at a level of mastery. Therefore, we would still consider this a skill acquisition deficit because she will require additional instruction to initiate successfully. That is, if we want her to perform the skill successfully, we need to continue to teach her how to perform the skill better. We also need to provide her ample time to practice and perfect the skill, just like an Olympic gymnast.

Some professionals who have written about skill acquisition deficits versus performance deficits categorize the two types of deficits as "Can't Do" (skill acquisition deficits) and "Won't Do" (performance deficits). Some have suggested that providing ample reinforcement is sufficient to enhance the performance of those exhibiting performance deficits. While I have used this terminology myself in the past, I no longer do so because of what the term "Won't Do" communicates.

What do you think of when you hear "Won't do?" When I hear "won't do," I think of willful disobedience. I think of skills that the child is refusing to perform because of stubbornness or lack of motivation. However, experience has demonstrated to me that lack of motivation is just one of many factors that impact our ability to perform skills and behaviors – even those we have already mastered. There are many behaviors that we have the ability to perform, and even the motivation to perform, but for some reason fail miserably at actually performing. In fact, sometimes when motivation to perform a behavior is at its highest, we perform at our lowest. Those of us who have ever made fools of ourselves on first dates know this well.

Below is a description of several factors that may affect the social performance of individuals with ASD, even after they have reached a level of mastery and autonomy with the skill. Many of these factors are closely related and can impact each other. For instance, sensory sensitivities can lead to heightened anxiety, which may lead to decreased motivation to participate in social situations.

**Factors Affecting
Social Performance**

- Motivation
- Sensory Sensitivities
- Anxiety
- Attention and Impulsivity
- Memory
- Self-Efficacy
- Movement Differences

As you read this section, continually think about the implications for social skills intervention. For instance, if we determine that the child is having difficulties joining in activities with peers, and that this difficulty can be attributed to a performance deficit (i.e., he has the ability to join in, but fails to do so), we can examine the following factors to determine what factor is contributing to this performance deficit. Furthermore, once we determine the factor (or factors) contributing to the performance deficit, we can (and should) select intervention strategies that address this factor directly. For example, if we determine that the child's joining-in difficulties are a result of anxiety, our intervention would focus on alleviating the anxiety that is negatively impacting his ability to join in activities with peers.

Motivation

Although motivation is not the sole factor contributing to lack of performance, it is an important factor to consider. There are many things that we have the ability to do, but simply do not do because we do not want to do them – for many of us, going to the gym comes to mind! Children who lack motivation to interact socially with their peers will likely avoid interactions with peers. Even if we teach these children the skills to interact effectively with others, they still may not interact with others. Thus, in addition to skill instruction, children need to be motivated to interact with peers.

A number of factors may diminish a child's motivation to interact with other children. For example, children who have experienced intense and prolonged peer failure and rejection will sooner or later begin to dread and even avoid social interactions with peers. Another reason why children with ASD lack motivation to interact with peers is that they lack common interests. They may be uninterested in the games and activities other children play and, therefore, have no interest in joining them.

Children with a history of negative peer relationships and peer failure need to be exposed to the positive aspects of peer relationships. Structured playgroups and peer awareness training that promotes a climate of acceptance and understanding among peers is a good start. Playgroups can be structured around shared or similar interests in an effort to pique the interest of the child with ASD. If all else fails, provide copious amounts of reinforcement (verbal praise, a favorite toy, a desired activity) contingent upon the child interacting (or attempting to interact) with peers.

Some might consider this type of delivery of reinforcement as bribery. I don't care what we call it as long as it achieves its desired result. In this case the desired result is facilitating a positive interaction between the child with ASD and her peers – a result that may, in the future, increase her intrinsic motivation to interact with peers. (See Chapter 9 for more information on reinforcing social performance.)

Sensory Sensitivities

Sensory issues can significantly impact social interactions by leading to social withdrawal, avoidance, and diminished social performance. Common sensory sensitivities in individuals with ASD include all five senses (sound, smell, taste, touch, and sight). For example, individuals who are hypersensitive to loud noises may avoid social settings where loud noises are likely to occur, such as school cafeterias, playgrounds, or sporting events. One young man I worked with was highly sensitive to smells, in particular women's perfumes. He spent most of his time in school avoiding those who wore these caustic toiletries. You can imagine how difficult it was for him to participate in social activities once he got to high school.

Sensory sensitivities may also diminish social performances by negatively affecting the child's ability to concentrate. The child may attend to the sensory stimuli, such as a ticking clock, wallpaper patterns, or the sound of another person's voice, and thus fail to read the relevant cues of the social interaction (nonverbal cues, timing and topic of the conversations, etc.). Often the sensory stimulation can so completely overwhelm the child who is engaged in an interaction that he abruptly terminates the interaction and flees the environment.

The clinical implications in this case would be to address the sensory sensitivities through sensory integration, self-relaxation, or environmental modifications, rather than to teach social skills that the child may already have in his behavioral repertoire. (See Chapter 9 for more information on modifying the environment.)

Anxiety

Anxiety can wreak havoc on our brains and bodies, and consequently our performances. The impact is often a matter of degree and severity. At mild to moderate levels, anxiety may serve as an adaptive response to external stressors in a person's life. Indeed, a moderate amount of anxiety is often an effective stimulus for motivating a person to withdraw from a harmful event, and may improve cognitive efficiency by increasing alertness. However, at high levels anxiety can be debilitating, significantly diminishing behavioral performance and cognitive processing. This type of negative impact on social performance is often experienced by those who have a speaking phobia, or fear of speaking. Anxiety of speaking can turn an otherwise eloquent and articulate speaker into a stammering, nervous wreck.

Those with public speaking fears can relate to this. The simple act of introducing yourself to a group of strangers may provoke enough fear and anxiety to make you virtually forget your own name! In this case, your speaking performance is not being impacted by your speaking skills, but by your anxiety. Therefore, the intervention would focus on alleviating your anxiety, not on teaching you how to introduce yourself.

The same is true for children with ASD. If our assessment determines high levels of social anxiety, we need to examine how this anxiety is impacting the child's social performance, and implement a plan to reduce anxiety. (See Chapter 2 and Chapter 3 for additional information on anxiety and ASD.)

Attention and Impulsivity

Attention and impulsivity also significantly impact various aspects of social performance. In particular, these factors impede social reciprocity and turn taking. Activities that involve turn taking, such as conversations and many social games, require that we stay alert and maintain attention to the task at hand. Perhaps your own attention has wandered in the middle of a conversation as you were listening to another person, or even worse, while you were speaking, causing you to lose your train of thought.

I see many children who have great difficulty playing turn-taking games because they cannot wait to take their turn. This results in a less than enjoyable experience for all involved. It also results in peers refusing to play games with these children in the future. Children who are impulsive also tend to repeatedly interrupt or talk over others during conversations. And they fail to plan their interaction strategies and purpose, resulting in interactions that appear haphazard and random.

It is not that these children need to be taught how to take turns or how to have a conversation (although both of these are possibilities that should be considered), what they need is an intervention (e.g., self-monitoring, self-regulation, or planning) that decreases their impulsivity and increases their attention to task.

Memory

Our social performance is also dependent upon our memory. I am not referring to memory of "how to do" something; I am referring to memory "to do" something. For instance, those of us who have locked our keys in our cars haven't forgotten "how to" take our keys out of the ignition prior to exiting. We have forgotten "to do" it.

To provide another example to illustrate this point, every Friday trash is picked up on my street. Every *other* Friday I drive away from my house, look in my rearview mirror, and see no trash can at the curb. Since my oldest son is only 3 years old as I write this, I am unable to blame him for this dereliction of duty. I am responsible for this chore. I haven't forgotten "how to" walk to our shed, grab the trash barrel, and wheel it to the curb. I've forgotten to do it! Furthermore, my failure to take the trash out would be considered a performance deficit as I clearly have the skills to do it. An intervention focusing on teaching me the specific skills involved in taking the trash out would be a waste of your time and mine. Instead, this performance deficit could be addressed by memory prompts and cues, or perhaps through organizational strategies (I am a disorganized wreck in the morning).

I see similar performance deficits in children with ASD. They may have developed the necessary skills to initiate an interaction with peers, but they forget to do so. They may know how to read the nonverbal cues of others, but forget to do so during the interaction. Again, prompts are effective in such situations as are behavior repetitions.

Self-Efficacy

The social learning theorist Bandura defined self-efficacy as: "people's beliefs about their capabilities to produce designated levels of performance that exercise influence over events that affect their lives. Self-efficacy beliefs determine how people feel, think, motivate themselves and behave" (Bandura, 1994, p. 2).

Individuals with strong self-efficacy are confident and self-assured. They approach new and difficult situations with vigor and purpose, and view failure as temporary obstacles to their inevitable success. Individuals with low self-efficacy, in contrast, are often fearful of and avoid new and difficult situations. They give up easily when faced with challenges and, perhaps most troubling, they view task failure as confirmation of their personal shortcomings. Not surprisingly, they are prone to anxiety and depression.

Many of the children and adolescents with ASD I have met over the years have very low opinions of their social abilities, the product of many years of social failure and peer rejection. Low self-efficacy leads to performance deficits when individuals refuse, or are hesitant, to initiate social interactions because they are convinced that they will not be successful. And when you are convinced that you will fail – you *will* fail.

Although it is important to establish strong self-efficacy when teaching children with ASD social skills, it cannot be artificially manufactured. That is, we cannot give another person a strong sense of self. The person must develop positive perceptions of self internally. However, there are several things that we can do to facilitate the development of positive self-efficacy. Bandura suggests four strategies to positively influence a person's self-efficacy: Mastery Experiences, Modeling, Social Persuasion, and Stress Management – all of which are central components of the social skills model presented in this book.

Strategies That Enhance Self-Efficacy

- Mastery Experiences
- Modeling
- Social Persuasion
- Management

According to Bandura, the most effective way to create a strong sense of self is by experiencing personal success and accomplishment – **mastery experiences** – and avoiding failure (at least until a strong self-efficacy has been established). There is no substitute for the feeling of accomplishment and success. Unfortunately, when it comes to social experiences, children with ASD are more like the Chicago Cubs than the New York Yankees (sorry, Cubs fans!).

The second strategy proposed by Bandura to improve self-efficacy is to observe **successful models**. Bandura believed that modeling is most effective when the observer perceives similarities between herself and the model. In other words, the "hey, if she can do it, I can do it" phenomenon. Indeed, modeling is an effective strategy for teaching skills to children with ASD, and it is a centerpiece of the intervention strategies to be discussed later.

The third strategy suggested by Bandura is **social persuasion**. Social persuasion involves the encouragement we provide the child to try otherwise difficult tasks, and the positive feedback that we provide to point out the positive aspects of his performance. I am in many ways a cheerleader for the children I work with, and always one of their biggest fans. However, social persuasion cuts both ways. Those who have been told that they lack the ability to establish and develop friendships with peers are likely going to believe it.

The fourth strategy for improving self-efficacy is to help the person **manage anxious responses**. Individuals with low self-efficacy tend to view their heightened physiological responses (e.g., increased heart rate) as signs of poor performance whereas individuals with high self-efficacy view their heightened physiological arousal as a sign of alertness and energy. For the latter group, performance is enhanced by stress, and for the former, it is severely diminished. The implications for intervention are to teach children how to better recognize and understand their physiological responses, and thus, how to better regulate their responses to this stress.

Movement Differences

Four movement differences experienced by individuals with ASD are most salient for social functioning: starting, stopping, switching, and combining (Donnellan & Leary, 1995).

Starting has to do with initiating movements. To use the line dance example again, perhaps you still remember how to do the line-dance that you learned at a previous wedding, but can't seem to get yourself started. In this case, all you typically need is to see the first step or two of the dance and you are on your way. Ever forget how a song goes even though you know the words to it? I bet if I gave you the first word to the song, you would be able to sing the rest. Sometimes our procedural memories need just one simple prompt to get the engine running. Sometimes we just need the first word to the song.

Stopping involves terminating activities or tasks. An example would be those times when you get a song stuck in your head and can't get rid of it! As stated earlier, individuals with ASD have great difficulties terminating conversations and often need concrete cues to signal the end of the conversation.

Switching, another movement factor, involves transitioning from one thought, activity, or even emotion to another. Transitions tend to be difficult for children with ASD, and shifting topics in conversations is particularly problematic.

Combining, the final movement difference that affects social performance, involves processing multiple sensory inputs at once. For instance, looking *and* listening. It is not uncommon for an individual with ASD to tell us, "If I have to look at you, then I cannot listen you." Ever turn the volume of your car stereo down to look for a street sign? If so, you have experienced the movement difference of combining.

Great effort must be expended on distinguishing between a skill acquisition deficit and a performance deficit. Unfortunately, there are no tests, or test procedures that will tell you with 100% accuracy whether a given skill deficit is a skill acquisition or a performance deficit. Instead, we are required to use a problem-solving approach that tells us with some certainty what type of skill deficit we are dealing with and, consequently, what type of intervention strategy to select.

---

1. Does the child perform the skill across multiple settings and persons?

2. Does the child perform the skill without support or assistance?

3. Does the child perform the skill fluently and effortlessly?

4. Does the child perform the skill when reinforcement is provided?

5. Does the child perform the skill when environmental modifications are made?

A good rule of thumb is to ask, "Can the child perform the task with multiple persons (including peers) and across multiple settings (including unstructured settings)?" For instance, if the child only initiates interactions with Mom at home and not with his peers at school, view the initiation difficulty as a skill acquisition deficit.

I hear the statement frequently from school personnel, "The child interacts fine with me, but does not interact with other children, so it must be a performance deficit, right?" Not quite. In my experience, children with ASD tend to interact better and more easily with adults, because adults typically make it easy for them. The adults do most of the conversational "work."

To use a baseball analogy, just because Tommy can hit Dad's soft, underhand pitches at home, doesn't mean he has mastered the skill well enough to hit pitches thrown by his peers on the playing field. If Tommy struck out 30 times in a row

Distinguishing Between a Skill Acquisition Deficit and a Performance Deficit

Five Questions to Ask

Performance Across Settings and People

on the playing field with peers, would you call it a performance deficit? No! Even though Tommy can whack the tosses from Dad, he still needs to be taught the necessary skills to hit the pitches of peers. It is a skill acquisition deficit, and intervention strategies should be selected accordingly.

Sometimes adult interactions with children with ASD are similar to throwing a child a soft, underhand pitch. Although they are positive and enjoyable, they do not necessarily prepare the child for more difficult peer interactions. Children with ASD also tend to have greater difficulties interacting with peers in unstructured settings (the playground, cafeteria, etc.), compared to structured settings (the classroom, structured playgroups, etc.). For this reason, I require that the child be able to successfully exhibit the particular social skill in both structured and unstructured settings prior to deeming the skill "mastered."

Independent Performance

The second key distinction between a skill acquisition and a performance deficit is whether the child can consistently perform the skill or behavior independently; that is, without the need for continual adult prompting or assistance. When you identify specific skill deficits, ask the following questions. "Does the child perform the skill?" And "Does the child perform the skill *with* assistance?" For instance, the child may respond to the initiations of peers, but only if he is prompted by an adult to respond. Skills that can only be performed with prompts and assistance are considered to be at a novice level of performance and, thus, are classified as skill acquisition deficits. Some children occasionally exhibit a skill or behavior independently, but still typically require a prompt to perform it. This inconsistency is typical of the Intermediate Level, and is still classified as a skill acquisition deficit.

Fluency

Task fluency is another distinguishing factor between skill acquisition deficits and performance deficits. When individuals with performance deficits perform a task (for instance, when reinforcement is provided, or anxiety is eliminated), they are able to perform it fluently, with little effort. In contrast, those with skill acquisition deficits (who are at an Intermediate Stage of learning) may perform a task successfully, but do so slowly and with great effort. They appear "locked in" to the task at hand as the skill requires a great deal of concentration, or cognitive effort, for them to perform. They may also be unable to perform multiple tasks or skills at once, such as dribbling a basketball and at the same time asking another child to play with her; or completing a math assignment while asking another child if she can hang out with her at recess. This is the most difficult way to discern a skill acquisition from a performance deficit, so be cautious about how you interpret this information.

Reinforcement

Another strategy for distinguishing between a skill acquisition and a performance deficit is to provide copious amounts of reinforcement to the child for performing the skill or behavior. This is a very simple, yet effective strategy for determining whether the child's skill deficits are a result of lack of motivation. For instance, prior to beginning the structured playgroup, tell the child that if he "plays" with his peers (always use terminology that is appropriate for the child's developmental level), he will be allowed to select a preferred toy or sensory item from a preselected assortment of toys.

If the child interacts appropriately with peers during this time, you can be confident that he has the necessary skills to interact with peers and that, therefore, you are dealing with a performance deficit. If the child is still having difficulties interacting with peers, even after being "bribed" with a favorite toy, you can be confident that you are dealing with a skill acquisition deficit.

Environmental Modifications

The final strategy for distinguishing between a skill acquisition and performance deficit is to modify the social and physical environment. This is most easily accomplished in structured play settings, but can also be done in naturalistic settings. The goal is to remove those sensory stimuli that may be leading to diminished social performance, such as visual clutter and excessive noise. Modifying the environment may also include using fewer peer playmates and allowing more time for the child to initiate and respond to interactions.

Children who successfully exhibit social skills when the environment is modified will need an intervention that focuses on sensory needs, stress management, and environmental modifications.

Chapter Summary

Successful social programming is dependent upon our ability to distinguish between a skill acquisition deficit and a performance deficit. A skill acquisition deficit refers to the absence of a particular skill or behavior. A performance deficit refers to a skill or behavior that is present, but not performed.

- ◎ *The skill acquisition/performance deficit dichotomy guides the selection of intervention strategies. Some strategies are designed to promote skill acquisition, while others are designed to enhance performance. The key to successful social skills programming is to match the type of intervention strategies with the type of skill deficit.*

- ◎ *Acquisition of social skills proceeds on a continuum from novice to intermediate, to mastery.*

- ◎ *Social performance can be negatively impacted by several factors, even after the child has reached a level of mastery with a given skill. These factors include motivation, sensory sensitivities, anxiety, attention and impulsivity, memory, self-efficacy, and movement differences.*

Selecting Intervention Strategies

5-STEP MODEL

1. **Assess Social Functioning**

2. **Distinguish Between Skill Acquisition and Performance Deficits**

3. **Select Intervention Strategies**

   - **Strategies That Promote Skill Acquisition**

   - **Strategies That Enhance Performance**

4. **Implement Intervention**

5. **Evaluate and Monitor Progress**

This is the point where I share some sobering news: *There is no **single** intervention strategy that will teach the child with ASD to be successful socially!* But don't fret, several strategies can be used in combination to teach the child to be successful socially. The social skill strategies that I implement primarily come from a behavioral, cognitive, cognitive-behavioral, and social-learning theory perspective.

In the field of autism spectrum disorders, professionals sometimes spend so much time arguing about what path to take, and not to take, that we often leave parents confused and frustrated regarding available service options. In social skills instruction a multitude of effective intervention strategies can be used to enhance and foster social success for children with ASD. The trick is to select strategies that are most effective for a given child's needs. Interventions that work for one child may not work well with another child. I spend countless hours reviewing the social skills strategies and programs that are on the market, searching for strategies to add to my ever-expanding intervention tool chest. In reality, it is a notebook of strategies and ideas that I keep. I recommend that you do the same.

Matching Intervention Strategies With Type of Skill Deficit

Strategies That Promote Skill Acquisition	Strategies That Enhance Social Performance
• Thoughts, Feelings, and Interest Activities	• Reinforcement/ Contingency Strategies
• Reciprocal Intervention Strategies	• Gaming Skills
• Social Stories™	• Environmental Modifications
• Role-Playing/Behavioral Rehearsal	• Peer-Mediated Instruction
• Video Modeling	• Increased Social Opportunities/Live Practice
• Social Problem Solving and Social Rules	• Disability Awareness/Peer Support Strategies
• Self-Monitoring	• Priming Social Behavior
• Relaxation Techniques/ Emotional Regulation	• Self-Monitoring*
• Prompting Strategies*	• Relaxation Techniques/ Emotional Regulation*
• Interaction/Conversation Planning	• Prompting Strategies*
	• Video Modeling*
	• Social Stories*

* These strategies may be used to promote skill acquisition and to enhance performance. They are covered in Chapter 8, *Strategies That Promote Skill Acquisition.*

The social skills program presented in this book is meant to be flexible and malleable. The goal is to provide a conceptual framework that helps you to select and reject strategies with purpose and, most important, with a logical rationale.

For instance, does the strategy target the skill deficits identified in the social assessment? Does the strategy enhance performance? Does the strategy promote skill acquisition? Is there research to support its use? If not, what is your plan to evaluate its effectiveness with your child? Is it developmentally appropriate for your child? Is the strategy consistent with what you know about social performance? That is, does it promise to teach social interaction skills (initiation and reciprocity) exclusively through the use of worksheets, or does it involve movement, or behavioral practice?

Furthermore, do not limit social skills strategies to those that you read about in books and research articles. Social performance is dynamic, changing with every moment, whereas many prepackaged social skill strategies are rigid and static. I hope that after reading this book you will have the knowledge base and confidence to take advantage of "teachable moments" as they arise in the natural environment. You may even find yourself developing your own effective social skills strategies.

<table>
<tr><td>

- What specific social skills will be targeted?
- Does the strategy match the type of skill deficit (for each skill)?
- What is the child's developmental level (language and cognitive functioning)?
- Is the strategy supported by research?
- If the strategy is not supported by research, what is the rationale/logic for using it?
- What components of social interaction skills (i.e., thinking, feeling, doing) does the strategy address?

</td><td>

Questions to Answer When Selecting Intervention Strategies

</td></tr>
</table>

Because of space limitations, I have included only strategies that I have found to be most effective for children with ASD in my own practice and research. Although this section will not cover every social skill strategy available, it is comprehensive enough to satisfy the pragmatic cravings of the most practical readers. My preference is to use intervention strategies that are supported by empirical research. However, like any good teacher (which I aspire to be some day), I have developed many strategies out of sheer necessity to meet the needs of my clients. Thus, some of the strategies have not yet been validated via empirical research. In such cases, I will provide a logical rationale for why I use these untested strategies, and in particular, why I believe they are useful for children with ASD.

The strategies presented in the following two chapters are designed to address either specific skill acquisition deficits (Chapter 8) or performance deficits (Chapter 9). However, some of the strategies (e.g., video self-modeling, Social Stories, and prompting) work equally well in addressing both performance deficits and skill acquisition deficits. Therefore, strategies that can be used to promote skill acquisition *and* enhance social performance are listed in both columns in the table on page 120. In addition, some of strategies may be used simultaneously with other intervention strategies, or are linked to other intervention strategies. For instance, I often use prompting strategies as the child is participating in a role-playing procedure. Or, quite commonly I use a social problem-solving technique while the child is watching himself on video (video self-modeling). In each case, suggestions for combining strategies are provided.

More space has been devoted to strategies that promote acquisition of skills. This is primarily because performance enhancement strategies, such as behavior contracts, token economies, and environmental modifications, have been covered extensively in other texts; especially those addressing behavior management (see Alberto & Troutman, 2006). Skill acquisition strategies, on the other hand, have been largely ignored in the literature. Nevertheless, I will describe performance enhancement strategies that will make a valuable addition to your social skills program.

Social Accommodation vs. Social Assimilation

Prior to selecting intervention strategies, it is important to consider the concepts of social accommodation and social assimilation. *Accommodation*, as it relates to social skills instruction, refers to the act of modifying the physical or social environment to promote positive social interactions. Examples include training peer mentors to interact with the child throughout the school day, conducting autism awareness training or sensitivity training for classmates, and signing the child up for various group activities, such as Little League, Boy or Girl Scouts, and so on. Whereas accommodation addresses changes in the environment, *assimilation* focuses on changes in the child. Specifically, it refers to instruction that facilitates skill development that allows the child to be more successful in social interactions. By their nature, social accommodations enhance social performance, and social assimilation involves promoting skill acquisition.

The key to a successful social skills training program is to address both accommodation and assimilation. For instance, one family that I worked with did a wonderful job of structuring playgroups for their child and keeping him active in social activities. However, they were becoming increasingly frustrated because their son was not making friends and continued to experience negative peer interactions. The problem was that they were putting the cart before the horse. They provided their child with ample opportunity to interact with others, but they weren't providing him with the skills necessary to be successful in those interactions.

Similarly, providing skill instruction (assimilation) without modifying the environment to be more accepting of the child with ASD also sets the child up for failure. This happens the moment an eager child with ASD tries out a newly learned skill on a group of non-accepting peers. The key is to teach skills *and* modify the environment.

Finding the Balance

The balance between accommodation and assimilation is determined by the child's developmental skill levels. For instance, children with lower developmental skill levels (for instance, severe cognitive difficulties and limited language) require a higher level of social accommodations to promote meaningful social relationships. That is, instead of spending hours trying to teach a nonverbal child how to initiate and maintain conversations, you would teach her how to use her augmentative communication system to join in activities with peers. In this case, a high level of social accommodations is required to ensure that peers are aware of the augmentative system and make an effort to include the child in social activities (via peer training and disability awareness training).

Please note that I am not suggesting that children with more significant disabilities do not need social skills programming or want meaningful social relationships. They absolutely do! However, the focus of the intervention has to be modified (i.e., more social accommodations) to promote their social success. Keep these concepts in mind as you implement the intervention strategies.

Strategies That Promote Skill Acquisition

5-STEP MODEL

1. Assess Social Functioning

2. Distinguish Between Skill Acquisition and Performance Deficits

3. **Select Intervention Strategies**

   ■ **Strategies That Promote Skill Acquisition**

   ■ Strategies That Enhance Performance

4. Implement Intervention

5. Evaluate and Monitor Progress

As stated in Tenet #2, and reiterated throughout, *if we want children to be successful socially, we must teach them the skills to be successful.* For example, if we want a child to join in interactions with peers, we must teach him how to join in. And if we want a child to maintain a reciprocal conversation, we must teach him how to maintain a reciprocal conversation. Sounds simple, doesn't it?

Unfortunately, we often apply faulty logic to our social skills programming. That is, children are reinforced for successful social interactions, but not taught the skills to interact socially. This simply sets the child up for failure. I have heard professionals insist that they were teaching social skills when in reality they were enhancing performance of existing skills via a behavior contract or other reinforcement system. Unfortunately, they were attempting to enhance the performance of a skill that did not exist.

The use of the skill acquisition deficit and performance deficit dichotomy typically helps these professionals see the errors of their ways – it did for me!

This chapter presents a broad collection of strategies designed to promote skill acquisition in children and adolescents with ASD. In most cases, I provide a basic structure or guidelines for using the strategy. The guidelines represent how I "typically" use the strategy, but as you are well aware, not all children with ASD are created equal. Therefore, I encourage you to modify the strategies to meet the individual needs of your child or client.

✔ Thoughts, Feelings, and Interest Activities

✔ Reciprocal Interaction Strategies

✔ Social Stories™

✔ Role Playing/Behavioral Rehearsal

✔ Video Modeling

✔ Social Problem Solving and Social Rules

✔ Self-Monitoring

✔ Relaxation Techniques/Emotional Regulation

✔ Prompting Strategies

✔ Interaction/Conversation Planning

Thoughts, Feelings, and Interests

Social Skills to Teach: Reading nonverbal cues, taking another person's perspective, inferring the interests of others, initiating interactions

This category includes a broad group of intervention strategies that address recognizing and understanding the emotions, thoughts, and interests of others. Specific strategies include:

- Use of Pictures and Videos to Read Emotions

- Thought Bubble Activity

- If-Then Statements

- Interest Inventory

- Mind Reading Worksheets

- Mind Reading Computer Programs

When I start working with a child, I typically devote the first session to ascertaining his or her ability to recognize and understand the feelings and thoughts of self and others, as this is essential to successful social interactions. For instance, we continually modify our behavior based on the nonverbal feedback we receive from others. We may elaborate on a story if the other person is smiling, looking on intently, or showing other signs of interest. On the other hand, if the other person repeatedly looks at her watch, sighs, or appears otherwise disinterested, we may cut the story short.

The ability to recognize and understand the feelings and thoughts of others is an area of weakness for many individuals with ASD. The good news is that children with ASD can be taught to read emotions and to take another person's perspective (Charlop-Christy & Daneshvar, 2003; Ozonoff & Miller, 1995; Stafford, 2000).

Effectively reading nonverbal behaviors is essential to reading emotions and being able to take another person's perspective. As mentioned, individuals with ASD often have difficulty recognizing and understanding these nonverbal cues. Consequently, they are less able to modify their behavior to meet the emotional and cognitive needs of others. Nonverbal cues reveal not only what the other person is feeling, but also what she is thinking.

Some children with ASD have no problems identifying and recognizing nonverbal cues – IF they actually look for them. The problem is that they either forget to look for nonverbal cues or fail to understand the importance of looking for them (because they have not been taught to do so). These children will require additional instruction to teach them the social rule(s) for how and when to look for nonverbal cues (see Social Problem Solving and Social Rules on page 153).

Many programs and resources have been designed specifically to teach children with ASD how to recognize nonverbal cues and how to take another person's perspective. I will present some of those programs in the following section. I will also present strategies that are not commercially available and, therefore, will require no additional purchase on your part to implement.

Though the entry level and progression of skills will vary from child to child, thinking, feeling, and interest activities typically progress in a systematic fashion. I recommend the following order.

Steps to Follow in Teaching Thoughts, Feelings, and Interests

1. Identify feelings based on facial expressions.

2. Identify feelings based on body language/gestures.

3. Identify feelings based on contextual cues (e.g., "How do you think the boy is feeling?").

4. Understand why a person is feeling a particular emotion (e.g., "why is the boy feeling sad?").

5. Identify the interests of others.

6. Identify the thoughts of others.

7. Infer the thoughts and interests of others based on available contextual cues (e.g., "what might he be thinking?" or "what might she like to do?").

Use of Pictures and Videos to Read Emotions

The most basic thought and feeling activity involves showing the child pictures of people exhibiting various emotions. Pictures can range from showing basic emotions such as happy, sad, angry, or scared, to more complicated emotions such as embarrassed, ashamed, nervous, or incredulous. Begin by asking the child to point to an emotion (i.e., "point to happy"), then ask the child to identify what the character is feeling (i.e., "how is he feeling?").

Many of the children I work with seem to pick up the ability

to identify emotions quite easily. When they do, it is time to move on to more advanced instructional strategies, such as teaching them to understand the meaning or "why" behind emotions. This requires the child to make inferences based on the context and cues provided in the picture. That is, based on the information in the picture, ask "why is the child sad?" The pictures should portray characters participating in various social situations and exhibiting various facial expressions or other nonverbal expressions of emotion.

You may cut pictures out of magazines, or download and print them from the Internet. You may also use illustrations from children's books, which are typically rich in emotional content and contextual cues.

Once mastery is achieved on the pictures, move to video footage of social situations. You can use the same procedure as for the pictures, only this time the child is making inferences based on dynamic social cues. Simply ask the child to identify what the characters in the video are feeling and why they are feeling that way. When the scenario moves too quickly for the child, press pause, and ask the question with a still frame. (Make sure your machine has a clear picture when on pause.)

Tone of voice is a source of emotional content that is often overlooked, and audio or video recordings may be used to recognize emotions in people's voices. The use of pictures and videos for inferring emotions can also be used in conjunction with social problem solving (see Social Problem Solving and Social Rules on page 153).

Note:

Since the world is three-dimensional, unlike pictures and videos, it is imperative to provide instruction on how to read nonverbal cues in natural settings. During the course of the day as opportunities present themselves, parents and teachers should routinely ask the child with ASD to identify how other children are feeling. Begin with obvious displays of emotion (e.g., a 2-year-old throwing a tantrum), then move to more subtle displays of emotion (e.g., an older child sulking or pouting).

Thought Bubble Activity

A thought bubble activity is an effective strategy for teaching children with ASD to infer the thoughts, or to take the perspective, of another person (Wellman et al., 2002). In this activity, children with ASD are asked to fill in the "thought bubble" (which represents what the person is thinking) of another person. Thought bubbles can be used with cartoon drawings or pictures of people. The idea is to teach the child that we can often determine what others are thinking by listening to what they are saying, or by watching what they are doing. For instance, if Michael is talking about baseball, he is probably thinking about baseball as well. Read statements (similar to the one just described) to the child and ask her to fill in the thought bubble for the character. For instance, for the example above, the child would write the word "baseball" in a thought bubble to describe what Michael was thinking.

If-Then Statements

The ability to read nonverbal (and verbal) cues is also essential to identifying the interests of others. I recommend using If-Then statements to teach the child to infer the interests of others. If-Then statements are effective for children with ASD primarily because they present information in a logical and linear fashion. For instance, *if* Michael is talking about baseball and wearing a New York Yankees baseball shirt, *then* he probably likes baseball. In addition, if the child can recognize feeling in the tone of another person's voice, he may be able to infer that *if* Michael's voice sounds excited when he talks about dinosaurs, *then* he probably likes dinosaurs.

Use pictures, videos, and real-life examples (other children in the class) as the primary focus of interest activities. Recognizing the interests of others is extremely important for initiating interactions, and ultimately developing friendships. That is, once the child knows that Michael likes baseball, he could then initiate an interaction with something as simple as asking, "Do you like the Yankees?"

An interest inventory is another way to help children use the interests of others to initiate conversations. An interest inventory requires the child to brainstorm possible interests of peers. The child begins by selecting peers she would like to make friends with. She is then asked to list all the things that she thinks the selected peer might be interested in. If-Then statements are used to facilitate the generation of interests. These interests are then used as potential conversational topics. That is, the child with ASD can use these topics to initiate conversations with the selected peer. The interest inventory may be used in conjunction with the Conversation Map discussed on page 179.

Child's Name: Danny

Interests (toys or games that he/she likes play with, or things that he/she likes to do):

1. Dinosaurs

2. Power Rangers

3. Basketball

4. Trains

Howlin, Baron-Cohen, and Hadwin's book *Teaching Children with Autism to Mind-Read* (1998) offers helpful information and resources to add to your intervention "tool chest." The worksheets and activities in this book require the child to infer emotions, take another person's perspective, and infer the interests of others. I find them most suitable for elementary-aged children.

One worksheet is my favorite because it seems to create an "aha" experience with many of my clients. The worksheet depicts a faceless child holding an ice cream cone. The caption on the picture reads, "*Alan's daddy buys him a chocolate ice cream.*" The child is then asked, "*How will Alan feel when his daddy buys him an ice cream?*"

Emotion Question Worksheet

Teacher: Describe the picture to the child and ask the child either to *say* how the person in the story feels, or to *point* to one of the emotion faces below.

Alan's daddy buys him a chocolate ice-cream cone.

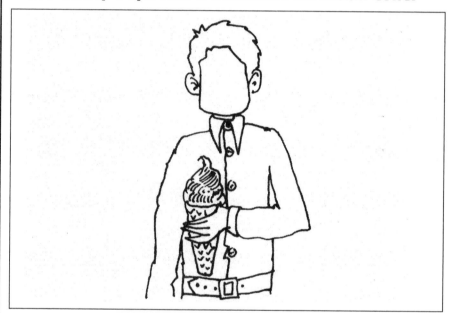

Emotion Question: How will Alan feel when daddy buys him an ice-cream cone. Prompt – will he feel happy/sad/angry/afraid?

Justification Question: Why will he feel happy/sad/angry/afraid?

From *Teaching Children With Autism to Mind-Read. A Practical Guide* by P. Howlin, S. Baron-Cohen, & J. Hadwin, p. 46. Copyright 1998. New York: John Wiley & Sons. Reprinted with permission.

The overwhelming majority of children with ASD who do NOT like chocolate ice cream will respond with "sad" or "angry." This is where it gets good. My response to the child is, "But ALAN (accentuating the name Alan and pointing to his picture) likes chocolate ice cream. How will ALAN feel when HE gets a chocolate ice cream?" This is when the aha experience happens – the look on the child's face is unmistakable. The response is typically, "Oh, Alan will be happy."

This one activity has required the child to:

- infer emotion

- take another person's perspective

- infer the interests of others

- integrate all three of these skills – most important of all

Mind Reading Computer Programs

Several computer programs address both emotions and perspective-taking abilities. My favorite is *Mind Reading: An Interactive Guide to Emotions* developed by Simon Baron-Cohen (2004). The program contains three areas to teach children how to recognize the thoughts and emotions of others, "emotions library," "learning center," and "game zone."

The emotions library contains an extensive collection of video clips depicting actors (children and adults) displaying a variety of emotions organized into a helpful collection of "emotion groups."

The learning center is divided into three sections. One section teaches the child about the various emotion groups by providing a pictorial and video example. This section also provides a video vignette depicting an actor displaying the emotion in a social setting. The other two sections in the learning center provide lessons and quizzes that can be tailored to match the child's individual needs and skill level. As the child progresses, he is presented with more challenging lessons.

The "game zone," the third part of the program, provides a collection of five emotions-related games that maintain the interest of most of the children that I work with. The highlight is a game called "famous face," which allows the child to "control the emotions" of famous teen/child actor Daniel Radcliff (Harry Potter). More information on this program may be found on the publisher's webpage at: http://www.jkp.com/mindreading/.

One Note of Caution *(this applies to all social-cognitive activities):*

Though I view the ability to read nonverbal cues and take another person's perspective as a necessary component of interpersonal relationship building, it is not sufficient in and of itself. That is, simply being able to read nonverbal cues and take another person's perspective does not ensure that the child will establish and keep meaningful social relationships. Indeed, there are many children (and adults) without ASD who have these skills, but still experience significant peer failure and rejection.

It is what you DO with this information that is important. That is why it is imperative that we view social interaction skills as three integrated components: thinking, feeling, doing. Perspective taking involves only one component. If we want the child to be successful socially, we must address these other areas of social functioning. In other words, now that the child knows how to take another person's perspective, it is time to teach her how to use it, and how to perform socially!

Reciprocal Interaction Activities

Social Skills to Teach: *conversational skills, reciprocity, reading nonverbal skills, processing speed, social problem solving,*

A prominent social difficulty for children with ASD is lack of reciprocal interactions. These children often engage in one-sided interactions that lack give-and-take. For example, in conversations, they ask questions of others or rarely talk about the interests of others. Or they ask repetitive questions, typically about topics that interest them. However, reciprocity is the key to maintaining successful social interactions. It requires an awareness of self and other, and sufficient flexibility to "think on your feet" to adapt to the flow of the interaction.

Strategies covered in this section include:

- Conversation Game

- Newspaper Reporter

- Improvisational Techniques

In this activity, the child with ASD is instructed to ask the therapist (in individual sessions) or another child (in group sessions) a question and then wait for a response. After answering the question, the other person then poses a question to the child with ASD. This back-and-forth interaction proceeds for a specified time period (typically 2-3 minutes). The activity may include two or more persons.

This reciprocal activity tends to be difficult for even the most verbally fluent adolescents, as they often fail to ask a question in return or provide long-winded responses. When the child fails to provide a response, or fails to ask a question in return, provide a gestural prompt to indicate that it is his turn. For instance, I typically point to the child and then point to myself in one motion. The prompt can be paired with a verbal prompt initially, and then faded to only a gestural prompt (see Prompting Strategies on page 174 for additional information).

If you are doing it correctly, the back-and-forth, back-and-forth, back-and-forth nature of this activity will appear contrived and mechanical. That's O.K.! Remember, the goal is to facilitate a give-and-take conversation, not necessarily a "natural" conversation – that will come later. Initially, keep questions as concrete and simple as possible (e.g., What did you eat for breakfast? What is your favorite movie?). You will find that many children will ask the same questions as the questions that are asked of them (e.g., "Do you have a dog?" "Yes." "Do *you* have a dog?" Or, some children will scan the room looking for things to ask about (e.g., "What color is the carpet?" "What kind of computer do you have?"). Again, this is O.K., as long as a back-and-forth exchange is occurring.

The Conversation Game leads to other more natural conversation tasks. For instance, once the children begin to master the back-and-forth nature of the activity, I place requirements on the types of questions that they may ask. For example, we (the group members) select a topic that they have to stick to, or they are only allowed to ask questions about the other person (as opposed to topics, facts, or self-interests). I find that after a few sessions (this varies depending upon the child), conversations begin to build naturally. I let this happen, but only towards the end of the activity (for instance, the last 30 seconds or 1 minute). During this time follow-up questions and more elaborate responses are allowed as long they maintain a reciprocal nature – no monologues allowed!

Newspaper Reporter

To facilitate reciprocal interactions, I also use an activity called Newspaper Reporter. Here the child is required to play the role of a newspaper reporter and ask questions of others. The form consists of rather simple questions about another person, such as:

Questions to Ask

- What is your name?

- How old are you?

- What is your favorite food?

- What is your favorite color?

- What is your favorite television show?

- What do you like to do for fun?

The goal of Newspaper Reporter is simply to get the child in the habit of asking questions, thereby increasing the give-and-take of conversations. The activity is particularly useful for children who rarely ask questions about others. Later in the sessions, the child should be encouraged to ask additional, probing questions to gain more information from the other person (in the spirit of great investigative journalism). The level of sophistication and complexity of this activity depends entirely on the developmental level of the children involved. This often becomes a favorite activity, as children ask for extra forms to take home.

Both the Conversation Game and the Newspaper Reporter activity can be used with video self-modeling. I regularly video record the activities, edit out the conversational mistakes or "bloopers" and then show the child positive and successful instances of his behavior. (The strategy of recording positive behavior will be discussed more extensively on pages 185.)

I have always been amazed at the social interaction skills of improvisational actors. With nothing more than a title or a theme to go on, these performers can create a song or an entire play, demonstrating the ultimate in cognitive flexibility and adaptability.

In my mind social interactions are also improvisational experiences. Rarely can we predict with certainty what a particular social interaction will entail. We may control the initiation, but not much else. The unpredictability increases considerably when we interact with people we do not know and in settings with which we are unfamiliar.

Thus, such interactions require the same skills as those of improvisational actors: We are drawing upon past experiences to guide our behavior and we are thinking on our feet – we are thinking of what to say next, how we will say it, and perhaps how and when the interaction will be terminated. Add a little anxiety (think of your first date), and all of these things become exponentially more difficult.

As I was watching an improvisational troupe perform one day, the light bulb came on. Improvisational skills would be extraordinarily useful for children with ASD to learn. Besides quick social decision making, improvisation requires the child to read the body language and nonverbal cues of her partner in order to anticipate the behaviors of the other person. As such, I consulted not my therapy and research textbooks, but a website on improvisational strategies and techniques (http://www.learnimprov.com).

Though not the cornerstone of my social skills program, I use improvisational exercises as warm-up activities for sessions. These exercises can also be used at home with family members or at school with classmates. The spontaneity of the exercises provides a nice complement to the more controlled Conversation Game described earlier. Further, a useful aspect of the improvisational techniques is that they can be modified to match most skill levels (i.e., developmental level and language level).

The three exercises presented in the following are particularly useful for teaching children with ASD to think on their feet, and to anticipate the behaviors of others by reading verbal and nonverbal cues. I prefer to begin these exercises in individual sessions (just me and the child), and then have the child perform them in group sessions after she has become more comfortable with the process. Beyond else, remember to have fun with it!

Free association. In free association one person starts by saying a word, any word. In response, the next person says the first word that comes to mind. The exercise continues in this fashion for a minute or two depending upon the size of the group. Instruct and encourage the children to say the first thing that "pops" into their head without thinking too much about what to say. Although similar, this is NOT the same psychoanalytical technique made famous by Sigmund Freud to detect repressed thoughts, so don't psychoanalyze!

Speaking with one voice. Once you get warmed up with the free association exercise, you may move on to the next, more difficult exercise called "speaking with one voice." In this activity (which can be performed by two or more people), the group is required to say words in unison.

Group members can take turns beginning the word. For instance, if you and I were doing this exercise, we would face each other, and I might (slowly) start to say, "Baahh" until you recognized that the word we will say together is "ball," or "bottle," or any other word that starts with the sound "baahh." Or, I could say "neeee" and you would join me to finish the word "needle." Once single words become easy, move on to creating sentences and stories.

This task requires careful listening, looking, and sharing with the other person in order to anticipate what he or she will say. A similar exercise requires group members to mirror the leader's gestures and body positions.

"Yes, and ..." The goal of this exercise is to get the children to add to, rather than control, a statement made by another player. One person starts out by making a statement. For instance, "dinosaurs are very big." The next person must add a statement of his own that begins with "yes, and ..." It might be, "yes, and they are now extinct." The other person will then follow with, for example, "yes, and if you dig in the right place, you can find fossils," and so on. This exercise tends to work best with only two people, but it may be used with larger groups.

Social Skills to Teach: reading nonverbal cues, taking another person's perspective, inferring the interests of others, initiating interactions, reciprocal interactions, making eye contact, social rules and concepts

A Social Story™ (Gray, 2000) is a frequently used strategy to teach social skills to children with ASD. The effectiveness of Social Stories has been supported by two independent studies (Bledsoe, Myles, & Simpson, 2003; Rogers & Myles, 2001). A Social Story presents social concepts and rules to children in the form of a brief story, and may be used to teach a number of social and behavioral concepts, such as initiating interactions, making transitions, playing a game, and going on a field trip.

Carol Gray (1995, 2000) emphasizes the following components as essential to a successful Social Story:

1. The story should be written in response to the child's personal need;

2. The story should be something the child wants to read on her own (depending upon ability level);

3. The story should be commensurate with the child's ability and comprehension level;

4. The story should use less directive terms such "can" or "could," instead of "will" or "must." (This last component is especially important for children who tend to be oppositional or defiant; i.e., the child who doesn't decide what to do until you tell him to do something and then does the opposite!).

(For a more comprehensive guidance on creating a Social Story, see Gray, 1995, 2000.)

There are a multitude of options for using Social Stories or more generic social narratives. For example, the Social Story may be paired with pictures and placed on a computer to take advantage of the child's propensity towards visual learning and interest in computers. The use of pictures adds context to the skill or concept that you are teaching; pictures of the child with peers adds a personal touch to the story. Social Stories may also be used in combination with other strategies. For instance, I use Social Stories to introduce relaxation strategies to children experiencing symptoms of anxiety (see page 169).

I have found that children with ASD learn best when Social Stories are used in conjunction with practice, or role-playing. That is, after reading a Social Story, the child practices the skill introduced in the story. For example, immediately after reading a story about raising your hand before speaking, the child practices raising his hand to be called on.

The following story was written for a kindergartner with ASD. Annie had average expressive language ability, but rarely spoke to peers. In fact, the school staff could think of no instances when Annie had initiated an interaction with her peers. The purpose of the story was to introduce the skill of initiating interactions, in particular, asking to join in an activity with other children. *Note:* Annie loved the monkey bars!

The Annie Story: Playing With Friends

I like making friends at school. There are a lot of kids at my school to play with. When I see other kids playing a game, I can walk over to them and say, "Can I play with you?"

Sometimes I want other kids to play a game I want to play. If I want a friend to play on the monkey bars with me, I could say "Do you want to play on the monkey bars with me?" It makes me very happy to play with other kids.

Since we wouldn't expect Annie to learn how to ask friends to play with her simply by reading her a story, she was given an opportunity to practice the skill introduced in the story. Notice that the story actually presented two skills, asking to join in an activity and asking another child to join an activity with her. Therefore, the story was read to Annie in sections to allow her to practice each skill separately. For instance, after reading the first paragraph, I stopped and allowed Annie to practice the skill by asking to play a game with me. After three behavioral repetitions we read the next paragraph, which introduced the skill of asking another person to play with her. Again, each role-play involved three behavioral repetitions. The story was read to Annie during the next session, only this time she practiced the skill with a peer buddy. The session also took place immediately prior to recess (see Priming Social Behavior in Chapter 9). The combination of Social Story and role-playing proved to be an effective strategy, increasing social interactions between Annie and her peers. It is a strategy that I have used regularly since, typically with similar results.

Role-Playing/Behavioral Rehearsal

Social Skills to Teach: *reading nonverbal cues, reciprocal conversations, initiating interactions, making eye contact, social rules, nonverbal communication*

Role-playing or behavioral rehearsal is used primarily to teach basic social interaction skills. It is an effective approach to teaching social skills that allows for the positive practice of skills (Gresham, 2001).

Role-playing involves acting out situations or activities in a structured environment to practice newly acquired skills and strategies, or previously learned skills that the child is having difficulties performing. Role-plays can be either scripted or spontaneous. In the latter, the child is provided with a scenario (e.g., asking another child to play with him), but not with the specific script. Typically, I combine scripted and unscripted elements to each role-play. For instance, the child might be provided with an opening statement or question, but the rest of the interaction would be spontaneous.

I use role-playing to teach a variety of interaction skills, particularly those involving initiating, responding, and terminating interactions. In one scenario, the child is required to initiate a conversation with another person, who is engaged in a separate task. Consequently, he would have to ask to join in, or ask the other person to join him in an activity. The latter typically proves to be most difficult for children with ASD.

Role-playing also complements the teaching of specific social rules, such as maintaining an appropriate distance during conversation, how to use eye contact to initiate a conversation, and waiting for another person to stop talking before initiating a conversation. Role-playing allows the child to execute the skill or behavior without the pressure and anxiety that sometimes is associated with real-life situations, and allows practice of the mechanics of a movement through multiple behavioral repetitions. Role-play activities can be performed with adults or with other children as participants.

During the first few sessions, it is not uncommon for the child to get "stuck" in conversations and interactions, often for 30 seconds to 1 minute, without knowing what to say or how to proceed. In such cases, use prompting to ensure that the child participates successfully in the role-play (see Prompting on page 174). During these early sessions, the child should be given ample time to process and respond to the role-play scenarios.

Note:

This "control" over the pace of the interaction is a strength of role-playing activities. For instance, if the child is practicing how to join in an activity with another person, the adult can wait while the child attempts to join in, which likely wouldn't happen in real-life situations. Also, there is no chance for rejection!

As the sessions progress, speed and proficiency should gradually increase. You can add difficulty and complexity as the child becomes more fluent with the skill. Repetition is a key aspect of role-playing, as is ending with an errorless (or at least a positive) performance. When introducing a new skill or concept, I typically require five repetitions of the role-play scenario. When practicing a previously learned skill or concept, I typically require three repetitions of the role-play.

It is important to encourage (and prompt if necessary) the child to apply skills learned via role-play to real-life situations. This may be encouraged by selecting role-play scenarios that the child is likely to encounter on a frequent basis, or by having the child rehearse skills or behaviors just prior to using them in the natural environment (see Priming Social Behavior on page 207).

Finally, it is imperative to keep the role-play fun and exciting. Let the child select skills and scenarios that he would like to practice, and skills and scenarios that he would like you or other children to practice. Regardless of the role he assumes (initiator or responder), the child will be practicing social interaction skills. For instance, if he instructs you to play the role of the child asking another child to play with him, he still has to respond to your initiation. In situations where the child is practicing how to talk to adults (e.g., requesting assistance in class), he may relish the opportunity to play the role of the adult – what child wouldn't?

1. Use both scripted and spontaneous role-play scenarios.

2. Select interaction skills or social rules that can be "acted out" or practiced.

3. Provide prompts to ensure successful performance of the skill during the role-play.

4. Add complexity and difficulty to the role-play as the child progresses.

5. Perform five repetitions of the role-play for newly introduced skills and three repetitions for previously learned skills.

6. Provide prompting to ensure that the child performs the behavior or skill in the natural environment.

Video Modeling and Video Self-Modeling

Social Skills to Teach: *reading nonverbal cues, reciprocal conversations, initiating interactions, making eye contact, social problem solving, self-awareness*

A video modeling intervention involves watching a video demonstration and then imitating the behavior of the model. Video modeling may be used with peers, adults, or self as a model (video self-modeling). The complexity of social interaction skills necessitates the use of multiple intervention strategies. Video modeling allows you to combine a broad range of strategies and can be used to promote skill acquisition, enhance skill performance, and reduce problem behaviors. Video modeling is without a doubt the most effective social skills intervention strategy that I have used with children with ASD.

This section provides a review of the research literature on video modeling and video self-modeling along with conceptual and theoretical information. The section concludes by providing practical information on how to design and implement a video modeling intervention, followed by three clinical examples of video self-modeling for children with ASD.

An emerging body of research demonstrates great promise for the use of video modeling (peer or adult as model) and video self-modeling (VSM) as a therapeutic modality for individuals with ASD. Bellini and Akullian (2006) conducted a meta-analysis of video modeling and video-self modeling research across 20 peer-reviewed studies and involving 63 participants with ASD.

Results suggest that video modeling and VSM are effective intervention strategies for addressing social-communication skills, behavioral functioning, and functional skills in children and adolescents with ASD. Specifically, these procedures promote skill acquisition and skills acquired via video modeling and VSM are maintained over time and transferred across person and settings. That is, video modeling and VSM appear to be effective interventions for children across the spectrum of autism from early childhood to adolescence. Perhaps most important to time-strapped educators, video modeling and VSM are relatively brief strategies. Thus, interventions produced rapid increases (or decreases in some cases) in targeted skills with a median intervention length of nine sessions. In addition, the median duration of the video clips shown to participants was only 3 minutes.

Benefits of Video Modeling and VSM

1. Promotes acquisition of new skills

2. Enhances performance of existing skills (increases mastery and fluency, and decreases anxiety)

3. May be combined with other strategies (coaching, social problem solving, self-monitoring, etc.)

4. Allows for the use of "hidden" supports and prompt fading

5. Increases self-confidence through the viewing of efficacious behavior

6. Promotes self-awareness

Video modeling and VSM are particularly effective strategies for teaching children with ASD social skills for the following reasons.

- **Incorporates visual learning.** The effectiveness of video modeling interventions, in part, may be attributed to the fact that video modeling and VSM integrate a powerful learning medium for children with ASD (visually cued instruction) with a well-studied intervention modality (modeling). Sherer et al. (2001) noted that VSM was most effective for the children in their study who enjoyed watching themselves on video, and who demonstrated prior preference for visual learning, such as video viewing and the use of visual support strategies.

- **Increases attention.** Attention is a necessary component of modeling (Bandura, 1977). That is, a person cannot imitate the behavior of a model if she does not attend to the model's behavior. Some individuals with ASD exhibit overselective attention or attend to irrelevant details of the environment (Happe, 1991; Koning & Magill-Evans, 2001).

   The use of video modeling allows you to remove irrelevant elements of the modeled skill or behavior through video editing, thereby enabling the individual with ASD to better focus on essential aspects of the targeted skill or behavior. Charlop-Christy et al. (2000) attributed the positive gains observed in their study to the fact that children with autism attended more closely to the video model than the live model.

- **Decreases anxiety.** Many individuals with ASD exhibit anxiety and distress related to social interactions, which may significantly impact their ability to attend to a learning task. Video modeling and VSM can be implemented with minimal human interaction, thereby reducing much of the distress and anxiety related to social interactions.

- **Increases motivation.** Anecdotal evidence and clinical experience suggest that watching videos is a highly desired activity for many children with and without ASD – leading to increased motivation and attention to the task. In VSM, motivation to watch oneself on the video may be enhanced by the portrayal of predominantly positive behaviors (Buggey, 1999), which may also increase attention and self-efficacy (Dowrick, 1999).

- **Increases self-awareness**. VSM allows the individual to monitor and evaluate his own behavior. Watching oneself on video provides a visual representation of self, which may assist in the development of self-awareness.

Two Types of VSM

VSM interventions typically fall within two categories: positive self-review (PSR) and video feedforward (Dowrick, 1999).

PSR refers to individuals viewing themselves successfully engaging in a behavior or activity that is currently in their behavioral repertoire. PSR may be used with low-frequency behaviors or behaviors that were once mastered, but are no longer. In this case, the individual is videotaped while engaging in the low-frequency behavior and then shown a video of the behavior.

An example of PSR can be applied to my golf game (which, by the way, may be characterized as a skill acquisition deficit). To implement the intervention, I can videotape myself hitting the ball 10 times, in hopes that I will hit at least one good shot (low-frequency behavior). After editing the tape, the positive self-review intervention would involve me repeatedly watching that one good shot. The goal would be for me to learn from what I did right, not from what I did wrong.

PSR is a relatively simple strategy to use from a technological standpoint. However, for very low-frequency behavior, it requires extensive amounts of raw video footage to capture even a small amount of the target behavior.

Video feedforward, another type of VSM intervention, is typically used when the individual already possesses the necessary skills in her behavioral repertoire, but is unable to put them together to complete an activity. For instance, the child may have the ability to get out of bed, brush her teeth, get dressed, and comb her hair (morning routine), but cannot perform these skills in the proper sequence. A video feedforward intervention would videotape her engaging in each of these tasks and then splice the segments together to form the proper sequence.

The same may be done with typical social interaction sequences. For instance, the child could be videotaped demonstrating three different skills: initiating an interaction, maintaining a reciprocal interaction, and appropriately terminating the interaction. The three scenes could then be blended together to portray one successful, and fluent, social interaction.

Feedforward is also a good option for individuals who need additional assistance, or support, to complete tasks successfully. The notion of "hidden supports" is an important component of video feedforward interventions. For instance, the child may be videotaped interacting with peers while an adult provides assistance through cueing and prompting. The adult prompt is subsequently edited out (i.e., hidden) so that when the child views the video segment, she sees herself as independent and successful.

Feedforward requires additional technological capabilities, as compared to PSR, but it typically requires a smaller quantity of raw video footage.

Guidelines for Implementing Video Modeling Interventions

1. ***Select a model and skill to teach.*** The model may be an adult, a peer, or the child himself. The next step is to select the behavior, skill, or social concept that will be presented to the child via the video. Do not try to address too many things at once. Keep it simple and keep it focused on one or two skills, behaviors, and/or concepts. In selecting a skill, remember, video modeling can be used to promote skill acquisition and to enhance performance of skills that the child is having difficulties performing.

2. ***Identify other actors.*** Once the star has been selected, you will need to select other cast members. Use peers whenever feasible when recording social behavior to provide context and ecological validity. After all, these are the children that the child with ASD interacts with most frequently.

   Note: In school settings, parental permission is necessary for all children appearing in the video. Check with the school regarding its policy on videotaping classrooms. Some schools have a blanket permission policy whereby parents are informed at the beginning of the year that their child's classroom may be videotaped for various educational purposes, such as feedback to teachers regarding their instructional practices and individual student interventions. If parents do not wish to have their children recorded, they are asked to contact the school directly to opt out of the recording policy.

3. **Plan the production.** You will need to decide if the behavior will be recorded in the natural environment or via a role-playing scenario. For role-playing productions, it is helpful to create a story board of the various scenes to help keep track of and to organize the production. A story board is extremely helpful in the editing stage as well. If the scenes will be scripted, a script must be written and the actors need an opportunity to rehearse.

   Story boards or outlines may also be used for recording behavior in the natural environment to help organize and set up the scenes. If behavior will be recorded in the natural environment, you must determine how to best capture the target behavior or some component of it.

4. **Determine the support or edits that will be necessary to portray the child as socially efficacious.** To capture low-frequency behaviors, a large amount of raw footage has to be collected and then edited to show just the target behavior. Also, certain behaviors will require support and assistance to perform. For instance, the child might respond to the social initiations of peers, but only when prompted by an adult. If "social response" is the target behavior, these adult-prompted social responses are recorded, but the prompts are edited out to portray the child as responding independently, without the need for adult assistance (hidden supports).

5. **Prepare for the filming stage.** Assemble your cast, but before you yell, "ACTION," you will need to consider a few more things. First, make sure that your camera is set up in a location that will clearly capture the target child. Also make sure that lighting in the room is adequate enough to see the actors. Do a test recording in the room (at the same time of the day as the actual filming) to avoid dark recordings. Finally, sound quality is important. Do a test run to determine if the actors' voices will be captured by the video camera. If voices are not audible, move the

camera closer to the actors, or use a separate microphone that can be placed closer to them. Cordless microphones are also an option. Keep in mind that the editing process will allow you to increase voice volume to a certain degree, but don't take chances. There is nothing worse than having to discard 30 minutes of raw footage all because your sound was imperceptible.

6. **Edit.** The editing process is by far the most challenging and time-consuming aspect of the video modeling intervention. Determine who will edit the raw footage. This does not require a degree in video production, but the person who does the editing must be knowledgeable about computers, and be wiling to learn the editing software. If you and the other team members are technophobic, you will need to find colleagues or family members who can provide a tutorial.

   One obstacle prevents many from conducting video modeling interventions – technical skills. Please do not let your technological limitations impede implementation of this very effective intervention. Ask around for help. One teacher that I worked with enlisted the assistance of the local high school video editing class to edit her videos. Others have asked their teenage sons or daughters to help them learn the software.

   This leads us to the selection of software. Most digital video cameras are sold with software that allows you to do basic editing. Don't expect to win an Academy Award for editing. In fact, the technical quality of the video is of little importance to the outcome of the intervention. Remember, children are learning by watching visual representations of the target behavior. A harsh cut here or a bad splice there will not diminish the outcomes. Plan on producing enough videos clips so that you do not have to show the same clip on consecutive days. Also, keep the video clips short. Two- to 3-minute clips will suffice.

7. **Share the video.** This step involves showing the child the video clips. If the editing step is the most laborious of the video modeling procedure, showing the video must be considered the easiest. In fact, once the editing is done, the VSM intervention is as easy as any intervention that I have ever implemented, especially those that can be carried out in the natural environment.

As part of this process, you need to determine where the video will be shown: at school (in the classroom, or resource room), at home, or in the therapeutic setting? You will also need to determine when the video will be shown. If you are using the video clip as a primer, you will want to show it immediately before the child is expected to perform the behavior (e.g., immediately prior to recess, or immediately prior to a difficult transition). Also decide who will show the video to the child (consider having the child do this himself). Ideally, the video clip should be shown daily, but once or twice a week will typically suffice. In some situations this is not feasible, however. In these cases, show the video clip as frequently as possible, even if this means once a week, or every other week. Results may not be as quick and dramatic as if you show the video on a daily basis, but you should still see benefits.

Make sure the instructions are simple and straightforward. There is no need to explain to the child the theory underlying video modeling, or to provide overly detailed instructions prior to watching the video. If you wish, share with the child the purpose of the video modeling intervention prior to the first viewing or prior to the video recording (i.e., "We will be making/showing a video that will help teach you how to ..." Or "... to show you how well you ..."). Simply state that you want the child to watch his behavior on the video (be specific; for instance, if you want the child to watch social initiations, say that). If you plan feedback, wait until the child has viewed the entire video clip, then rewind and provide feedback on specific scenes as necessary (pause while providing feedback). If you are using video modeling in conjunction with a social problem-solving or self-monitoring strategy, procedures and instructions must be modified accordingly. At the end of the video viewing, reinforce the child for attending to the video.

8. ***Collect social validity and treatment fidelity data.***
   The final step of the video modeling process is to collect data from either parents or teachers on implementation of the intervention, and to elicit their feedback regarding the child's progress (see Social and Treatment Fidelity in Chapter 11).

The following are three examples of video self-modeling interventions that I have found effective with children and adolescents with ASD. They illustrate the variety of VSM applications available. The length of each intervention depends on the child's needs, as well as the skill or behavior chosen. The rate of skill acquisition varies from child to child, but you can typically expect to see some change/progress during the first week or two of the VSM intervention.

Tina

Tina was a 5-year-old child with autism who seldom initiated or responded to the social approaches of other children, resulting in a high degree of social withdrawal. She did, however, occasionally initiate and respond to other children when specifically prompted by an adult.

A VSM intervention was set up to increase spontaneous social initiations and responses. Tina was videotaped interacting with peers in her preschool classroom. The teacher was instructed to prompt Tina to initiate and respond to as many peers as possible during the video recording phase.

After sufficient video footage was collected (about one hour of footage), the video was edited to remove all instances of non-interaction and negative behaviors, so that Tina viewed only footage of positive social interactions. In addition, the footage was edited to remove all evidence of teacher prompting. That is, the audio of the teacher's verbal prompts was reduced so that Tina did not hear them as she watched the video. Instead she viewed video footage that depicted her as fluent and independent in her interactions with peers. Three 2-minute video clips were produced. Tina watched one clip per day. The teaching staff told Tina that she would be watching a video that showed her "playing with her friends."

Michael

Michael was a 12-year-old child with Asperger Syndrome who frequently blurted out answers in class and engaged in a variety of other impulsive behaviors.

A VSM intervention was set up to teach Michael an appropriate replacement behavior (i.e., raising his hand). A role-play scenario was arranged with Michael, three peers, and his teacher. The students were told that they would be making a video to show their classmates how to raise their hand and how to wait patiently to be called on in class. During the role-play, the teacher asked the students various questions as they remained seated at their desks. (The students had received the answers ahead of time.) The students were directed to raise their hands and wait to be called on. The teacher was directed to take turns calling on each student in the classroom, and to provide verbal praise to each child for raising his hand.

The role-play scenario was videotaped; it depicted Michael raising his hand to answer a question and waiting patiently for his turn. The video was edited to remove all miscues, bloopers, or any other unwanted footage. It was then shown to Michael, who was designated as the "host" of the classwide showing. Michael was asked to show the video to the class. Prior to showing the video, Michael shared with the class the purpose of the video (i.e., to show them how to raise their hands). Following the viewing, Michael demonstrated to the class the proper way to raise one's hand before answering a question.

Artie

Artie was an 8-year-old boy with autism who had difficulties transitioning from one activity to the next at school. His greatest difficulty was transitioning from computer class to gym class. When the teacher provided a directive for Artie to shut the computer off and line up for gym, her requests were often ignored or were followed very slowly and with considerable prompting on her part.

A VSM intervention was implemented to increase Artie's compliance with teacher directives, and to increase the speed of his transition from computer class to gym class. The video recording took place in two parts. In the first part, the teacher was videotaped asking the class to shut down their computers and to line up for gym. In the second part of the video recording, the students (with a focus on Artie) were recorded shutting down the computers and lining up for gym class. Artie was provided reinforcement (at the discretion of the teacher) for lining up quickly during the recording. The video was edited to depict him lining up quickly and without the need for teacher prompting. The two recording scenes (i.e., teacher providing directive to line up and Artie shutting off the computer and lining up) were spliced together to appear as though Artie and the class were transitioning promptly as a result of the teacher's directive. The video clip lasted approximately 30 seconds. Artie watched the video each day prior to computer class.

For additional instruction on conducting VSM intervention, please refer to the Video Futures Project at the University of Alaska, Anchorage, http://www.alaskachd.org/video/. For information on editing home movies, check out the helpful website, How Stuff Works, at: http://computer.howstuff-works.com/video-editing.htm

For additional information on video editing software, check out Adobe Premiere" at http://www.adobe.com/products/pre-miere/main.html or Apple iMovie at: http://www.apple.com/ilife/imovie/

Social Problem Solving and Social Rules

Social Skills to Teach: *social problem solving, social rules and concepts, conversation planning, considering multiple viewpoints*

The primary purpose of social problem solving and social reasoning activities is to teach the child how to make sense of her social behavior and the (often unwritten) rules of the social world (see Difficulties With Social Cognition on page 41). For the purpose of clarity, the section is separated into two broad categories: (a) analysis of social behavior and social situations (social problem solving) and (b) knowledge and understanding of social rules and customs. However, as for many areas of social functioning, these two areas are inextricably related. For instance, in order to successfully analyze our social behavior and make subsequent behavioral decisions, we often need sufficient declarative and procedural knowledge (see Chapter 2) regarding social rules. Keep in mind that the ultimate goal of teaching social problem solving and reasoning is to help the child make effective behavioral decisions.

The strategies covered in this section include:

- A Step-by-Step Process for Analyzing Social Situations

- Strategies That Promote Cognitive Flexibility and Considering Multiple Viewpoints

- Teaching Social Rules

- Coaching

The first two strategies are designed to teach social problem solving, while the latter two are designed to teach social rules.

A Step-by-Step Process for Analyzing Social Situations

Many children with ASD have difficulties interpreting social situations. This is due to a number of factors, including lack of self-awareness, failure to read nonverbal and contextual cues, and difficulties with perspective taking. It is also due to the fact that they lack the necessary skills and strategies to analyze social situations. Therefore, social problem-solving (SPS) strategies should be implemented in combination with other social skill strategies, such as those described under Thoughts, Feelings, and Interests on pages 126-134.

Research has demonstrated that social problem solving can be effectively taught to children with ASD (Bernard-Opitz, Sriram, & Nakhoda-Sapuan, 2001). Many different methods and techniques have been used to facilitate the development of social reasoning in children. SPS strategies may be used in individual and group social skill programs, or they can be incorporated into a classroom curriculum.

To meet the unique needs of children with ASD, I have modified a commonly used SPS approach to incorporate the reading of nonverbal cues using picture cards, videos, live observations, and past social experiences (written stories may be used with some children).

Pictures that depict social situations provide an entry point for teaching SPS. Pictures tend to be the easiest for children with ASD to comprehend because they are static, stationary depictions of a social scenario. Everything that is happening in the scenario is frozen for the child to see and analyze.

As soon as the child is able to analyze pictures of social situations, I transition to the use of **video vignettes** in place of the pictures. The videos depict dynamic (moving) representations of social scenarios. Videos have the added benefit of allowing you to stop and play back a social situation. In addition, by combining SPS with VSM, we can teach children to analyze their own social situations, which is the primary goal of teaching social problem solving.

Once the child has demonstrated mastery of the SPS strategy on pictures and videos, he should be given the opportunity to apply the strategies to *real-life social situations* involving herself or others. The SPS strategy may also be used "live" or with behaviors or situations that have occurred in the past. If using it for past behavior or situations, make sure to do so immediately following the behavior.

Note:

It is important to use SPS strategies when the child makes good decisions, too! Imagine if your boss did an SPS strategy with you each day to help you "understand" each mistake that you made. Let the child analyze and learn from his appropriate and effective social decisions. The result will be increased social problem solving, self-awareness, and perhaps even increased self-confidence.

Six Steps of SPS Process

The following represents the six steps of the SPS process. The process is not rigid. It should be adapted to meet the unique needs of each child, including her cognitive ability, language ability, and present level of social functioning (e.g., perspective-taking ability, self-awareness, and ability to read nonverbal cues).

1. The first step in the SPS process is to provide a description of the social scenario depicted in a picture or video. What is happening or what has happened? If there is a problem, have the child identify it. If the child has difficulties answering general questions, you may need to initially ask more specific questions regarding the social scenario. You may also want to start the process by modeling appropriate answers for each step.

2-3. The second and third steps combine thinking and feeling instruction with social problem solving. It is impossible to effectively analyze social situations if you fail to read the nonverbal cues of the participants. Therefore, Steps 2 and 3 require the child to recognize the feelings and/or thoughts of the characters depicted in the social scenarios, and then infer why they might be feeling or thinking that way. (*Note:* Steps 2 and 3 may be omitted once the child has demonstrated sufficient mastery of reading the thoughts and feel-ings of others.)

4. The fourth step involves predicting consequences. That is, based on the contextual cues available to the child, what does he think will happen next to the char-acters in the social scenario? The goal here is to teach the child to see the consequences, or the cause and effect, of social behaviors.

5. The fifth step has two purposes. First, it teaches the child to select more adaptable behaviors, or make "bet-ter" behavioral decisions. Second, it teaches the child to view social scenarios from multiple viewpoints, which is an important aspect of social problem solv-ing, and an essential component of successful social relationships.

6. The last step involves predicting the consequences of the alternate behaviors. For example, "what would probably happen if he/she/you would have tried this other behavior?"

1. Describe the social scenario, setting, behavior, or problem (what's happening or what has happened?).

2. Recognize the feelings/thoughts of participants (How does he/she/you feel? What is he/she thinking?).

3. Understand the feeling of participants (Why is he/she/you feeling/thinking that way? Ask child to provide evidence).

4. Predict the consequences (What do you think will happen next? What will be the consequences of this behavior?).

5. Select alternative behaviors (What could he/she/you have done differently).

6. Predict the consequence for alternative behaviors.

For more information on social problem-solving strategies, see *Social Decision Making/Social Problem Solving: A Curriculum for Academic, Social, and Emotional Learning,* by Elias and Butler, with Bruno, Papke, and Shapiro (2005).

***Strategies That
Promote
Cognitive
Flexibility and
Consideration of
Multiple
Viewpoints***

SPS strategies may also be used to address "narrow-mindedness" or rigid thinking. The goal is to promote cognitive flexibility by providing practice in viewing problems from multiple perspectives and generating multiple solutions. I will discuss three strategies that target rigid thinking: brainstorming, pro/cons, and Test of Evidence (TOE).

Brainstorming. When brainstorming potential alternative viewpoints, the child is required to list as many viewpoints as possible without evaluating them along the way. That is, he should be encouraged not to determine whether the viewpoint is right or wrong – this will be a challenge with a child with ASD! For instance, the child could list all the possible ways in which people view broccoli, such "broccoli is tasty," broccoli is awful," broccoli is good for you," and "broccoli makes me sick."

Pros/cons. Another strategy is to generate a list of pros/cons or advantages/disadvantages of engaging in a particular behavior or activity. For instance, if the child cannot understand why he must wear a helmet when riding his bike, the parent or teacher can have her make a list of advantages to wearing a helmet and disadvantages to wearing a helmet.

Test of evidence. Friedberg and McClure (2002) describe a cognitive behavioral strategy for helping children recognize and process their faulty beliefs, called a Test of Evidence (TOE). A TOE is particularly useful for children who make sweeping overgeneralizations and faulty conclusions that are based on faulty assumptions. It is also valuable for children who cannot recognize the errors in their logic. A TOE can be used for faulty beliefs about self, or the child's rigid beliefs about the world. For instance, consider the case where the child insists that "everybody hates me."

Steps of TOE

1. ***Help him analyze the assumptions and the logic behind this belief.*** The first step of TOE is to help children access and reveal the facts that support their belief. This is very enlightening for child and adult alike. This is the "just the facts" stage. Ask the child "what makes you absolutely certain?" or "what facts support your belief?" For the example above, "what makes you certain that everybody hates you?," responses might be "because everybody picks on me," or "nobody ever plays with me."

2. ***Generate contrary evidence, or facts that might disconfirm the child's faulty conclusions.*** In this step you want the child to try and prove himself wrong – the child will need assistance with this step. Present instances when other children played with him, or when other children were nice to him.

3. ***Ask the child to consider alternative statement or belief.*** Here you want the child to "try on" an alternative statement or belief that is different than the original. For instance, instead of "everybody hates me," he would have to consider the possibility that "everybody likes me." In this stage, the child will base his conclusion only on the contrary beliefs generated in Step 2.

4. ***Have the child draw another conclusion based on both the confirming evidence (Step 1) and the disconfirming evidence (Step 2).*** It is helpful to represent this evidence in two columns ("supporting evidence" and "contrary evidence"). Keep in mind that the goal of this tech-

nique is not necessarily to prove the child wrong, which you may never do. The goal is to teach the child to identify multiple or conflicting explanations, and to examine the facts that make up his belief system. In the example above, the child should come to the conclusion that "some people are mean to me, but many people like me."

Belief or Statement: "Everybody Hates Me"

Step One: Supporting Evidence

    1. "Everybody Picks on Me"

    2. "Nobody Plays With Me"

    3. "My Teachers Are Always Mean to Me"

Step Two: Contrary Evidence

    1. "Timmy Does Not Pick on Me"

    2. "Michael Played on the Computer With Me"

    3. "Cindy Helped Me Find My Notebook"

    4. "Ms. Ortiz Helps Me With My Math Assignments Without Yelling"

Step Three: Alternative Statement or Belief

    1. "Other People Do Like Me"

Step Four: Final Conclusion

Supporting Evidence	Contrary Evidence
"Everybody Picks on Me"	"Timmy Does Not Pick on Me"
"Nobody Plays With Me"	"Michael Played on the Computer With Me"
"My Teachers Are Always Mean to Me"	"Ms. Ortiz Helps Me With My Math Assignments Without Yelling"
	"Cindy Helped Me Find My Notebook"

Final Conclusion

"Some People Like Me and Some People Don't Like Me"

Teaching Social Rules

In addition to faulty social problem-solving strategies, difficulty interpreting social situations may also be due to lack of knowledge (both declarative and procedural) about social rules and conventions. Social rules include social customs, such as maintaining an appropriate distance and voice volume during conversations, not interrupting others when they are talking, looking for nonverbal cues, and maintaining eye contact during conversations. Social rules also require the comprehension of slang and idioms. For example, when I sneeze, most people say, "Bless you." Most people don't know that "Bless You" originated from the belief that sneezing expelled evil spirits from the body, but they say it anyway because it is a social custom. That is, it is just something that we do, perhaps to be "polite." If we are at a baseball game and somebody says "keep your eye on the ball," most of us know that that idiom means "to watch the ball closely."

Most children learn these social rules quite easily through experience and perhaps trial and error. However, children with ASD are not learning them by simple exposure to social situations and often need explicit instruction. In many cases, social rules should be taught to children with ASD the way we would teach social customs to visitors from other countries ... one at a time and with sufficient context. The most effective teaching strategy for introducing and teaching social rules will depend upon the child's developmental level.

Steps of Teaching Social Rules

Typically, social rules should be taught to children with ASD in the same way as we teach any complicated or abstract concept:

1. Provide a clear description of the concept

2. Include relevant contextual information

3. Use multiple exemplars

4. Make connections to the child's prior knowledge

5. Include hands-on demonstrations and modeling

In other words, you may teach social rules through good teaching! A number of strategies are particularly useful in teaching social rules and concepts. A Social Story™ (see Social Stories on page 139) is a valuable strategy for introducing and teaching social rules. Use of literature, (film) videos, and role-playing are also effective media for learning social rules. Selected social rules can also be used as the focus of the SPS strategy discussed earlier in this chapter. For instance, the concept of personal space could be taught by providing a picture of a child violating somebody's personal space. The child would then be required to analyze the picture via the SPS steps (e.g., what's happening in the picture, how are the characters feeling, what could they do different, etc.).

Myles, Trautman, and Schelvan (2004) have written an extremely insightful book on this topic, *The Hidden Curriculum: Practical Solutions for Understanding Unstated Rules in Social Situations*. The book is filled with helpful strategies and hundreds of curricular items that I refer to often in my clinical practice. It also contains additional suggestions for SPS.

In my social skills groups, I typically have children select one rule each from the book that they are required to teach to the other members of the group (e.g., "when you leave a situation or place, always say good-bye"). I place no parameters on how they teach it. I just ask them to "teach it." The creativity has been extraordinary and the questions that they ask create wonderful opportunities for teachable moments! For example, a child with ASD might ask "why do I have to say good-bye if I am going to see the person again?" The response to this question might be, "because it lets the other person know that you enjoyed talking with her and that you want to talk with her again some time."

Another book, *Social Awareness Skills for Children* (Csoti, 2001), also presents a wide variety of teachable social rules and skills ranging from body language, personal space, greetings, to the concept of friendship.

One social rule in particular, eye contact, is a common target of social and behavioral interventions. Eye contact is an important component of social reciprocity. If you have ever had a conversation with somebody who does not make eye contact, you will undoubtedly understand its importance.

First, it is difficult to determine, at least initially, if the person is talking to you. Second, when a person does not make eye contact, it is hard to determine whether she is finished talking and that it is your turn to speak. Although I do not insist on the child maintaining eye contact for the duration of the interaction, I teach the child to use eye contact to initiate, maintain, and terminate an interaction.

Teaching a Social Rule (Eye Contact)

The concept of eye contact is first introduced to the child via a story or through direct instruction. The story or instruction includes information on why eye contact is important and when to use eye contact. In particular, the child is taught to use eye contact to initiate and to end (or punctuate) the social initiation. The child is taught that eye contact allows him to determine whether he has the other person's attention; and also lets the other person know that what he is about to say is directed to the other person. The child is then taught to make eye contact when he is done talking to let the other person know that it is her turn to speak.

This simple technique significantly improves initiations and reciprocity of interactions. This rule and many others are best learned by supplementing them with role-play or behavioral rehearsal (i.e., practice!). In this case, we would have the child practice making eye contact to initiate and terminate an interaction.

Coaching

Another effective approach for teaching social rules (and other social interaction skills) is coaching. Coaching utilizes verbal and visual instruction to facilitate the development and performance of social skills (Elliott, Racine, & Busse, 1995). A flexible teaching strategy, coaching may take many shapes and forms, but typically contains three basic steps:

1. A social rule or skill is introduced to the child.

2. The child is provided opportunities to practice or rehearse the application of the rule or skill with the coach.

3. The coach provides immediate feedback to the child regarding her performance.

Like most strategies presented in this book, coaching may be combined with other strategies. For instance, the skill or rule presented in Step 1 can be introduced via a Social Story™ or through modeling (video or live). The second step should initially be performed as a behavioral rehearsal, but should eventually be performed in a naturalistic environment with the coach present. This is important for facilitating generalization, or transfer of skills across settings. The final step, feedback, may include reinforcement via verbal praise and acknowledgment. In the case of performance errors or difficulties, the feedback should be followed by the coach modeling or guiding the child through a successful performance. *Do not end this or any social skill activity with failure.*

Self-Monitoring

Social Skills to Teach: *self-awareness, self-management, self-knowledge*

In addition to a general lack of awareness of their bodies' physiological responses, children with ASD demonstrate limited awareness of their thoughts, feelings, and behavior, including how their thoughts, feelings, and behavior impact those with whom they interact.

Self-monitoring strategies have demonstrated considerable effectiveness for teaching children with and without disabilities to both monitor and regulate their own behavior (Carter, 1993). Strategies can target a number of externalizing behaviors, such as time-on-task, work completion, and disruptive behaviors, as well as internal processes, such as thoughts (self-talk) and feelings (both positive and negative affect).

Self-monitoring strategies have also been used effectively to address the social and behavioral functioning of children with ASD (Coyle & Cole, 2004; Shearer, Kohler, Buchan, & McCullough, 1996). Shearer et al. used self-monitoring to increase the social interactions of preschool children with ASD. Coyle and Cole used self-monitoring in combination with video self-modeling (positive self-review) to decrease off-task behavior in school-aged children with ASD.

Self-monitoring strategies may involve having the child record the occurrences, duration, and frequencies of behaviors (whether the behavior was performed, for how long, how frequently it was performed) and the quality of the behavioral performance (how well the behavior was performed). The self-recording of behavior can be used during the behavioral performance or after the performance (or both).

Self-Monitoring Strategy

The following self-monitoring strategy was designed to increase self-awareness of behaviors, thoughts, and feelings in the context of social interactions. The goal of this "interactional" self-monitoring is to teach the child to be aware of her behavior during social interactions and to improve social performance by teaching her to modify her behavior as necessary to ensure a successful interaction. Self-monitoring strategies support generalization of skills because they teach children to independently monitor their own behavior.

Whereas the ultimate goal for some children without autism is to change a specific target behavior, the ultimate goal of self-monitoring strategies for children with ASD (in the context of social skills training) is to teach self-awareness. That is, to teach them how to self-monitor. Therefore, a key component of the self-monitoring evaluation is to reinforce the child's accuracy of recording as opposed to a specific behavioral performance.

Steps in Implementing a Self-Monitoring Strategy

1. *Identify behavior, skill, or emotion.* Initially, select overt behaviors (personal space, voice volume, asking questions during conversations, etc.) that can be observed by both the child and another person. Once the child learns how to successfully monitor overt behaviors, you may shift the training to cognitive processes such as thoughts. Expressions of feelings (facial expressions, body language, and gestures) may be targeted from the onset as long as they are observable.

2. *Define behavior, skill, or emotion.* Define the behavior you have targeted for the intervention clearly enough so that the child can understand it and identify it. This is the behavior that the child will be monitoring.

3. *Introduce behavior, skill or emotion to child.* Modeling (both live and video) is a great way to introduce the skill as it provides a visual representation. If the child does not already possess the skill or behavior in her behavioral repertoire, teach the skill before implementing the self-monitoring portion of the intervention.

4. *Select self-monitoring procedure.* Many different self-monitoring forms may be used; some are available on

the Internet or in textbooks. You may also create your own forms to address the individual needs of the child (see pages 167-168). Once you have determined the type of monitoring form to use, you need to decide where behavior will be recorded, and how often.

Again, self-monitoring does not have to be used exclusively with overt behaviors; it may also be used to help the child monitor his thoughts and feelings. However, it is virtually impossible to ensure accuracy of the child's monitoring of covert processes (with the exception of emotional expressions). Therefore, I recommend that you refrain from addressing self-monitoring of covert behaviors until the child has demonstrated proficiency in the use of self-monitoring for overt behaviors.

When selecting a self-monitoring procedure, it is also important to decide how you will measure the accuracy of the child's self-monitoring. Accuracy can be measured by having another person record the child's behavior simultaneously with the child, or by videotaping the child during the recording interval.

In addition, you will need to determine the prompting or cueing strategy to be used. The purpose of cueing is to remind the child to record the behavior. Typical cueing strategies include a clock, timer, a gesture from the teacher or other adult, or a natural cue such as a school bell.

The final consideration for this step is whether the child is to monitor his behavior live or on video. I prefer to begin self-monitoring strategies by having the child record behaviors that she sees on video. This gives the child a visual representation of the behavior and practice using the recording form. Besides, it allows the adult to provide feedback on the child's accuracy of recording. Live recording should begin as soon as the child is ready.

Some forms require the child to record the frequency or presence of a behavior during or immediately following a predetermined period of time, for instance, during recess.

Typical forms ask the child to "place a check-mark in the box each time you respond to questions from peers," or "how many times did you initiate an interaction with your peers at recess?" The use of paper forms is most appropriate when the child is monitoring behavior that he is viewing on a video screen because the child will be stationary (i.e., seated in front of the television screen). When counting frequencies, the child may use a counter that he can click each time he performs the behavior (i.e., click the counter each time you initiate with peers). This is the preferred method in situations where you want the child to monitor his behavior as it is occurring, but do not want him to carry around a rating form or notepad.

Other forms require the child to rate the quality of his performance, or how well he performed the behavior ("How successful were your initiations?" Or "Did you maintain an appropriate personal space when initiating the interaction?"). The child might also be asked to rate his performance on a scale of 1 to 4 (from very poor to very successful).

5. *Teach self-monitoring strategy.* Show the child the forms that she will be using, provide verbal instructions, model how to use the form, provide opportunities for practice, and prompt when necessary, until the child has demonstrated mastery of the procedure.

6. *Implement self-monitoring strategy.* Though ideally you want the child to self-monitor his behavior through-out the day, and in multiple settings, you need to deter-mine a specific time and location for the use of the self-monitoring procedure; for instance, at morning recess, during social skills group, during circle time, etc. Start with short intervals (5-15 minutes) and work your way to longer intervals (an hour or a day). Provide ample praise and encouragement for the child's attempts to use the self-management strategy. Remember, self-moni-toring is a difficult process for children with ASD. Their efforts should be acknowledged accordingly.

7. *Provide feedback.* The final stage of the interactional self-monitoring strategy is to provide feedback to the child on the accuracy of her recording. Compare the child's behavioral measurements with those of the adult selected in Step 4 to assess the accuracy of the record-ings. Initially, feedback should be provided after each

recording interval and then slowly faded so that the child does not require adult monitoring. If you have videotaped the recording interval, the child's measurements may be compared directly to her behavior portrayed on the video. This visual representation provides an effective mechanism for feedback. If you choose to provide reinforcement, it should be contingent upon accuracy of recordings and not based on a specific behavioral outcome. For instance, provide reinforcement for 80% accuracy (based on adult recordings), as opposed to successful completion of a particular behavior. Remember, the ultimate goal of this strategy is to teach self-awareness.

Personalized Information

Child's Name: Brian

Targeted Behavior or Skill: Initiating Interactions with Peers (initiations interaction is selected as an example; other target behaviors may be used).

Where behavior will be monitored: Morning Recess

Examples of Recording Strategies:

- **Frequency Recording**

    Please place a check in a box each time you **initiate an interaction** (on actual form, you will state the target behavior):

    How many times did you **initiate an interaction** with a peer at recess today (if a clicker was used, how many clicks did you record?)?_____

• Weekly Monitoring Form

Did you **initiate an interaction** with a peer today (please circle yes or no)?

Monday	Tuesday	Wednesday	Thursday	Friday
Yes/No	Yes/No	Yes/No	Yes/No	Yes/No
Total Number:	Total Number:	Total Number:	Total Number:	Total Number:

• Please rate how well you **initiated interactions** with peers today:

1 = Not very well

2 = I did well

3 = I did VERY WELL!

• Please answer the following questions by circling yes or no (you may also ask the child to rate how strongly she agrees with the statement):

I maintained an appropriate distance from others when I **initiated the interactions?**

Yes/No   ☐Disagree   ☐Agree   ☐Strongly Agree

I looked at the other person's eyes when I started my **initiation**?

Yes/No   ☐Disagree   ☐Agree   ☐Strongly Agree

I was anxious/nervous/scared/happy (use language that the child understands) when I **initiated interactions** with peers today?

Yes/No   ☐Disagree   ☐Agree   ☐Strongly Agree

Note: Emotional icons may also be used to record range of feelings. They may be used in combination with or in place of the words above.

For more information on self-awareness related to social interactions, please see *Social Awareness for Children* (Csoti, 2001).

Social Skills to Teach: *emotional regulation and self-awareness*

Relaxation techniques have been used for many years to teach children with ASD to regulate their physiological arousal and stress (Cautela & Groden, 1978). Elevated physiological arousal and stress significantly diminishes social performance and leads to increased social withdrawal. In the context of social skills training, the goal of relaxation training is to teach the child effective coping strategies to reduce the stress and arousal that impedes the development of social skills and negatively affects social performance.

A thorough discussion of cognitive behavioral techniques to reduce the cognitive component of anxiety in individuals with ASD is beyond the scope of this book. For more information on cognitive behavioral therapy for anxiety, please see *Exploring Feelings* (Attwood, 2004).

The following section will focus exclusively on relaxation techniques to help alleviate the physiological arousal and stress often experienced by children with ASD. Specific relaxation techniques include:

- Tension Release and Breathing Exercises

- Biofeedback

- Self-Awareness Training

Tension Release and Breathing

To help children regulate their physiological arousal, I recommend instruction in the areas of tension release and breathing. The level of complexity of the instruction should be matched to the child's developmental level. It is a good idea to supplement the instructions with visual cues and supports. *When My Worries Get Too Big!* by Kari Dunn Buron (2006) is an example of a relaxation book for young children presented in a picture book format. (Reprinted with permission.)

All relaxation strategies should be practiced by the child in therapy sessions and at home for at least 10 minutes per day. Eventually, the child should be encouraged to use relaxation strategies whenever she encounters a stressful situation (for about 1-2 minutes).

Then I can sit down,
rub my legs and close
my eyes. Now I feel more
like a **3** or a **2**.

I can think about happy things,
like my dog or my stuffed lion, or our
family cabin in the summer.
Now I am at a **1**.

This is when I need to fight back!
First, I can squeeze my hands together.

Next, I can take three really slow,
deep breaths. Slow in – slow out,
slow in – slow out, slow in – slow out.

Tension release:	Make a tight fist for 5 seconds. Release. *This should be done for a total of five sets.*
Breathing exercises:	Breathe deeply during stressful situations. Breaths should be slow and deep, inhaling through the nose and exhaling through the mouth.
	It helps children to visualize smelling a rose as they inhale (about 3 seconds) and blowing on a candle without blowing it out on the exhale (about 2 seconds). Use a real candle and flower if necessary to practice.

I recommend introducing the relaxation techniques to the child via a Social Story™ (Gray, 1995). The Social Story may also instruct the child as to when and where to use the relaxation techniques.

Example of Relaxation Intervention

For one child with ASD, Charlie, I developed a Social Story about relaxing during bad weather. The Social Story was paired with pictures of bad weather and a picture of Charlie exhibiting a "nervous" expression. After Charlie read the story, we engaged in a role-play activity to practice the information in the story. Charlie was encouraged to utilize these skills whenever he felt himself becoming nervous (a feeling discussed during the sessions).

Charlie was also given opportunities to practice his new skills during the sessions and in naturalistic situations outside of my office. After all, the proving ground is in the real world! For instance, in one session, I read Charlie a Social Story about taking a ride on an elevator (an anxiety-provoking activity for Charlie). I then told him that the two of us were going to take a ride on the elevator together and that I wanted him to first practice his relaxation strategies.

After the tension release and breathing exercises, Charlie and I walked to the elevator. As we approached the elevator, I again asked Charlie to practice his breathing and tension release strategies, and did so once more after we entered the doors. On this occasion, we did not take a ride on the elevator, but we did on the next session. I prefer graduated over sudden exposure to stressful situations as it allows the child to gradually practice his relaxation strategies.

Biofeedback

Biofeedback is another promising strategy for reducing stress. This therapeutic tool teaches clients to recognize and control physiological responses and subsequent psychological and behavioral responses. The form of biofeedback that I recommend for children with ASD involves the use of a heart rate monitor. By providing instant feedback about the child's physiological responses to stressors, the monitor presents a concrete example. That is, children learn that their feelings of anxiety are directly related to their physiological responses, in particular their heart rate, and that if they can regulate the physiological response, they will be better able to regulate the anxious response. Children who see their heart rate actually decreasing seem to take on renewed appreciation for their newly learned relaxation techniques. The heart rate monitor can also be used in naturalistic settings where stressful responses are likely to occur.

Self-Awareness Training

Self-awareness is an integral part of relaxation training. Self-awareness training involves teaching children to become aware of and detect both the stressors and anxiety-provoking stimuli (triggers) and their physiological and behavioral response to these stimuli.

I use an awareness training technique from Azrin and Nunn's early work on habit reversal and regulated breathing (1973). These steps may be modified or supplemented to meet the individual learning needs of the child (i.e., by using visual supports, such as pictures or videos to depict the behavioral responses, or by using Social Stories™ to introduce the awareness training technique).

Steps of Awareness Training

1. Response description

2. Response detection

3. Early warning

4. Situation awareness training

Response description requires the child to describe his anxious response in both physiological and behavioral terms: my heart races; my palms feel sweaty; my hands shake; I run away; I have trouble concentrating.

Response detection involves teaching the child to recognize when the response is occurring. For many children, recording instances of the response via self-monitoring is an effective way to teach response detection. I recommend that the therapist, teacher, or parent, record the responses along with the child to measure accuracy and provide feedback. The self-monitoring strategy may be discontinued once the child reaches a level of 90% accuracy compared to the adult's rating.

Early warning is intended to teach the child to recognize early warning signs so that relaxation strategies can be used quickly and before the anxious symptoms become intense and unmanageable. If the response description in Step 1 is thorough, the adult and the child need only to put the responses in sequence from early responses to later responses (e.g., "heart races," then "hands shake," then "I have trouble concentrating," etc.).

Situation awareness training involves teaching the child to identify situations or stimuli that evoke anxious responses. Severe weather, social interactions, public speaking, going to the dentist, and dogs are examples of common situations or stimuli that evoke anxious responses in many children with ASD. If children are made aware of these situations, they can use relaxation techniques prior to encountering the stressful situation, rather than as a reaction to these situations.

The following Stress Scale from *The Incredible 5-Point Scale* (Buron & Curtis, 2003) provides a simple tool for children to identify and then self-regulate common stressors.

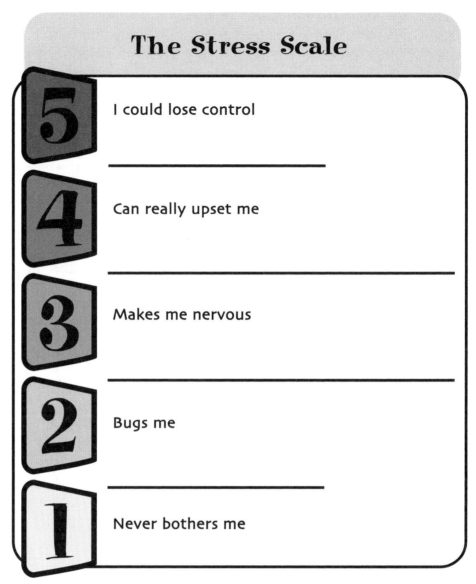

The Stress Scale

5 I could lose control

_____

4 Can really upset me

_____

3 Makes me nervous

_____

2 Bugs me

_____

1 Never bothers me

From *The Incredible 5-Point Scale* by K. D. Buron & M. Curtis, p. 65.
Copyright 2003. Shawnee Mission, KS: Autism Asperger Publishing Company.
Reprinted with permission.

Prompting

Social Skills to Teach: *reading nonverbal cues, reciprocal conversations, initiating interactions, making eye contact, responding to initiations*

Prompts are highly effective for teaching social interaction skills to children with ASD. In fact, I expect you to join in chanting the following mantra, "Prompts are our best friends … prompts are our best friends!"

Prompts are supports and assistance provided to the child to help her acquire skills and successfully perform behaviors.

Prompts can be used to teach new social skills and to enhance performance of previously acquired skills. In addition, they may be used with novice or advanced performers; in individual sessions or in group sessions; with verbal children or with non-verbal children; with preschoolers or with adults. Finally, prompts may be delivered by adults or by other children.

Five primary types of prompts may be used to facilitate social behavior. They are discussed here from "most" to "least" supportive. The most supportive prompts require the greatest amount of adult support and the least amount of independence on the part of the child, whereas least supportive prompts require more independence on the part of the child and less adult assistance. The goal is to use the prompt that provides "just enough" support – or the least supportive prompt necessary for the child to successfully complete a task. The order of prompts will have great importance as we discuss the specific guidelines for using and subsequently fading prompts.

Types of Prompts

Most Supportive   **Least Supportive**

Physical Prompt ... Modeling Prompt ... Verbal Prompt ... Gestural Prompt ... Natural Prompt

---

1. **Physical prompts** consist of physically guiding a child's performance of a target skill or behavior and are the most supportive type. Physical prompts range from hand-over-hand guidance (most supportive), to a simple physical touch to facilitate a specific movement (least supportive).

2. **Modeling prompts** consist of demonstrating or performing all (most supportive) or part (least supportive) of the desired skill or behavior to the child, who imitates the skill or behavior immediately. Both physical and modeling prompts can be used to teach new skills or behaviors.

3. **Verbal prompts** are a common prompting procedure. Verbal prompts include specific verbal directives (most supportive) or instructions, or single words and phrases designed to trigger or jog a child's memory of how to perform a task (least supportive). This type of prompt can be used to teach new skills or behaviors and also to enhance performance of existing skills or behaviors.

4. **Gestural prompts** involve providing a nonverbal gesture that visually directs or reminds an individual to perform a task. Gestural prompts typically consist of various hand signals but may also include visual cues and supports (pictures, cards, etc.). They range from elaborate (pointing to a location and pantomiming an activity) to simple (pointing to another student to facilitate a social initiation).

5. **Natural prompts** are the least supportive type of prompt. These are stimuli that naturally occur in the child's environment that direct a behavior to occur. This may include a bell ringing or kids lining up to go outside. There are many natural prompts for social interactions. A common natural (and direct) prompt occurs when a person initiates an interaction with us (i.e., asks us a question). This prompt naturally directs our behavior to respond. Unfortunately, this prompt is sometimes not enough for children with ASD, who often need a more supportive prompt (gestural or verbal) to respond.

Guidelines for Using Prompts

Although prompts can be used for a variety of behaviors and skills addressed during a social skills program, the following guidelines are specifically designed to facilitate social interactions. They may be used during structured playgroups or in natural settings, such as the playground or classroom.

- **Use of prompts to facilitate positive social interactions.** The primary purpose of prompting is to promote POSITIVE interactions. Make a particular effort to prompt skills and behaviors that are the target of the intervention. That is, focus on the child's treatment and IEP objectives. Be patient with your prompts. Wait before providing a prompt to allow the child ample time to process various social situations. Only prompt if absolutely necessary. A rule of thumb in structured play sessions is to prompt after 30-45 seconds of non-interaction, or solitary behavior. Prompts should be provided to both children with ASD and their nondisabled peers to facilitate initiations and responses (reciprocal interactions).

Note:

You may prompt any skill that the child is working on, but focus primarily on initiations and responses to increase social interactions.

- **Prompt sequence.** Begin by providing the least supportive prompt necessary to promote successful completion of the behavior. (There is no need to use physical prompts when a gestural or verbal prompt will suffice.) Allow 20-30 seconds for the child to respond to the prompt. If the child does not respond, provide a more supportive prompt (or more specific prompt if using verbal prompts). Twenty to 30 seconds will test your patience, but be patient. Give the child ample time to process the prompt within the context of the social situation. If he does not respond to the second prompt after 20 seconds, provide an even more supportive prompt. Proceed in this fashion until a physical prompt is necessary. If the child does not respond to the physical prompt, simply redirect him to a new activity or move on to another child (if working with groups).

Note:

Remember the focus of the social interaction groups is to facilitate positive interactions; therefore, do not get caught up in trying to manage problem behaviors. If the child does not feel like interacting or is being non-compliant, simply move on to another child and wait for an opening to return to the target child.

Verbal prompts should be as specific as necessary to promote performance of the skill. For instance, it might be necessary to provide specific instructions such as, "Tommy, hand the ball to Jimmy," or "Tommy, ask Jimmy to play blocks with you." However, for some children a general verbal prompt will suffice, such as "Jimmy, it's time to play with Tommy" or "What are we supposed be doing?"

- **Prompt fading.** As the child progresses from novice to mastery performance of a specific skill, fade the prompts as quickly as feasible from most to least supportive. Prompts typically need to be faded gradually. If a child requires a modeling prompt, first proceed to a less supportive modeling prompt (e.g., from modeling the whole behavior to modeling a part of the behavior). From there, fade to a verbal prompt (which is less supportive than the modeling prompt). If you are fading verbal prompts, fade the prompt from specific to general (e.g., from "Tommy hand the ball to Addison" to "Tommy play with Addison" to "Tommy time to play," and so on).

An effective way to fade prompts from most supportive to least supportive is to pair the prompts prior to fading them. This is done by providing the less supportive prompt just before or simultaneously with the more supportive prompt; for instance, providing a verbal directive prior to modeling the behavior, or providing a gestural prompt prior to providing a verbal directive. The more supportive prompt would then be withdrawn during subsequent performances of the skill or behavior. For instance, you would no longer use the verbal prompt after the delivery of the gestural prompt.

Interaction/ Conversation Planning

Social Skills to Teach: *reciprocal interactions, initiating interactions, planning interactions*

Many children with ASD have great difficulty planning and initiating social interactions and getting other children to engage in activities with them. They are often dependent on the advances of other children, which can be infrequent. As a result, these children only engage in activities with other children if the other child initiates the interaction. Other children with ASD have no problems initiating interactions, but their initiations are often poorly planned. These ill-timed and ill-conceived initiations lead to interactions that appear random and capricious, and almost always one-sided.

Most of us initiate interactions with a specific purpose in mind. It may be to ask a question, to join in an activity, or perhaps to just chat with another person. Some of us even rehearse (cognitively or behaviorally) how the interaction might go, or what we will say to other person. This is particularly true for conversations or interactions that are stressful to us. For instance, you may at some point in your life have engaged in cognitive and/or behavioral rehearsal prior to asking a question in front of a large group (i.e., going over in your head what you will say). If so, you were using an active conversation or interaction planning strategy to make sure you got your message across. Most children with ASD are not using active planning strategies prior to initiating interactions and, therefore, tend to be unsuccessful.

This section will describe a procedure I developed for teaching a child with ASD how to plan and initiate an interaction with peers, called the Conversation Map.

The Conversation Map provides the child with a guide, or pathway, to follow when she initiates interactions. The map helps integrate perspective taking, social problem solving, and inferring the interests of others with specific initiation skills. Because it involves perspective taking, social problem solving, and inferring the interests of others, this activity is most appropriate for older elementary- through high-school-aged children, but some younger children may do just fine with it. If necessary, remove the cognitive processing components, and focus on the concrete aspects of the map. In these cases, you would spend less time having the child brainstorm the interaction, and more time practicing the interaction.

The structure provided below presents general guidelines for planning an interaction. Each of the questions should be modified to meet the developmental level and dialect of the child.

1. ***Select child to play with***. The Conversation Map begins by asking the child to identify a specific child whom the child with ASD would like to talk with (or "play with," "hang out," "chill with"… use terminology the child will understand). The selection of a specific child provides a frame of reference for the child to facilitate skill instruction. Encourage the child to apply a similar map (formally then informally) to initiations with other children.

2. ***Determine reason for playing with child***. The next step is to have the child identify why he wants to interact with the selected child; that is, to ask a question or request assistance; to play or hang out with child; or just to talk with her.

3. ***Identify other child's interest.*** After the purpose of the interaction has been identified, ask the child to identify the target child's interests. This step will incorporate the Interest Inventory discussed on page 131. (This will flow naturally into the next section, which involves having the child brainstorm what he might say or talk about with the other child.)

4. ***Select topic of planned conversation.*** Next, have the child select a specific topic, which will be the initial focus of the conversation. Ideally, the child will have the option of selecting a topic that is of mutual interest to both himself and the other child. At this stage, the child is just brainstorming topics, not the specific initiation statement or question. Also during this step, ask the child to consider whether the other child will be interested in the topics he selects. That is, do they match the interests listed in the previous step? This may create a teachable moment – to help the child see the relationship between the other child's interests and potential topics of conversation.

5. ***Develop scripted initiation and expected response.*** The next step in the Conversation Map is to ask the child to create a list of ways in which he will initiate the interaction with the other child based on the topic selected above. The initiation will typically include a greeting (verbal or nonverbal) and an opening statement or question.

   Have the child be specific with his initiation (e.g., "what's up, Brad?" followed by, "do you like Yugi-oh cards?"). The child is then asked to consider how the child might respond to his initiation (e.g., "yeah, I like Yugi-oh"). Have the child try to select three potential responses to his initiation. Once potential responses are identified, have the child generate his response to the other child's potential responses (e.g., "want to see my cards?").

6. ***Select best setting to initiate conversation.*** Have the child consider the best setting in which to initiate the conversation with the target child; for instance, in class, at recess, in the hallway, in a group with other children or when she is by herself, and so forth. This is also the point where you might review specific rules regarding initiating interactions, such as waiting for the other person to stop talking, using eye contact to initiate, maintaining appropriate personal space, and so on.

7. ***Practice.*** At the risk of sounding like a broken record, when the map is completed, it is time to practice the interaction covered in the map via a role-playing activity.

1. Person you would like to talk to or play with?

   Name of person:

   Grade/class of person:

2. Reason you would like to talk with the person?
   - To ask a question
   - To play with or hang out with the person
   - Just talk with the person

3. Person's interests?
   - Things he/she likes to do
   - Things he/she likes to talk about

4. Things you might say or talk about?
   - Would the other person be interested in talking about this?

5. How might you begin conversation?
   - What will you say?
   - How might the other child respond (3 possible responses)?

6. When would be the best location to talk to this person?
   - In class
   - In the hallway
   - At recess
   - When he/she is with other children
   - When he/she is by herself

7. Practice!

Chapter Summary

This chapter provided a broad collection of social skill intervention strategies designed to promote skill acquisition in children with ASD. As such, these strategies are most appropriate for teaching skills that the child does not already possess, or possesses at a novice level. Though the strategies were presented separately in the text, in many cases they may be used in combination with other strategies. In addition, some of the strategies (e.g., Social Stories™, video modeling, and prompting) can be used to promote skill acquisition AND to enhance performance. The strategies covered in this chapter included:

◎ Thoughts, Feelings, and Interests

◎ Reciprocal Intervention Strategies

◎ Social Stories

◎ Role Playing/Behavioral Rehearsal

◎ Video Modeling

◎ Social Problem Solving and Social Rules

◎ Self-Monitoring

◎ Relaxation Techniques/Emotional Regulation

◎ Prompting Strategies

◎ Interaction/Conversation Planning

Strategies That Enhance Performance

Performance enhancement strategies serve to enhance the performance of existing or newly learned skills and behaviors, not to teach new ones. For instance, if you can't speak Spanish, all the reinforcement in the world won't help you deliver a speech in Spanish next week. While it might increase your motivation to learn, it will not teach you how to speak Spanish. Performance enhancement strategies facilitate performance by either addressing the factor that is diminishing performance (lack of motivation, anxiety, sensory sensitivities, etc.) or by providing opportunities to perform newly learned or existing skills.

Though they do not teach skills by themselves, perform- ance enhancement strategies are often necessary companions to skill acquisition strategies. For example, while we are teaching a child a new skill, it is necessary to reinforce both effort and/or performance of the skill. To use another example, if we teach a child to join in activities with peers, but do not provide opportunities for social participation, the child is unlikely to ever perform his newly learned skill of joining in. The strategies in this chapter cover performance enhancement strategies that should be incorporated into an effective social skills program.

- ✔ Reinforcement/Contingency Strategies
- ✔ Gaming Skills
- ✔ Environmental Modifications
- ✔ Peer-Mediated Instruction
- ✔ Increased Social Opportunities/Live Practice
- ✔ Disability Awareness/Peer Support Strategies
- ✔ Priming Social Behavior

Reinforcement/ Contingency Strategies

This section will cover basic principles of reinforcement and contingency, followed by descriptions of two commonly used contingency systems: group contingency systems and behavioral contracts.

Basic Principles of Reinforcement

Positive reinforcement is a powerful motivator of human behavior. Most of us are driven by positive reinforcement, both internally and externally. From our paychecks to our leisure activities, we select activities that hold the promise of positive reinforcement. We are more likely to perform, or attempt, a behavior if we think we will be reinforced for it. For instance, if you are told repeatedly that you look great wearing blue, you will probably wear blue again, and again.

In social skills parlance, a child who receives reinforcement for initiating an interaction with another child is likely to initiate interactions again in the future. The opposite is also true, a child who does not receive reinforcement for initiating an interaction (e.g., the other child rejects his initiation attempt) will be less likely to initiate interactions in the future. Specific types of reinforcers include attention (from peers or adults), social praise, sensory items, tangible items (toys, stickers, food, etc.), and preferred activities (playing a video game or extra recess time).

Reinforcement ...

- Increases desired behaviors. Simply put, if you promptly deliver copious amounts of reinforcement (desired reinforcement) to target behaviors, the target behaviors will increase.

- Forces us to monitor the child's behavior, and communicates to the child that we are monitoring his behavior. This is a very important concept for reducing problematic behaviors.

- Provides feedback to the child about his behavioral performance. Since it is the delivery of positive reinforcement, it will involve feedback regarding positive behaviors rather than the negative ones. And we all could use that.

Social interactions can be stressful and excruciatingly difficult for children with ASD, at least until they acquire sufficient skills and confidence. Therefore, reinforcement and specific reinforcement strategies should be woven into your social skills program and ALL your social skill activities and strategies. The timing of the reinforcement is paramount. Typically, reinforcement should be delivered immediately following the successful performance of the target behavior. However, use caution with your delivery of reinforcement for two reasons.

Timing of Reinforcement Delivery

1. ***Do not provide reinforcement or verbal feedback while the children are actively engaged in a social interaction.*** It may break the momentum of the interaction and create a distraction. This is especially important for those who are expending a great deal of cognitive resources on the task at hand. In other words, once you facilitate the dance (through prompting if necessary), get off the floor! You can reinforce and provide feedback at the end of the play sequence.

This is another reason I recommend that you frequently video-tape interactions. If you can catch it on tape, you can show it to the child later and provide immediate reinforcement and feedback without interrupting the original interaction.

2. ***Remember that social interactions may have an inherently reinforcing quality.*** Even children with ASD who experience intense peer failure and rejection may still find great satisfaction in participating in positive social interactions. Even children who are fearful and tend to avoid social interactions may still be intrinsically motivated to engage in successful social interactions with peers. Therefore, it may be unnecessary or even detrimental to provide external reinforcement when the behavior or activity is naturally reinforcing to the child (Deci, Koestner, & Ryan, 1999). The following story captures this well.

External Reinforcement and Intrinsic Motivation: A Classic Tale

An elderly man was awoken from his slumber by the sound of trash cans banging outside his window. This was the fourth night in a row that this had occurred. He had had enough!

The man slipped on his house coat and hurried down the stairs and out his front door to put an end to the infernal racket. As he exited his building, he noticed three young lads smiling and shouting gleefully, evidently thrilled with their late-night drum performance. As he approached the boys, the leader of the group snapped, "What do you want, old man?"

The man replied, "I was just appreciating how well you kids banged those trash cans. In fact, I was hoping that you would come back each night at this time to bang them some more. And if you do, I'll give you each $5."

Taken aback, the leader of the group graciously accepted the offer. Sure enough, the next night the boys were back, louder than ever, evidently invigorated by their new business opportunity. Upon hearing them outside his window, the elderly man sauntered down the stairs to meet them.

As he approached them, his expression turned to anguish as he said, "Listen boys, I'm afraid I have some bad news for you. My car broke down this morning, so unfortunately I will have less money to pay you for your valuable services."

The boys were a bit disappointed with the news, but nonetheless, they showed up the next night to perform their duties. Again, the man was there to meet them with a distressed look – the bearer of bad news.

He bowed his head as he told them, "I regretfully have to terminate our business relationship. It seems that my car repair costs were far greater than I had anticipated. Consequently, I simply have no money to pay you. However, I would be grateful if you would consider continuing your can-banging services for free."

But the boys were having none of it. The leader spoke for the group as he said firmly, "Listen, old man, you're crazy if you think we're going to waste our time, standing on this corner, banging trash can lids for free." With that, the boys left ... as did their motivation to bang trash can lids.

The question of whether external reinforcement diminishes intrinsic motivation is a contentious issue in the fields of education and psychology. My belief is that most children do not get enough reinforcement during the course of their day, so rarely do we run the risk of over-reinforcing. However, if the child does find social interactions with other children enjoyable, and is highly motivated to interact with other children, it is not necessary to provide reinforcement for the successful performance of social behaviors. If, on the other hand, the child is not motivated to interact with other children (i.e., disinterested), it might be necessary to reinforce the performance of social behaviors.

In either case, it is imperative that the child be reinforced continually for his effort and participation, especially if she is socially anxious or has low self-efficacy. Be a coach, be a teacher, and if necessary, be a cheerleader!

Group Contingency Systems

Group contingency systems involve providing reinforcement to groups of children (i.e., classwide, schoolwide, etc.) for performing specific behaviors. Group incentive programs typically establish a list of target behaviors (cooperation, encouragement, helping, etc.) that children are expected to perform during the course of the school day. Children who are "caught" performing a target skill are acknowledged through praise, stickers, coupons, or a token system. When the entire group accumulates a pre-established number of tokens, the group earns the reinforcement.

A group contingency system makes a great complement to classwide social skills instruction. As social skills are introduced and taught to the class, they may be targeted via the group contingency system.

Example of Group Contingency Systems

One teacher that I worked with introduced three social skills a month to her class as part of a group incentive program. She kept a jar on her desk, and each time she observed a student performing a target skill, such as helping a classmate, she handed the student a marble and asked her to place it in the jar. When the class filled the jar, they earned a popcorn and movie party. Like any good teacher, she manipulated the system so that all the students had an opportunity to contribute to the jar – not just the teacher's pet.

Behavior Contracts

A behavior contract is a contingency strategy whereby reinforcement is provided contingent upon the performance of a predetermined level of behavior. It is a written or informal agreement between the child and an external agent (parent, teacher, or therapist) (Polsgrove, 1979). For example, if the child turns in all homework assignments for one week, he will be allowed to rent a video game on Friday night.

I use behavior contracts exclusively with children who demonstrate little to no intrinsic motivation to interact with peers, or with children who are reluctant to interact with other children because of anxiety or low self-efficacy. I recommend using them with any child who needs an extra "push" to perform the skills that she is learning in the social skill program.

Behavior contracts work best when the child plays an active role in writing the contract as it improves her motivation to uphold it. This may be accomplished by allowing the child to negotiate the specific elements of the contract. Behavior contracts can be a link to self-monitoring strategies as they require the child to take an active role. Eventually, support the child as she develops self-contracts that do not involve adults, and focus on self-reinforcing strategies, where the child selects and delivers her own reinforcement.

According to Polsgrove (1979), the elements of the behavior contract include the selection of target behaviors, the establishment of performance criteria, agreed-upon consequences for meeting performance criteria, when the consequences will be delivered, consequences for failure to meet performance criteria, methods for evaluation of performance, and performance feedback.

1. *Select target behaviors.* Behaviors should be selected based on your treatment/social objectives and should be defined clearly enough for the child to understand.

2. *Establish performance criteria.* Performance criteria refer to the specific criteria that the child must reach in order to earn the consequence (e.g., "ask one child per day to play with you at recess for one week"). A key is to push the child while also setting her up for success (do not establish unrealistic performance criteria!), particularly early on in the intervention.

3. *Agree on consequences.* Let the child determine the potential consequences for reaching the performance criteria. It is wise to develop a list of reinforcers (i.e., items or activities that the child finds reinforcing) beforehand.

4. *Determine when consequences will be delivered.* Clearly spell out when the consequence will be delivered. This could be a teachable moment, especially if flexibility is a focus of the intervention, but I would not suggest using this until after the behavior contract system has been fully established. That is, only after she has successfully performed behaviors and earned consequences using the behavior contract.

Note:

If you say you are going to deliver a consequence on Friday afternoon to the child with ASD, you'd better deliver the consequence on Friday afternoon!

----

5. ***Agree on consequences for failure to reach performance criteria.*** Some behavior contracts provide an alternative consequence (i.e., punisher) for failure to reach the performance criteria. I do not advocate for the use of punishers for failing to reach a performance criteria. I might recommend it if you were contracting to address problem behaviors. However, social skill contracts are not written to manage problem behaviors; they are written to enhance successful social performance.

I have included this step only to highlight the fact that it is a common element of behavioral contracts. If the agreed-upon positive consequence is highly desired, failure to earn it will be painful enough for the child without adding punishment.

6. ***Determine methods of evaluation.*** The next element involves determining how the child's performance will be evaluated. This could be through work products, behavior observations, or self-monitoring forms.

7. ***Provide performance feedback.*** The final element is often the most important facet of the behavior contract – providing feedback on performance. The feedback provides valuable connection between the contract and the teaching of skills. Be specific with the child. Let her know what skills need to be improved, and how you will help her improve those skills. And no feedback loop would be complete without telling the child what she did well and why the behavior is important to perform.

Steps in Using Behavior Contracts

1. Select the target behavior.

2. Establish performance criteria.

3. Reach an agreement with the child on consequences for meeting performance criteria.

4. Determine when the consequences will be delivered.

5. Reach an agreement with the child on consequences for failure to meet performance criteria.

6. Determine method for evaluation of performance.

7. Provide performance feedback.

Gaming Skills

I know what you are probably thinking. No, I am not suggesting that we teach children with ASD to play black jack, poker, or any other "game of chance." The gaming skills that I am referring to involve the typical games that children play. Rarely do children participate in social interactions that consist solely of conversation. Usually, children are involved in social interactions that involve activities, movement, games, or other shared tasks. For instance, children can spend hours planning a club house, playing wiffle ball, playing with action figures, or playing video games together without asking one single personal question about the other person. It is a rudimentary level of social interaction, but it is a meaningful interaction nonetheless. It is also a rather simple way to facilitate nonstressful social interactions for children with ASD. Finally, it does not require professional involvement.

The following steps are helpful for incorporating gaming skills into a social skills program.

Find out What Games Are Popular

The first step to teaching gaming skills is to ascertain what games are popular for your child's age group. Start by asking your son or daughter what games other children are playing. If they are unsure, ask teachers or other children.

Rule of Thumb:

If your school has banned a game, it is probably an extremely popular game. As I write these words, "Yugi-oh" is a wildly popular card game among older elementary-school children and adolescents. Many schools have banned these cards from their campuses because they have "distracted from the educational mission" of the school. The game also involves the loser relinquishing cards to the winner – as you could imagine, this would cause a disagreement or two.

Try to select games that other children may not have played yet. This will allow your child to teach other children how to play a new, yet popular game.

Determine Who Will Teach the Game to the Child

After selecting a potential game to teach the child, you will need to determine whether you have the ability to teach the game, or if you will have to consult with an expert – that is, another child! Peer mentors can be selected from the neighborhood, school, or they can be family friends or siblings.

Invite Another Child to Play

Once your child has mastered the game, allow him to invite a peer over to your house to play. Have the game ready. Although they do not have to play the game for three straight hours, playing it might make a nice ice-breaker to get your child comfortable with the interaction and confident in his skills.

Suggestions for Incorporating Gaming Skills Into a Social Skills Program

1. Find out what games are popular.

2. Determine who will teach the game to the child.

3. Invite other children to play.

Also look for opportunities to facilitate your child's interest in games or activities that are age appropriate. One of my young clients with ASD enjoyed collecting and gathering action figures, which he carried with him in a box. The problem was, his figures were Pokémon characters, and Pokémon was no longer a "cool" game for children his age. So his parents encouraged him to collect super-hero action figures, such as Batman and X-Man characters, which were very "in" among his peers.

Imagine how much more popular he was with a box of super-heroes than a box of Pokémon! For a child with many difficulties with social initiations, all he had to do was open the box, and he would have many willing dance partners. I like to refer to the phenomenon as an "initiation in a box."

Environmental Modifications

Although environmental modifications are not a direct focus of my social skills program, the impact of environmental stimuli on the child with ASD must be considered. I am speaking of the physical environment here, not the social environment.

As addressed in Chapter 6, sensory processing deficits, including hypersensitivities to sensory stimuli and difficulties integrating multiple sensory inputs (e.g., listening while looking) are common in children with ASD, and may significantly impede social performance by negatively affecting concentration and attention, increasing anxiety, and leading to avoidance or withdrawal from social situations.

In the context of social skills programming, sensory sensitivities may be addressed using the following strategies:

- Relaxation Techniques

- Sensory Integration

- Modification of the Physical Environment

Relaxation techniques are covered earlier in this chapter (see pages 169-174) and sensory integration strategies are covered in great detail elsewhere (see, e.g., Yack, Sutton, & Acquilla, 2002). This section will focus exclusively on modifications of the physical environment.

Modifications of the Physical Environment

Modifications to the physical environment may be made in the therapeutic setting (therapist's office, resource room, etc.) and/or in the child's natural environment (home, classroom, etc.).

One young man I worked with had great difficulties concentrating on the strategies and activities of the session because, as he said, the "clock was too loud." He was referring to a clock that I hardly noticed in the room. In fact, I didn't think it was working until I held it up to my ear to hear its faint ticking noise. Sure enough, I removed the clock and the student's concentration improved considerably.

Davis (2005) and Davis and Dubie (2004) provide a series tips for modifying the physical environment to address the sensory processing needs of children with ASD. I have modified some of these tips to make them particularly relevant for social interactions. Not all modifications are appropriate or necessary for every child with ASD. Be sure to select environmental modifications that meet your child's or client's sensory needs.

Tips for Modifying the Physical Environment

✔ Limit the amount of visual material on the walls or ceiling.

✔ Keep the amount of visual material on activity sheets to a minimum.

✔ Desensitize a child to an area by slowly integrating him on numerous visits.

✔ Wear minimal amounts of perfume or cologne.

✔ Seat the child away from bright windows.

✔ Seat the child away from doors or hallways to reduce distractions.

✔ Minimize interactions and increase proximity to children and adults with loud voices.

✔ Use carpet squares or tape to mark spaces where the child will sit or stand during activities.

✔ Have a rocking chair, bean bag chair, or favorite sensory item available to support relaxation.

✔ Keep the classroom or therapy area organized and free of clutter.

✔ Use visual timers to reduce stress related to how long an activity will last.

✔ Use earphones to reduce auditory sensitivities.

✔ Have child wear weighted vest to promote relaxation and awareness of body in space.

Peer-Mediated Interventions (PMI) is an effective strategy for facilitating social interactions between young children with ASD (and other disabilities) and their nondisabled peers (Laushey & Heflin, 2000; Sasso, Mundschenk, Melloy, & Casey, 1997; Odom, McConnell, & McEvoy 1992; Strain & Odom, 1986). In PMI programs, nondisabled children in the class are selected and trained to be "peer buddies" for a child with ASD. As such, the nondisabled peers participate in the intervention by making social initiations or responding promptly and appropriately to the initiations of children with ASD during the course of their school day. PMI allows children with ASD to perform social behaviors through direct social contact and by modeling the social behaviors of peers.

PMI allows us to structure the physical and social environment so as to promote successful social interactions. PMI can be used in naturalistic settings (classroom and playground), and also in structured settings (structured playgroups). For maximum effectiveness, it is recommended that PMI programs be used in both settings. The use of peer mentors allows the teacher and other adults to act as facilitators, rather than active playmates. That is, instead of being a third wheel in child-child interaction, the teacher prompts the peer mentors to initiate and respond appropriately to the child with ASD. The use of trained peer mentors also facilitates generalization of skills by ensuring that newly acquired skills are performed and practiced with peers in the natural environment.

PMI differs from general "peer buddy" or "peer mentor" programs in the level of training provided to the peers. That is, PMI involves systematically training peer mentors on how and when to initiate and respond to their peers with ASD. General "peer mentor" or "peer buddy" programs typically have no such requirement for training.

Peer-Mediated Interventions

Characteristics of PMI Programs

- Nondisabled peers are systematically taught to initiate and to respond to peers with ASD

- May be used to enhance performance of skills in the natural environment

- Allow adults to serve as facilitators rather than as playmates for the child with ASD

Peer Mentors

Peer mentors in PMI programs should be classmates of the child with ASD, demonstrate age-appropriate social and play skills, have a record of regular attendance, and have a positive (or at least neutral) history of interactions with the child with ASD. Peer mentors should be made aware of the behaviors associated with ASD in a manner that is respectful and developmentally appropriate for the age group. For instance, they may need to be taught that the child with ASD sometimes needs additional time to respond to their questions or play requests. It is also helpful to give the peer mentors advanced warning regarding any stereotypical behaviors that the child with ASD might exhibit (hand-flapping, rocking, sound sensitivities, etc.) during their interactions.

Guidelines for Selecting Peer Mentors for PMI Programs

1. Select only socially competent peers!

2. Select peers who are approximately the same age or grade as the child with ASD.

3. Make sure peer mentors have a neutral or positive history with child with ASD.

4. Choose peers who exhibit age-appropriate play.

5. Select socially responsive peers.

6. Select peers who are likely to follow adult instructions.

7. Ensure peers are willing to participate.

Peer Mentor Training

After peer mentors have been selected, they must be trained. At the onset of training, teachers (or therapists when implemented in non-classroom settings) should describe the peer mentor role to each child and also to their parents (don't forget to get parental permission). In classroom settings, two children per class should be trained as peer mentors.

Training for the peers could occur in small-group lessons outside the classroom to avoid distractions. In these lessons, teachers or therapists should briefly describe the importance of being a good peer mentor, provide information regarding the behavior of their peer with ASD, review peer mentor skills previously introduced, and introduce new skills or practice a previously introduced skill. The content and scope of the lesson should be presented in a developmentally appropriate manner. At the beginning of each lesson, the school team member should describe how the individual children might use the skills they have learned. Skills to be taught may include initiating and responding appropriately and promptly to their peer with ASD.

A social coaching procedure (Strain & Odom, 1986) may be used to teach a new skills to peer mentors, consisting of

- verbally introducing the social skill

- soliciting a verbal response in which children describes the skill

- providing a short series of positive examples of the use of the social skill with a child in the group, and

- having each child demonstrate the use of the skill with another peer in the group

<table>
<tr><td>

Prior to Beginning Program

1. Describe role of a peer mentor.

2. Provide a detailed description of roles and responsibilities (to parents too).

3. Teach peer mentors about autism spectrum disorders (be child-specific).

Every Week (Ongoing Training)

1. Reaffirm importance of peer mentors (provide verbal praise).

2. Introduce new skills and review previously learned skills or topics (provide verbal description and model demonstration of skill).

3. Have mentors practice skills with adult facilitator and other peers.

</td></tr>
</table>

Implementing a PMI Program

Note:

For more information on peer-mediated interventions, see Vanderbilt/Minnesota Social Interaction Project Play Time/Social Time: Organizing Your Classroom to Build Interaction Skills *(Odom & MCConnell, 1993) and* S.O.S. – Social Skills in Our Schools: A Social Skills Program for Children with Pervasive Developmental Disorders, Including High-Functioning Autism and Asperger Syndrome and Their Typical Peers *(Dunn, 2006).*

Increased Social Opportunities/ Live Practice

When children learn news skills, it is imperative to provide them ample opportunities to practice and perform them as frequently as possible. According to Elliot and Gresham (1991), lack of opportunity to interact socially and lack of opportunity to practice social skills are two factors that contribute to the development of social skills deficits. These two factors are also responsible for the failure of many social skill programs, especially those being conducted in clinical settings or resource rooms. Too often, our social skills instruction, and consequently the child's social performance, ends the moment the child leaves the therapy room.

It shouldn't be this way. The natural environment is filled with rich social opportunities and experiences. As a therapist I have to keep in mind that I am not preparing my clients to interact successfully with a 30-something-year-old psychologist in a sterile therapy room. I am preparing them to interact with real children in real environments. Similarly, in any formal social skills training, children need opportunities to practice their newly learned skills with other children in natural settings.

Many parents that I work with do a wonderful job of providing social opportunities for their child, including playdates with other children, Boy Scouts, horse-back riding, Little League, 4-H, group music lessons, community theatre, chess clubs, choir, and martial arts.

Parents often ask what activity is best for their children. The answer is: It depends. The right activity for your child will depend upon her interests, skills, and temperament. The key is to select activities that provide your child with opportunities to interact socially with peers, and to practice the skills that she is learning in her social skills program.

1. ***Select opportunities that the child is interested in participating in.*** I have seen parents sign their child up for one activity after another only to create great distress for both the child and the rest of the family. Of course, many children with ASD will need a little push to select and to be a part of social activities; especially children with social anxiety. Provide encouragement, support, and reinforcement as necessary.

   If the child is highly anxious, ask teachers and therapists for suggestion on how to include her in social activities. Another suggestion is to provide the child with a selection of activities from which to choose. Though you are pushing her to be part of a social activity, she is ultimately deciding which activity to participate in. Team sports are wonderful experiences for many children, but do not feel obligated to sign your child up for tee-ball or Little League just because the neighborhood kids are playing. Often team sports turn into nightmare experiences for children and families. However, if your child enjoys the experience, regardless of his ability level, let him play!

2. ***Let the child's strengths and weaknesses guide your selection of activities.*** I played the trumpet for a year when I was in the fourth grade. Though I was very excited to play the trumpet, I was very bad. Thankfully, my parents pulled the plug on it after one year. I simply have no musical ability, or perhaps it is well hidden. Taking trumpet lessons was a mismatch with my abilities. If my parents would have kept signing me up for lessons each year, I would have been miserable, and I would have resented them for making me be a part of it. Select activities that leverage your child's strengths, not accentuate his weaknesses.

3. ***Consider the child's temperament.*** If the child has great difficulties sitting or standing in one place for more than a minute, baseball is not the sport for him. Try soccer or basketball instead. If the child is highly anxious around large groups, try 4-H, horse-back riding, or small-group musical lessons. If the child has great difficulties with ball games, try martial arts. If the child is creative and likes to be the center of attention, sign her up for community theatre.

Playdates are also a great way for children with high social anxiety and sensory sensitivities to interact with peers in a safe environment. My recommendation is first to invite other children to your home to benefit from the home field advantage. If the kids enjoy each other's company, schedule a "road game" at the other child's house.

There are no limits to the activities that can be selected. If the activities provide ample opportunities for social interactions, they will make a nice supplement to the child's formal social skills programming.

Things to Consider When Setting up Social Activities

1. Select activities that match the child's interests.

2. Select activities that leverage the child's strengths and minimize his weaknesses.

3. Select activities that match the child's temperament.

Disability Awareness and Peer Support Strategies

Chapter 2 introduced a developmental pathways model (see page 27) that proposed a path from social skill deficits to social anxiety. Briefly, the path suggested that social skill deficits lead to peer failure and other negative peer relationships, which in turn leads to anxiety regarding subsequent social interactions.

This model applies especially to children with social anxiety; it does not apply to all children with ASD. That is, not all children with social skill deficits experience peer failure. And not all children who experience peer failure develop social anxiety. Why is that?

The best explanation is that these children are fortified by the presence of various protective factors (Bellini, 2006). Protective factors serve not only to protect against the development of anxiety, they can even remediate symptoms after their onset. Besides internal qualities such as temperament and coping strategies, two external factors play critical protective roles in the development of social anxiety – adult and peer support. I will present strategies to leverage these factors in this section.

Perhaps the most rewarding aspect for me in teaching social skills to children with ASD is the look of excitement and wonderment on their faces as they begin to learn and understand the importance of effective social interaction skills. It sometimes seems as though they have a new toy to play with. Teachers and parents often report that the child is labeling emotions of others in the classroom, expressing emotions through words, and attempting to initiate interactions with other children.

As exciting as this is, it makes it even more devastating when children with ASD try out their new social skills in environments that are insensitive and unsupportive. Their sense of excitement and wonderment deflates the moment that their social overtures are unwittingly rejected by adults and peers. My work with an 8-year-old boy, Dalton, illustrates this point well.

Dalton came to my clinic with essentially no social initiation skills and high levels of social anxiety. We worked for months in individual and group sessions teaching Dalton how to initiate interactions with others (asking other children to play, requesting assistance from adults). Dalton's progress was slow, but steady.

Promoting an Accommodating Environment

One session his parents brought in a videotape of Dalton sitting in the school cafeteria at lunch. They wanted me to help them process a "meltdown" that Dalton had during the video recording. The video began with Dalton sitting at a lunch table with his classmates (unfortunately, there was no sound). After Dalton removed his sandwich from his lunch bag, he began fumbling with his juice box – those tiny straws can be frustrating! After a few moments of attempting to insert the straw, Dalton had had enough, and raised his hand to request assistance (a time for celebration!).

After a few seconds the lunchtime supervisor appeared at Dalton's side and immediately took corrective action, skillfully inserting the straw into the juice box. As the lunchtime supervisor started to walk away, Dalton looked up at the man, smiled, and attempted to say something to him (another cause for celebration). Unfortunately, the lunchtime supervisor did not notice Dalton's social overture.

He walked swiftly away, probably to take care of another juice-box crisis.

Dalton's face quickly turned from a smile to a frown. Ten seconds later he was in tears. Five minutes later he was crying hysterically in the arms of this teacher. He was inconsolable.

This episode was not the fault of the lunchtime supervisor, who was unaware of Dalton's needs or the skills that Dalton was working on in a therapist's office 50 miles away. This episode was the fault of the therapist, and his failure to address issues in the child's natural environment. In this case, Dalton's school was in dire need of disability awareness and sensitivity training. We don't know for certain what it was Dalton tried to say to the lunch supervisor. Even if the lunchtime supervisor had heard him, he probably wouldn't completely have understood everything Dalton was saying. However, if he had known that Dalton was working very hard to learn initiation skills such as requesting assistance and asking questions, he would have been more likely to have taken a few moments to acknowledge Dalton's initiations. A meltdown would have been avoided, and Dalton would have received a natural reinforcer for performing a targeted social skill in a real-life setting.

This episode provided the catalyst for the parents to design and implement disability awareness training for children in Dalton's classroom and every adult in the school building.

Disability Awareness – Then and Now

When I was in school, there were no children with significant disabilities in my classes. When I ask audience members over the age of 25 to raise their hands to signify that they had children with disabilities in their classroom, few hands go up. In my case, children with disabilities were clustered in two classes at the far end of the school building. We would occasionally see these children walking to lunch or on the playground, both at separate times than the general school population. When these children would occasionally mingle with nondisabled children, they were frequently the object of teasing and ridicule. Although there is no excuse for this behavior, it was probably to be expected given the lack of experience the rest of us had interacting with those who had disabilities.

Thankfully, times have changed. When I ask college students to raise their hands to signify that they had children with disabilities in their classroom, most, if not all, raise their hands. Inclusion is truly a beautiful thing, but it is not perfect.

Many children with ASD are still objects of teasing and bullying. I do not blame the children who are teasing; I blame many schools for failing to implement disability awareness and sensitivity training to both their students and staff. Children seem prewired to notice differences. Anyone with children knows the embarrassment of the first time their child pointed out a person with obvious physical characteristics that were different from their own (color of skin, physical disabilities, etc.).

My own personal embarrassment came at a Cincinnati Reds baseball game when my 3-year-old noticed a little person, a man in his 30s, walking up the aisle past our seats. Zachary stood up, pointed his finger, and shouted gleefully, "Daddy, look at that silly little guy!" I looked at the gentleman with all the shame and regret a bad parent could possibly muster under the circumstances. For his part, the gentleman gave me a knowing, and forgiving, wink of the eye. For Zachary and his father, this was a critical teachable moment about human differences.

Note:

A number of disability awareness and sensitivity programs are available for both adults and children. Some specifically target autism awareness, whereas others target general disability awareness. Some focus on the specific needs of the child in the classroom, others present general information on the disability. Some are schoolwide trainings, others focus on the classmates of the child with the disability. An extensive list of disability awareness resources may be found on National Dissemination Center for Children with Disabilities webpage, at http://www.nichcy.org.

Child-specific vs. general awareness. A common question from parents and teachers is whether to conduct a disability awareness program that is child-specific or one that covers general disability awareness and appreciation of differences.

Many parents are afraid to stigmatize or single out their child as having a disability, or as being different. They are afraid that if other children find out that their son has ASD, he will become the object of teasing. I remind them that their child is already the object of teasing and that other children already view him as being "different." Only now – after training – they might refer to him as the boy with autism rather than the multitude of other horrible names children sometimes call those who are different.

A Rule of Thumb:

If the child blends in well with the other children, and other children have no idea that he is "different," it is probably not necessary to conduct a child-specific intervention. Further, I recommend that schoolwide programs focus on general disability awareness and sensitivity training, while classroom programs might focus more on issues relevant to specific classmates.

There is no research to support the use of a child-specific over a disability-specific program. However, Baker (2003) recommends child-specific disability training in situations where the child is displaying noticeable behavioral differences, especially if those behaviors upset other children. Baker further recommends talking with the child with ASD prior to talking to his classmates to make sure that the child understands something about himself before he hears it from other children. Let the child know that you will be talking with the class about things he does well and things that he needs help with, such as talking and playing with other children. Finally, Baker recommends not having the child with ASD present during the sensitivity training with classmates.

Regardless of the type of program that you choose to implement, remember to keep it developmentally appropriate and allow children ample time to process the information you are sharing. Encourage questions; all questions!

Follow-Up

In the end you might want to confirm that your message had its intended affect. That is, that the children fully understood what you were attempting to communicate to them. You can do this through activities, or via small-group or individual questions. The importance of this type of follow-up was illustrated by a friend of mine, who relayed the story of his 10-

year-old coming home from school one day and asking, "Dad, what is ass-burgers, and how do you catch it?" And this was coming from an extremely bright kid. As it turned out, his son had a classmate with Asperger Syndrome and that day the class participated in an "Asperger awareness training" – a training that apparently missed its mark.

The use of peer mentors or peer buddies is another great way to develop a safe and supportive social environment for children with ASD. Unlike PMI described earlier in this chapter, which systematically trains peers to initiate and respond to children with ASD in specific social situations, the use of peer mentors is typically less structured and less formal.

Peer Mentors and Peer Buddies

The goal of peer mentors is to provide a layer of social support to children with ASD across the school day, and across various school settings. Pratt (2000) recommends the following strategies for using peer support programs for children with ASD:

Strategies for Using Peer Support Programs

✔ Pair elementary-age students with ASD with peer mentors during transitions, when playing on the playground, and during other unstructured times of the day.

✔ To prevent dependence on one peer, vary peer mentors across time and activities.

✔ Assign peer mentors to help the child with ASD become acclimated to the new setting when transitioning to a new school or classroom.

✔ Pair children with ASD with a peer mentor during special school events, such as school assemblies.

✔ Allow students with ASD to assist and support their classmates. Utilize the strength of the child with ASD to build relationships with peers. For instance, the child with ASD who excels at computers can teach classmates how to use a particular computer program.

From *Peer Support Programs* by C. Pratt. Copyright 2000. Bloomington: Indiana Resource Center for Autism Training. Used with permission.

Even though systematic training is not a component of utilizing peer mentors and peer buddies (as it is with PMI programs), it is still important to provide peer mentors with information regarding ASD and the specific behaviors of the child they will be assisting. Peer mentors can be the same age or older than the child with ASD and may be used in environments and situations that are especially difficult or stressful to the child. Peer mentors should always be willing participants.

Moreno and Pratt (1994) suggest that the following advice be given directly to peer mentors prior to involvement with their peer with ASD. (The suggestions should be tailored to meet the individual needs of the child with ASD.)

Directions for Peer Mentors

✔ Be consistent in how you refer to your classmate with ASD. Use whatever name he/she prefers. Avoid calling them by their name one time and a nickname (e.g., "buddy," "dude," etc.) the next.

✔ Be specific when discussing plans or directions. For example, do not say "I'll meet you near the room after class." Instead say, "I'll meet you at locker number 220 at 12:05 pm."

✔ DO NOT BE LATE! Many people with ASD have a hard time understanding concepts of time and waiting. The result is that they may feel confused, upset, and insulted if they think you are late. If necessary, plan to be early and wait for him/her.

✔ Remember that taking a little extra time or trouble to include your classmates with ASD in your social plans could be very important to them. They need and want friends and social opportunities, and do not always know how to show that need to others.

✔ Do not tease or be sarcastic with your classmate with ASD. In order to understand the humor in teasing or sarcasm, people must be able to detect double meanings. The person with ASD may not have that knowledge. Besides, teasing has probably been a very unpleasant part of that person's experience.

✔ If you see others teasing, laughing, or making fun of a person with ASD, try explaining a little about the person to them. They may only be laughing because they do not understand the person or the disability. However, if the teasing persists, talk to an adult about it.

✔ Do not make promises that you cannot keep. Avoid phrases like, "maybe we'll go to the show together some day." This may be interpreted as a promise. They seldom process all of the qualifiers, such as "maybe" or "some day."

From *Advice for Peer Tutors* by S. J. Moreno & C. Pratt. Copyright 1994. Bloomington: Indiana Resource Center for Autism Training. Used with permission.

In addition, I recommend providing specific information on any stereotypical behaviors that the child with ASD might exhibit, such as hand-flapping, rocking, vocalization, and so on. Explain these behaviors in terms of sensory needs and calming strategies and relate them to behaviors that we all engage in, such as fingernail biting, foot tapping, knuckle cracking, and pencil tapping. Finally, these tips for peer mentors can also serve as the foundation for class-wide awareness training provided that they are modified to match the developmental level of your students.

Priming Social Behavior

Priming is widely defined as the act of making something/ someone ready, as in "priming a pump" or "the team was primed for the championship." Priming from a social-cognitive perspective has a similar meaning. In this context priming refers to the "incidental activation of knowledge structures" (Bargh, Chen, & Burrows, 1996, p. 230), which facilitates memory recall or task performance. For instance, if we had had a brief conversation about your high school experience, you would have a much better chance of remembering your class president than if I asked you out of the blue, "Who was your class president in high school?" The same is true for task performances. Having a conversation about your high school drama experience, or seeing a commercial for *Arsenic and Old Lace* might activate knowledge or memory structures that instantly have you reciting your lines from a play you starred in 20 years ago.

What is perhaps most fascinating (and disturbing) about priming is that the activation of knowledge or memory structures often occurs outside of our awareness, or consciousness, producing "automatic" social behaviors. That is, our behavior is being primed and we do not even know about it.

Priming Research

Bargh, Chen, and Burrows (1996) primed college students with words associated with elder stereotypes and secretly measured their walking speed as they left the laboratory room. The results were astounding. Participants who were primed with elder stereotypes walked significantly slower than those primed with neutral words. In a separate experiment these researchers found that college students who were primed with words associ-

ated with rudeness were considerably more likely to interrupt a subsequent conversation (which was staged by research accomplices unknown to the participants) than were participants who were primed with positive and neutral words.

———————

The use of priming does not only occur in psychological research laboratories. Turn your television on, and you may suddenly have the impulse to buy something!

Priming has proven to be an effective strategy for children with ASD (Koegel, Koegel, Frea, & Green-Hopkins, 2003; Schreibman, Whalen, & Stahmer, 2000; Zanoli, Daggett, & Adams, 1996). Specifically, video priming has been used to reduce problem behaviors during transitions for children with ASD (Schreibman, Whalen, & Stahmer, 2000). The researchers selected transitions in settings deemed most problematic by the children's parents. The researchers then videotaped the settings to show the environment just as the child would see it (moving through the store, getting ready in the morning, etc.). The children were not depicted in the video.

The positive effects of priming to facilitate social behavior is supported by other researchers, who used priming to increase the social initiations of preschool children with ASD (Zanoli et al., 1996) and to decrease problem behaviors in the classroom (Koegel et al., 2003).

The usefulness of priming procedures to activate knowledge structures and to facilitate social cognition and social behaviors makes it a valuable intervention component in social skill programming. Social cognitions and social behaviors can be primed by presenting cognitive or behavioral "primes" just prior to performance of the skill or behavior in the natural environment.

Cognitive Priming

Cognitive priming strategies can be either visual (e.g., pictures, videos, modeling, or visual prompts) or verbal instruction (e.g., verbal description of the behavior, discussion of the behavior, or verbal prompts).

Behavioral Priming

Behavioral priming strategies involve behavioral rehearsal, or practicing the skill or behavior just prior to performing it in the natural environment.

Many of the social skill strategies previously discussed can be used as a primer. For instance, we can prime the use of social problem solving by using an SPS strategy (see page 153) with the child prior to him entering into a social situation, such as recess, a Boy Scout meeting, or chess club. The goal in this case would be to activate his knowledge structure for social reasoning and analysis, so that if he were confronted with a difficult social situation, he would be more likely to utilize his problem-solving skills. Or, we could use a simple, generic SPS strategy with a child prior to asking her to problem-solve a more complicated social situation that the child was directly involved in.

Similarly, social rules can be primed by introducing them (via a Social Story™) prior to the child confronting a social situation involving the rule (e.g., what to do at a birthday party). Social behavior can be primed by rehearsing or role-playing specific social interaction skills, such as reading non-verbal cues, initiating interactions, and maintaining reciprocal conversations immediately prior to exposing the child to social opportunities. Finally, social behaviors may be primed by showing a video of the child skillfully and successfully interacting with peers, again, prior to being exposed to a social situation.

Priming does not teach new skills or behaviors, but it is a powerful strategy for activating skills and behaviors already in our behavioral repertoire.

- Pictures

- Videos

- Modeling

- Verbal Description of Behavior

- Behavioral Rehearsal

- Social Problem Solving

- Social Stories™

Note:

Strategies to Prime Social Cognitions and Behaviors

Chapter Summary

The strategies covered in this chapter are designed to enhance the performance of existing or newly learned skills. These strategies enhance performance by either addressing the factor diminishing performance (low self-efficacy, lack of motivation, inattention, impulsivity, etc.), or by providing opportunities to perform newly learned skills. Performance enhancement strategies should be used to supplement skill acquisition strategies. The performance enhancement strategies covered in this chapter include:

- Reinforcement/Contingency Strategies

- Gaming Skills

- Environmental Modifications

- Peer-Mediated Instruction

- Increased Social Opportunities/Live Practice

- Disability Awareness/Peer Support Strategies

- Priming Social Behavior

Implementing Intervention Strategies

5-STEP MODEL

1. **Assess Social Functioning**

2. **Distinguish Between Skill Acquisition and Performance Deficits**

3. **Select Intervention Strategies**

   - **Strategies That Promote Skill Acquisition**

   - **Strategies That Enhance Performance**

4. **Implement Intervention**

5. **Evaluate and Monitor Progress**

Now that we have assessed social skill functioning and identified skills to teach, distinguished between skill acquisition and performance deficits, and selected intervention strategies, it is time to implement the strategies that were introduced in Chapters 8 and 9. That is, it is time to teach social skills!

This chapter will detail guidelines for planning and implementing the intervention phase of the program, including how to structure and format both individual and group social skill sessions. I will refer often to the specific strategies and concepts that we have discussed to this point, so have your bookmarks, paper clips, or sticky-notes ready.

The chapter consists of the following sections:

- Planning the Program – Before You Start

- Structuring and Implementing the Program

- Special Considerations for Conducting Group Social Skills Training

- Examples of Session Structures

- Facilitating Generalization of Skills

Planning the Program (Before You Start)

A number of considerations must be addressed prior to beginning the social skills program. Proper preparation and planning is essential to successful outcomes. This section will cover the following areas of planning:

1. Determining which children will benefit from a social skills program

2. Determining the format for the social skills program (individual, group, or classwide instruction)

3. Selecting peer models

4. Assembling and training the team

5. Selecting materials and resources

6. Determining where the sessions will take place

7. Developing the schedule

Selecting the Target Child

The first step is to determine who will be the focus of the intervention. If you are developing a social skills program with one or two children in mind, or if you are a therapist in private practice, this step will probably not apply to you.

This step applies to those who already have a program in place or those responsible for identifying at-risk children. Always keep your eyes open for children who may benefit from social skills programming. Teachers and therapists should communicate to parents which children will benefit from the program. Will you be targeting preschool-aged children, elementary-aged, or adolescents? Will the social skills program include children with significant cognitive disabilities or higher-functioning children? Verbal or nonverbal children? If you are structuring the program around one child, these questions are obviously irrelevant.

Individual and/or group instruction? The first consideration in planning the intervention is to determine whether the child will benefit from an individual or group social skills program, or perhaps a combination of both. This decision should be based on the child's needs. Those with significant social skill deficits usually benefit from one-on-one programs, which allow more intensive, individualized instruction. The disadvantage of the individual sessions is that the child is not exposed to same-age peers, as she would be in group sessions. Group sessions, on the other hand, do not allow you to target every child's individual needs during each session. For instance, if there are three children with ASD in the group, all with five treatment objectives, only two or three objectives may be shared across group members.

The group format also diminishes the amount of time you can spend on any one child. But the benefit of practicing skills with other children, rather than with an adult, balances these disadvantages. Remember that this is a social *skills* group. The focus is not necessarily on facilitating relationships and friendships between group members, although this frequently happens and should be encouraged. The goal for the children is to learn social skills and to improve their social performance. I encourage parents to find opportunities for the children in the groups to play together outside the therapeutic environment. I am happy to say that his has led to many burgeoning friendships between my child clients.

My suggestion is to use both individual and group instruction. This allows you to focus on individual skill development, while allowing the children the opportunity to practice their skills with peers in the group setting. If the child has particular difficulties performing a skill in the group session, that skill will be the target of the individual session. Group sessions also allow us to video tape a large quantity of social interactions to be used for the VSM procedure. The VSM segments are then shown to the children in their individual and group sessions. Suggestions for structuring individual and group sessions will be presented later in this chapter.

Determining the Format of the Program

Advantages of Individual and Group Instruction

Type of Instruction	Advantages
Individual	▪ More intensive instruction ▪ More individualized instruction
Group	▪ Opportunity to practice newly learned skills with same-age peers ▪ Opportunity to video record social behaviors with peers for use with VSM

A Note on Group Composition:

Group members should be selected carefully based on the type of skill deficits they exhibit. Too often children with ASD are thrown into social skills groups with children with behavior difficulties, who typically have very different needs. The result is a group that focuses on behavior management, rather than social interaction skills.

Children with skill acquisition deficits should be grouped with other children with skill acquisition deficits (excluding peer mentors who should have few social skill deficits). This allows you to introduce and teach specific skills to all group members. If a child in the group is experiencing predominantly performance deficits, the skill instruction would be unnecessary and could lead to boredom and potential behavior problems.

I have also seen group social skills program that unwittingly consist of bullies and their victims. This might be an appropriate arrangement for conflict resolution, but it is not a conducive environment for the development of social interaction skills, especially for the victim.

Social skill groups should consist of two to five children in each session. I prefer smaller groups for children with more intensive needs. Groups may consist of children with ASD and their nondisabled peers, or consist exclusively of children with ASD. When using

> *nondisabled peers, time will need to be set aside prior to each session to provide additional training to these children. For child groups (ages 3-11), I recommend that the groups consist of no more than three children with ASD at any given time, unless multiple therapists are working together in teams. Adolescent groups (ages 12-18) may consist of as many as five individuals with ASD, particularly when the group is comprised of older adolescents.*
>
> *Group members should be matched by chronological age. For child groups, my recommendation is that the age of the oldest group member should not exceed the age of the youngest group member by 12 months. For adolescent groups, the age difference can be expanded to 18 months for younger adolescents, and 24 months for older adolescents.*

Classwide instruction. Some professionals suggest that social skills training be taught exclusively in the natural environment and as part of the general classroom curriculum. Without a doubt, social interaction skills should be taught in the natural environment and should be infused in the general classroom curriculum. However, we are dealing with children with significant social skill deficits, whose needs may not be sufficiently met by classwide instruction alone. In addition, unlike children with ASD, it is doubtful that the majority of the students in the classroom would benefit from a social skills curriculum that focused on promoting skill acquisition. Though many general education students need social skill instruction, these children primarily benefit from a program focusing on performance enhancement of existing skills.

Teaching social interaction skills to older children or adolescents only in the natural environment would be both ineffectual and extremely frustrating to the child. Would you like to learn a new dance routine, or your part in a play, on stage in front of an audience? We don't even ask children to play baseball games without providing adequate skill instruction via a controlled practice and individualized instruction, so how could we expect children with ASD to develop social interactions skills without it? The answer is that we shouldn't.

This does not mean that that skill instruction could not be provided in the natural classroom environment. On the contrary, the natural environment is a great place to teach new skills and promote social performance. We just can't rely on it as the only place to teach social skills.

When using a classwide social skills curriculum, select social skill strategies that target both skill acquisition deficits and performance deficits, such as video modeling, Social Stories™, role-playing, and prompting. In addition, make the introduction of social rules and concepts a regular part of the school day. It will serve as skill instruction for students with ASD (and other students with skill acquisition deficits) and "refreshers" and primers for the rest of the students in the class. Suggestions for structuring classwide social skills instruction is presented later in this chapter.

Selecting Peer Models

If you plan to implement group social skills instruction, you will have to decide whether to use nondisabled peers as part of the group. If you will use nondisabled peers, what criteria will you use to select them? Will the nondisabled peers need to be trained or prepared for the group sessions? If so, how will this be done? (See selection and training criteria for peer mentors and peer-mediated instruction in Chapter 9 for further guidance.)

My preference is to include nondisabled peers whenever feasible as they can provide models of efficacious social behavior. They can also be easily trained to initiate and respond to their peers with ASD, which is invaluable as children attempt to perform their newly learned skills. One word of caution, however: Make sure to select peers who are capable of demonstrating appropriate social behavior!

The Trials and Tribulations of Finding Peer Models

One day a client of mine and his mother showed up with a neighborhood kid, whom we will call Ethan. Ethan seemed to be a nice enough lad, bright smile, and eager to explore his environment; and explore the environment he did! I spent 30 minutes chasing Ethan around my office, under desks, over tables, and behind filing cabinets, which left very little time to focus on my client.

That was the point when I started asking parents not only to find nondisabled peers, but to find nondisabled peers who could listen and respond to directives, and who are able to model appropriate and efficacious social behavior.

If peer training is required, I follow the procedures covered in the sections on peer-mediated instruction and peer mentors in Chapter 9. If training is not required, I still spend a minute or two talking to the peer about why he is there and what will be expected of him. After praising the peer for being there, I typically provide the following instructions and briefing (adjust for the child's developmental level):

"Do you know why you are here? [If yes, listen carefully to his explanation, and adjust your instructions accordingly.] *You and Michael are here to play with each other (or "hang out" with each other). Michael has been working on some things that will help him to be a better friend. There might be times during our games and activities that I will ask you or Michael to do something. It is important that you listen carefully and do as you are told. But the important thing is that you and Michael have fun playing together. Do you have any questions?"*

Assembling the Team

Next, determine which adults will be involved in the intervention. What staff members or other professionals will take part in the intervention?

At a minimum teachers and parents should be actively involved. Ideally, every adult who comes into contact with the child on a regular basis should also be trained. Staff members should meet regularly to share their thoughts and concerns about the social skill program. Once strategies are selected, the intervention plan should be presented to all stakeholders (parents, teachers, principal, other therapists working with the child) to determine feasibility and acceptability. This is especially important for staff members who will be actively involved in strategy implementation (see Chapter 11 for more information on social validity and treatment fidelity).

Training. Parents and teachers should be trained to look for opportunities to prompt and reinforce performance of the targeted skills and behaviors. They may also need to be trained on how to look for "teachable moments" – that is, naturally occurring opportunities for the child to apply social interaction skills.

A brief introduction and training in the use of prompts and reinforcement may suffice, but in certain circumstances team members will need more advanced training. If the team member will be required to monitor and record social behaviors, she will also need to be properly trained to use the selected recording method (see Chapter 11).

In-service trainings combined with demonstrations of how to implement the intervention strategies with the child, coaching and continual feedback, are powerful techniques for teaching adult learners.

Gathering Materials and Resources

Next you will determine which materials and resources you will need in order to implement the intervention strategies. This book is a good start, but you'll need a bit more. What other items or resources do you and the other team members need to be successful? Will you be using activity sheets as part of the SPS strategies? What social skills checklist will you be using to monitor progress? What forms will you provide to parents to inform them of their child's progress? Will you require a television and DVD to play videos? Will you need a video camera? How about editing software? And what about toys and other object props?

I suggest making a "wish list" with two columns of materials. One column lists materials that you absolutely have to have prior to implementing the program, the other includes things that you would like to have in order to make your program better. (This is the list that you bug your principal or clinical director with each day.)

Have the setting organized and ready before the child comes in. You do not want to spend 5 minutes looking for a particular game or object when you could be delivering instruction.

Play materials. I have one word to describe the most appropriate play items for child groups: hands-on! O.K., that was two words joined by a hyphen, but you get my message. For younger children, play items should be infused into the instructional activities. After all, you are in essence teaching the child how to play!

Make sure that toys and activities are developmentally appropriate and that they are conducive to reciprocal interactions. One-player games that last 30 minutes should be left out of the therapy room. Provide plenty of manipulatives that promote sensory exploration. Liquid, sand, objects with rich textures, and clay all fall under the category of sensory exploration. Also have plenty of functional play items that promote constructive play. Legos, Lincoln Logs, and blocks all represent good choices in this category. The final category of play items is symbolic-pretend. These items promote socio-dramatic play and include puppets and puppet stages, dress-up items, dolls, tea sets, and action figures.

Games and activities for adolescent sessions should also be conducive to reciprocal interactions and be infused into the instructional activities. Use board games, card games, multiple-player video games, building supplies, models (built collaboratively), or other age appropriate games.

Other teaching materials. In addition to games and play items, you will need a number of other teaching materials during your social skill sessions. These mostly consist of the materials necessary to teach various social-cognitive skills, such as social problem solving, inferring the interests of others, and perspective taking. These materials include activity sheets and computer software. A television with a VCR or DVD player is also necessary for use with the video modeling strategies.

Materials and Resources Checklist

✔ Books, worksheets, pictures of emotions and social situations, Social Stories™, Conversation Map, self-monitoring forms, etc.

✔ Computer programs

✔ Evaluation forms to monitor progress and to provide feedback to parents

✔ Television and DVD to play videos

✔ Video camera and editing software if you are using VSM

✔ Toys and other play items that are developmentally appropriate and that are conducive to reciprocal interactions

Determining Where the Sessions Will Take Place

I'm often asked, "Where is the best place to teach social skills?" My answer is typically, "Everywhere!" Every environment that the child enters into – from the classroom, playground, therapy room, back yard, to the local Wal-Mart – presents a great opportunity for teaching social skills.

Social skills programming can take place in a private clinic, school resource room, or classroom. Social skills instruction take can also take place throughout the day in the child's natural environment such as the playground or at home? (See Individual and/or Group, and Classwide Instruction on pages 213-216.)

As you consider the best setting for the social skills intervention, keep in mind the child's sensory processing needs (see Environmental Modifications in Chapter 9). If the training will take place in a portion of the classroom, make sure that it is not distracting to the child with ASD or the other children. Also, the program involves a great deal of movement (or doing!), not just worksheets and board games, so keep this in mind when you select the location. If sessions are implemented in a private clinic or school resource room, look for opportunities to prompt and reinforce the performance of the skill in the child's natural environment.

Determining the Schedule

The next step is to create a consistent schedule for the sessions. When will they take place and how long will they last? The schedule should be coordinated with each of the team members to ensure they are available as needed. In school settings you must balance the time of the sessions with the child's academic schedule.

Sessions should be divided into three-month periods. This allows ample opportunity for skill development. It also coincides with the length of a school quarter. At the end of each three-month period, progress is assessed and treatment objectives are rewritten as necessary.

Number of sessions. Rate of skill development differs greatly from one child to the next. Some children will begin utilizing their new skills after only two or three sessions, while others may require over three months before they begin to "get it" and start using their newly learned skills.

Of course, simply using or trying a skill is just the first step towards social success. The child will take additional time to master the social skills that he is learning and developing. I recommend 36 social skill sessions per year (at least one per week). This could include a combination of individual and group instruction.

If that sounds like too much, think of it this way. Over the course of the three-month Little League season, children receive approximately 20-30 practice sessions (if they practice an average of twice a week). We are not teaching children to hit baseballs here; we are teaching children with significant social skill deficits how to be socially competent. Do not expect dramatically quick results and do not expect the process to be easy!

Separate the program into four, three-month periods (I refer to them as "quarters"). This will allow ample time for the child to learn and develop the skills that she is working to acquire. The child's current level of social functioning should be assessed at the end of each three month period and treatment objectives modified as needed.

Session length. Sessions should be approximately 30-50 minutes long, but the exact length will depend on whether the sessions are being conducted in a school setting or a clinic setting, the age of the child, and whether it is an individual or a group session. Staff resources and caseloads often prevent school practitioners from committing more than 30 minutes per week to a single child. In addition, some children, especially younger ones, may not have the attention span to last longer than a half-hour.

The longer the session, the more opportunity you have to work on additional skills and implement more strategies, provided that the child is attending to the task and hasn't fallen asleep on you. Individual sessions typically last longer because they involve a parent feedback and training component at the beginning and end of the session.

Structuring and Implementing the Program

Now that the planning details are out of the way and you have identified the target child, gathered resources, determined where you will implement the program, and who will be responsible for implementation, it is time to structure the sessions and implement the program.

This section will provide information on structuring the social skill sessions, including information on:

- Using play materials

- Connecting treatment objectives with targeted skills

- Introducing skills

- Teaching skills

- Providing parent/teacher training and feedback

Though this section is best suited for professionals who are directly responsible for implementing the strategies (e.g., therapists), the information has great relevance to those who are responsible for facilitating generalization of social skills to the natural environment, such as parents and teachers.

Session Structure: Two Age Ranges

The sample session structures presented on pages 230-233 are separated into two age categories: child sessions (age range, 3-11) and adolescent sessions (ages 12-18). There will be much overlap in structures, and the age requirements are not rigid. For instance, a 12-year-old might be better suited for the child session, or a 10-year-old might be ready for the longer sessions of the adolescent structure.

The distinction between the two session structures reflects the developmental differences in these two age ranges. The adolescent sessions are longer and involve more social-cognitive strategies commensurate with more advanced cognitive processing. There is also much variation within each age group, which will be reflected in the strategies used and the social skills and concepts addressed. Although the needs of a 12-year-old are quite different from those of an 18-year-old, the structure and format of the sessions will be quite similar. When conducting group sessions, group members should be matched by chronological age. That is, 11-year-olds should never be grouped with older adolescents. See section on suggested age ranges when conducting groups on pages 214-215.

Limit the child to one or two play themes and activities per activity (except for periods of "free" play). Providing the child with multiple play themes and numerous play items can become distracting and derail the focus of the intervention activity. Although the child should have a good time during games and activities, the focus is to teach social interaction skills. Specifically, the games and activities allow the child to perform and practice the skills introduced at the beginning of the session.

If used correctly, the separation between the activities and the instruction will be seamless, and the child will hardly notice that he is learning new skills. Include a period of free play at the end of each individual session to allow the child to play with that favorite object that you have been keeping from him. Free play also allows the child to talk about any additional topics that he would like to discuss, or to show the therapist that new computer game or action figure that he brought in. Use feedback at the end of the session to help the child make the connection between the skills introduced in the session and his performance of those skills during the activities.

Using Play Materials

Start slowly by selecting three treatment objectives the first quarter a child is involved with social skills instruction, especially younger children. If he reaches his objectives before the quarter is over, celebrate! Then rewrite your objectives to meet the child's developing skills. For instance, if the child reaches the objective of joining in interactions with peers during structured activities, you might change the objective to joining in activities on the playground. Or, if the initial objective involves joining in activities with one child, you might revise the objective to include joining in group activities.

Connecting Treatment Objectives and Targeted Skills

The use of fewer treatment objectives in the beginning also allows the parents and school team to get acclimated to the social skills process, which is important as they will be asked to prompt and reinforce the target skills during the course of the social skills program. Each session should address one or two objectives or topics.

Note:

As the child progresses in the social skills program, treatment objectives may be added, but do not use more than five at a time, as it becomes too difficult to manage the program, teach the skills, and monitor progress. It is important to note that you are not obligated to ONLY teach the skills that have been targeted in the treatment objectives. On the contrary, teach as many skills as you can find time to teach, but do not lose sight of the treatment objectives. In fact, it is impossible (and incomplete) to teach a skill in isolation without also teaching other component or related skills that are required to perform the target skill. For instance, in order to take another person's perspective, the child must also look for, and understand, the nonverbal cues of others and integrate this information with contextual cues from the environment. Similarly, to properly initiate a conversation with another person, one must think of something to say to the person (perspective taking, inferring interests, etc.), identify the correct moment to approach the person (social rules, timing), position the body properly (movement skills), and then make eye contact (nonverbal communication) – and all that is before the child even says a word! So although the treatment objectives represent accountability and, therefore, determine whether or not the child is making progress in the program, they will not represent every skill that you will be teaching the child during the quarter.

Introducing the Skill

Each session will involve introducing one or two social skills or social concepts that you will be addressing during the session (joining in, asking others to play, reading nonverbal cues, perspective taking, etc.). The introduction of the skill is an important aspect of the session as it provides an advanced organizer to the child with regard to what to expect during the session. The introduction of the skill also allows you to provide a context for the skill or concept, such as when, where, and why the skill or concept will be applied.

To capitalize on the propensity of children with ASD towards visual learning, present skills and concepts in visual or pictorial form whenever possible. Social Stories™, literature, magazines, modeling, video modeling and video self-modeling, newspaper stories, and behavioral rehearsal/role-playing are all effective strategies for introducing social skills and concepts.

Once you have developed the treatment objectives and determined the skills or concepts the child will be learning, it is time to decide how the skills will be taught, and thus what strategies will be used (see Chapter 7 for a detailed description of how to select social skill strategies). Depending upon the type of skill deficit the child is exhibiting (to promote skill acquisition and/or to enhance skill performance), the social skills program will consist of numerous intervention strategies, many used in combination.

Put much thought into the selection of intervention strategies prior to implementation. Ask yourself the following question for skill acquisition deficits: Which strategy will best *teach* the target skill(s) to this child at this time? For performance deficits, ask: Which strategy will best promote the performance of the target skill for this child at this time? Your answers to these questions will determine the intervention package that you select. Simply reach into your intervention tool-chest and get to work. Warm-up activities (e.g., improvisational exercises and the conversation game) are also recommended to help get the child's motor started, so to speak.

Teaching the Skill

Teaching social skills should not be confined to a specific place and time. Every setting the child enters presents an opportunity to teach a new skill or to enhance the performance of an existing one. Similarly, licensed therapists do not hold exclusive rights to deliver social skills instruction. Anybody can teach social skills provided that they have the necessary training and support.

Providing Parent/Teacher Training and Feedback

Time must be set aside at the beginning of the program and during each session for parent or teacher training. In most cases, parents and teachers should be trained to deliver social prompts and reinforcement to enhance the child's performance of targeted skills in the natural environment. The beginning (or conclusion) of each session may also be used to discuss concerns or issues that the parent or teacher may have regarding the child's social performance or the social skills program in general.

I recommend using a "Parent Update" form (see page 226) to spark communication between parents and professionals and to promote consistency across settings. The form communicates to parents what skills are currently being targeted in the program. The form is meant to be a dynamic document; that is, as targeted skills change, parents receive a new "Update." The form also suggests strategies that the parents may use at home to enhance the performance and generalization of the targeted skills to other settings. A similar form could be provided to teachers to help facilitate their involvement in the social skills program.

Time should be set aside each session to discuss the form and the strategies used at home. The targeted skills should be clearly defined and training provided to ensure that the parent or teacher has the necessary skills to implement the suggested strategies. If necessary, I sometimes have the parent or teacher practice the strategy with me. It is important to select strategies that can be implemented by parents and teachers to take advantage of "teachable moments" in the child's natural environment. The following is an example of the "Parent Update" form.

Sample Parent Update Form

Child: Tommy

Date: August 7

Skills currently being targeted:

1. Joining in play activities with peers

2. Asking questions about other people

3. Identifying feelings

Strategies to enhance performance of the skills at home:

1. Set up playdate with other children

2. Reinforce effort

3. Provide prompts for "joining in" and "asking questions about others"

4. Ask Tommy to identify feelings of characters in books or television shows

Please use the space below to share your experiences using the strategies:

There are some important distinctions between individual and group social skills training that should be considered. This section will provide information on special considerations for conducting group social skills training. In group training, warm-up activities and skill introduction will involve the same components and features as the individual sessions. Play materials will also be similar to those used during the individual sessions.

Parent training is typically not a feature of the group sessions because of the time commitment required to address the individual needs of all parents. However, the therapist should always find time to deal with a crisis or other urgent need as it arises. I recommend scheduling separate sessions with parents to provide ongoing training and consultation.

In group sessions, prompting is the primary teaching strategy used during structured play activities (see group session structure later in this chapter). The primary purpose of the prompting is to facilitate positive social interactions between group members. The therapist should focus her attention (for 1- to 2-minute intervals) on one child, or a child pair at a time, during structured play activities. That is, prompting is only provided to the target child and his play partner. After 1-2 minutes, the therapist then shifts her focus to the next child in the group and his partner. This process is repeated for the duration of the structured play activity.

This strategy of rotating focus is preferable to trying to observe and prompt all the children at once. What typically occurs is that your focus becomes divided, limiting your ability to fully focus your efforts on the child's needs. Or, you may spend your time prompting the child with the greatest need, thereby decreasing the attention you provide other children in the group.

Special Considerations for Conducting Group Training

Using Prompts to Facilitate Social Interactions

Suggestions for Delivering Prompts During Group Sessions

1. Provide prompts to facilitate positive social interactions between group members.
2. Focus attention on one child, or one child pair, at a time.
3. Provide prompts to focus child, or prompt other children to play with focus child.
4. Shift focus (prompts) to next child in the group after 1-2 minutes.

Using Reinforcement

As mentioned when discussing the use of reinforcement, I recommend that you do not provide reinforcement or verbal feedback while the children are actively engaged in a social interaction as it may break the momentum of the interaction. Instead wait until after the interaction has terminated, or if you are video recording, you may provide reinforcement and feedback as the child watches herself on video.

Using Play Items and Play Themes

During the structured play activities, select one shared play theme at a time. The play theme should involve mostly reciprocal activities, and incorporate the various categories of play items discussed earlier.

It is helpful to assign roles and responsibilities to the group members that facilitate reciprocal interactions, such as assigning one child to take orders and pass out materials; assigning another child to be the therapist's spokesperson (all questions go through this child); and assigning a child to be the group helper, whose job it is to provide assistance to others (this may require finding another group member to help out).

Assigned group roles for adolescent groups may consist of an order-taker, a consensus builder (this child seeks input from all group members), a spokesperson, and a group decision maker (this child makes all decisions for the group, and all decisions are final). Group roles should be rotated each session.

Collecting Data

Time should be set aside each group session for free play. Free play is an important component of group social skills instruction as it allows the child to interact in a relatively unstructured, yet safe environment. During the free-play activity, children are provided additional games and play items and given just one directive, "Have fun!"

Most important, the free play allows the therapist an opportunity to collect data on specific social interaction skills. The therapist can focus on the social interactions of one child per session, or if she feels brave, collect data on multiple children each session. Since data will be collected, the therapist should refrain from prompting social interactions during the free-play activity. The goal is to determine how the child is interacting with peers without the benefit of adult assistance (see Chapter 11 for more information on data collection).

Structure of Sessions

Though the strategies used during social skill sessions, and the time allotted for social skills instruction, will vary from child to child, and from setting to setting, the structure of the sessions will be fairly consistent. In addition, the individual and group session structures are separated by age group and may also be modified to match the time allotted for social skills training. If time is of the essence (which it typically is), simply change the time allotments placed next to each step in the examples on the following pages.

The individual and group session structures are most applicable for therapists who conduct social skills training outside the classroom. However, I have included a classwide session structure to meet the needs of teachers who would like to implement a social skills program in their classrooms. This structure is presented with the knowledge that the time and resources allotted to social skills instruction vary considerably from classroom to classroom and is dependent upon student, instructional, system, and time demands. As such, the structure should be modified to meet the unique needs of the classroom. If you are forced to modify the structures presented in this section, I strongly recommend that you maintain the basic progression of steps for the session (i.e., introduce skill, teach skill, practice skill, facilitate performance and generalization of skills to other settings, etc.).

Individual Child Session (Ages 3-11)

1. Parent or Teacher Feedback/Training (5-10 minutes)
   - Parent Concerns and Comments
   - Issues/Concepts/Rules to Address
   - Parent Training

2. Child Feedback and Conversation (5 minutes)
   - Child's Concerns and Feedback
   - Time to Chat (what has been happening in the child's life?)

3. Warm-Up Activity (2-3 minutes)
   - Improvisation Activity

4. Conversation Game (2-3 minutes)

5. Introduce Skill, Rule, or Concept (5 minutes)
   - Potential Strategies: Social Story™, children's literature, VM or VSM, modeling or verbal description, reading a story
   - Materials: Video and television, books, Social Story, picture cards, children's books

6. Teach Skill, Rule, or Concept (10-15 minutes)
   - Potential Strategies: Social Story, VM or VSM, modeling, SPS strategies, conversational mapping, thinking, feeling, and interest activities
   - Materials: SPS activities, computer software, thinking, feeling, interest worksheets, videos and television, picture cards, conversational maps

7. Practice Target Skill (5-10 minutes)
   - Potential Strategies: Role-playing/behavioral rehearsal, prompting, coaching
   - Materials: Play items

8. Reinforcement and Feedback (1-2 minutes)

9. Free Play (1-10 minutes)
   - Additional play items

10. Additional Parent or Teacher Feedback/Training (as time permits)
    - Homework (What do you want parents to focus on? What data would you like them to keep?)

Individual Adolescent Session (Ages 12-18)

1. Parent or Teacher Feedback/Training (5-10 minutes)
   - Parent Concerns and Comments
   - Issues/Concepts/Rules to Address
   - Parent Training
2. Adolescent Feedback and Conversation (5 minutes)
   - Child's Concerns and Feedback
   - Time to Chat (what has been happening in the child's life?)
3. Warm-Up Activity (2-3 minutes)
   - Improvisation Activity
4. Conversation Game (3-5 minutes)
5. Introduce Skill, Rule, or Concept (2-3 minutes)
   - Potential Strategies: Social Story™, VM or VSM, modeling or verbal description, reading a story
   - Materials: Video and TV, Social Story, picture cards, books, magazines, or newspaper articles
6. Teach Skill, Rule, or Concept (15-20 minutes)
   - Potential Strategies: Social Story, VM or VSM, modeling, SPS strategies, conversational mapping, thinking, feeling, and interest activities
   - Materials: SPS activities, computer software, thinking/feeling interest worksheets, videos and television, picture cards, conversational maps
7. Practice Target Skill (5-10 minutes)
   - Potential Strategies: Role-playing/behavioral rehearsal, prompting, coaching, natural conversations
   - Materials: Games and play items
8. Reinforcement and Feedback (2-5 minutes)
9. Free Play (1-10 minutes)
   - Additional games and activities
10. Additional Parent or Teacher Feedback/Training (as time permits)
    - Homework (What do you want parents to focus on? What data would you like them to keep?)

Child Group Sessions (Ages 3-11)

1. Group Discussion (2-5 minutes)
   - Goal is to help children adjust to session
2. Introduce Skill, Rule, or Concept (5 minutes)
   - Potential Strategies: Social Story™, VM or VSM, modeling or verbal description, role-playing/behavioral rehearsal, reading a story, priming
   - Materials: Video and TV, books, Social Story, picture cards, children's books
3. Structured Play Time (20 minutes)
   - Teaching Strategies: Prompting
   - Focus on One Child at a Time (or child pair)
   - Prompts to Facilitate Performance of Target Skills
   - Materials (one play theme at a time): Play items
   - Assigning Group Roles
4. Free Play (5-10 minutes)
   - Additional play items
   - No prompting
   - Data collection on interactions
5. Verbal Reinforcement and Feedback (2-5 minutes)

Adolescent Group Session (Ages 12-18)

1. Group Discussion (5-10 minutes)
   - Help Children Adjust to Session and Address Social Issues (use these issues if possible as topic for SPS)
   - Teaching Strategies: Social Problem Solving, Prompting
   - Materials: SPS activity sheets
2. Conversation Game (5 minutes)
3. Improvisational Activity (5 minutes)
4. Introduce Skill, Rule, or Concept (10 minutes)
   - Potential Strategies: Social Story™, VM or VSM, modeling or verbal description, role-playing/behavioral rehearsal, reading a story, priming, SRS
   - Materials: Video and television, books, social story, picture cards, books, magazines, newspapers, SPS activity sheets
5. Structured Activity (10-20 minutes)
   - Teaching Strategies: Role-playing, prompting
   - Focus on One Child (or child pair) at a time
   - Prompts to Facilitate Performance of Target Skills
   - Materials: Games and play items
   - Focus on One Play Theme at a Time
   - Assigning Group Roles
6. Free Play (5-10 minutes)
   - Additional Games and Play Items
   - No Prompting
   - Data Collection on Interactions
7. Verbal Reinforcement and Feedback (2-5 minutes)
8. Homework and/or Information Regarding Next Session

Classwide Session Structure

1. Warm-Up Activity (to get the child's attention)
   - Improvisation Activity
2. Introduce Skill, Rule, or Concept (3-5 minutes)
   - Potential Strategies: Social Story™, VM or VSM, modeling, verbal description, reading a story, priming
   - Materials: Video and TV, books, Social Story, picture cards, children's books, newspaper articles
3. Practice/Teach Skill (in pairs or small groups) (5-10 minutes)
   - Potential Strategies: SPS activities, role-playing/behavioral rehearsal, prompting, coaching
4. Verbal Reinforcement and Feedback (2-3 minutes)
5. After the Session
   - Provide prompts to facilitate performance and generalization of skill in multiple settings and with multiple persons

A critical aspect of all social skills programs is to develop a plan for generalization, or transfer of skills. Generalization refers to performance of skills across settings, persons, situations, and time. Remember, it doesn't really matter how well the child performs socially with adults in structured settings – the ultimate goal is to teach the child to interact successfully with peers in natural environments.

From a behavioral perspective, the inability to generalize a skill or behavior is a result of too much stimulus control. That is, the child only performs the skill or behavior in the presence of a specific stimulus (person, prompt, directives, etc.). For instance, the child may respond to the social initiations of other children, but only if his mother is there to prompt him. If Mom is not there, he does not respond. Therefore, the skill has not been generalized.

A number of strategies may be used to facilitate generalization of skills across settings, persons, situations, and time, including both behavioral and cognitive perspectives.

Generalization Strategies From a Behavioral Perspective

1. ***Reinforce the performance of social skills in the natural environment.*** This will require that multiple team members are aware of the child's treatment objectives and that the child has access to social opportunities in natural settings.

2. ***Train with multiple persons and in multiple settings.*** This includes changing the physical setting, varying therapists, and using multiple peer mentors.

3. ***Ensure the presence and delivery of natural reinforcers for the performance of social skills.*** For instance, if the child attempts to initiate an interaction with a peer, the peer's response and acceptance are considered natural reinforcers. For many children, social interactions are inherently reinforcing, provided that they are positive. Social accommodations, such as training peers to be responsive, help ensure that natural reinforcers are available and delivered.

4. ***Practice the skill in the natural environment.*** Skill instruction doesn't end at the therapist's door; it should be carried over to the home, playground, classroom, fast-food restaurant, or any other setting where social interactions take place.

5. *Fade prompts as quickly as feasible.* This decreases the child's reliance on specific prompts to perform a skill or behavior. Students may also be taught to provide their own prompts ("self-prompting"), which again lessens the child's dependence on another person.

6. *Train social skills loosely.* "Training loosely" means to vary the instruction, directives, strategies, and prompts that you provide the child during skill instruction. Sometimes we structure classrooms and therapy rooms too rigidly, which further increases the incongruity between these settings and the natural environment.

7. *Provide multiple exemplars for social rules and concepts.* The use of multiple scenarios and examples facilitates a broad application of social rules across multiple situations. This can also be accomplished by using multiple role-play scenarios that require the application of the social rule.

8. *Teach self-monitoring strategies.* Self-monitoring strategies are highly effective for facilitating generalization of skills and behaviors across settings because they lessen the child's dependence on others (see Chapter 8 for more information on Self-Monitoring).

9. *Provide "booster sessions."* To facilitate generalization across time (also referred to as maintenance), the child must continually practice previously learned skills that he does not regularly use. Social interaction skills, like other movement-based skills, operate on the "use it or lose it" principle. As such, I recommend "booster sessions" for children even after regular sessions are no longer necessary.

Generalization Strategies From a Cognitive Perspective

A cognitive perspective has particular relevance for the generalization of social-cognitive skills and related behaviors. According to cognitive psychologists (Pressley & McCormick, 1995), generalization of skills fails to occur because the child does not recognize that a skill that she has learned can be used in a new situation. Or, she may recognize that the skill can be used, but has difficulty using it because she lacks mastery of the skill.

Another reason why children fail to generalize skills is that they do not think that the outcome is worth the effort required to obtain it. That is, if the child has no interest in interacting with peers, he probably will not exert much effort to be part of a social interaction. Finally, failure to generalize skills also occurs when the child does not understand why the strategy is useful and how it might benefit social performance.

Based on this cognitive perspective on failure to generalize skills, the following suggestions are provided to promote generalization of social skills.

1. ***Encourage application of skills in multiple situations.*** When teaching a new skill, have the child brainstorm situations where the skill might be applied. Create novel role-play situations for the child to apply the skill or have the child create the role-play scenario.

2. ***Increase mastery of skill performance.*** Perhaps the best way to facilitate generalization is to teach to a level of mastery. That is, if we want skills to generalize, we must do a better job of teaching them! Those who have mastered skills typically have few difficulties performing the skill across settings, situations, persons, and time.

3. ***Encourage and facilitate an interest in interacting with others and developing relationships.*** Help children see the benefits of having friends and participating in shared activities. Have the child with ASD identify children he would like to be friends with and work to facilitate a relationship between the children.

4. ***Build self-efficacy related to social performance*** (see Chapter 6). A child with strong self-efficacy related to social performance will approach social interactions with confidence and a sense that his effort (no matter how strenuous) will result in social success.

5. ***Provide information on why the skill is useful.*** Help the child see how the skill will help him establish and maintain social relationships. Also help him see how the skill (or absence of the skill) might impact another person. Finally, show him via video self-modeling how performing the skill will benefit social interactions, that is, show him successfully using the skill to effectively interact with another person.

Chapter Summary

This chapter provided guidelines for planning and implementing the intervention phase of the social skills program (Step 4). In addition, information was provided on conducting group social skills programming and facilitating the generalization of skills across settings and persons.

- Planning the program involves determining which children will benefit, the format for the program (i.e., individual, group, or classwide), selecting peer models, training the team, selecting materials and resources, determining where the sessions will take place, and developing a schedule.

- Implementing the program involves effectively using play materials, connecting treatment objectives with targeted skills, introducing and teaching skills to the target child, and providing parent/teacher training and feedback to facilitate generalization.

- Special considerations for conducting group social skills programming include using prompts to facilitate positive social interactions between group members, withholding reinforcement until after the interaction has terminated, using play items and play themes to promote reciprocal interactions, and using free play to collect data.

- The generalization, or transfer, of skills to multiple settings and situations and with multiple persons is an essential aspect of social skills programming. Therefore, it is critical to develop a plan for generalization.

Evaluating and Monitoring Progress

11

5-STEP MODEL

1. **Assess Social Functioning**

2. **Distinguish Between Skill Acquisition and Performance Deficits**

3. **Select Intervention Strategies**

   - **Strategies That Promote Skill Acquisition**

   - **Strategies That Enhance Performance**

4. **Implement Intervention**

5. **Evaluate and Monitor Progress**

Although "Evaluate and Monitor Progress" is listed as the last stage in the intervention process, it is not the least important. In addition, it also is not the last thing to think about when designing a program. As social skill deficits are identified during assessment, methods for evaluating the efficacy of the intervention should also be determined. That is, progress monitoring measures should be linked directly to the treatment objectives selected in Step 1: Assess Social Functioning. To use a basic example, if the target of the intervention is initiating conversations with peers, baseline data on the frequency of initiations with peers and adults must be collected. Data on social initiations are subsequently collected throughout the implementation stage.

Measuring Social Performance

In school settings, accurate data collection is a legal imperative. School teams should focus on integrating the social skills assessment with the child's behavioral and social objectives. As such, Step 5 (Evaluate and Monitor Progress) is typically an important aspect of IEP development, implementation, and integrity. And though professionals are primarily responsible for monitoring progress, parents should take a keen interest in how their child's progress is being evaluated, and whether their child is making progress in the program.

The methods used to monitor progress are similar to those used to assess social functioning described in Chapter 5. A key distinction is that in Step 1 (Assess Social Functioning) we were assessing social functioning for the purpose of identifying social skill deficits that would be the target of the intervention. That is, skills that would need to be taught. Progress monitoring, on the other hand, involves evaluating the child's present level of social performance. The present level of performance is continually monitored and compared with past levels of performance to provide a measure of intervention progress. It is important to note, however, that the initial social skills assessment (Step 1) provides an opportunity to collect valuable baseline data (i.e., child's level of performance prior to beginning the program).

Social performance should be measured at the beginning of the social skills program (baseline) and, at the very least, at the end of each three-month quarter. Ideally, some measure of social performance should be collected each month, and even each week, during the course of the intervention. Social performance may be monitored via observation (both naturalistic observation and structured), interviews (parent, teacher, and student) and standardized and nonstandardized rating scales of social, emotional, and behavioral functioning (see Chapter 5). Finally, it is imperative to collect data across settings and across informants.

The following is an example of a progress monitoring form to help track progress and communicate results to parents and other professionals. The form includes the targeted objectives and performance criteria, and the results of baseline data and follow-up data collection. (A blank form is included in the Appendix.)

Social Skills Progress Monitoring Form (Sample)

Child's Name: Tommy

Child's Age: 9 years, 6 months

Date of Services: March 1, 2006   **to**   May 31, 2006

Type of Programming (individual, group, and/or classwide): Group

Social Objectives (See Chapter 5 for more information on social objectives):

1. Tommy will join in activities with peers at recess in 30% of observed intervals

2. Tommy will respond to the social initiations of peers during classroom free-play activity in 50% of observed intervals

3. Tommy will ask one question about other people during conversations in 25% of observed conversations

Baseline Data: (Beginning of Program or 3-month quarter)

Social Objective 1: 15% participation

Social Objective 2: 25% response ratio

Social Objective 3: 0% of conversations

Additional Baseline Data: Autism Social Skills Profile (Total Score) = 84
(Note: This could be any rating form that you choose)

Follow-up Data: (End of program or 3-month quarter)

Social Objective 1: 35% participation   *(Note: Increase criteria)*

Social Objective 2: 15% response ratio *(Note: Perhaps try a different strategy)*

Social Objective 3: 90% of conversations *(Note: Select new objective)*

Additional Follow-up Data: Autism Social Skills Profile (Total Score) = 92

Observation

Observations provide a direct measure of how a child is functioning in real-life social settings. Observations may be conducted in both structured (structured playgroups, social skill groups, etc.) and naturalistic settings (classroom, playground, home environment, etc.). Systematic recording methods should be used to ensure that the observational data are both reliable (accurate and consistent) and valid (measuring what we think it is measuring). Data are collected during free-play activities without the use of adult prompting and reinforcement.

Types of Recording Systems

The following provides a description of basic systematic recording methods that are useful for measuring social behaviors. (For a more thorough discussion of systematic recording, see Alberto & Troutman, 2003.) The recording systems covered in this section include frequency recording, duration recording, time sampling procedures, latency recording, and response ratio.

The following sample recording form was developed to measure frequency of social engagement (via partial interval), frequency of social initiations, and response ratios. These terms will be described in the following section. I suggest that you refer to the form as you read this section. The form can also be modified to record other behaviors and to incorporate other recording strategies, such as duration or latency recording.

Social Interaction Recording Form

Child: _____

Date: _____

Time: _____

Observer: _____

Social Engagement With Peers (Partial Interval, 1 minute in length)

1 = Participation

0 = No Participation

1	2	3	4	5	6	7	8	9	0	1	2	3	4	5	6	7	8	9	0	1	2	3	4	5	6	7	8	9	0

Social Initiations and Responses (Event/Frequency Recording)

Record each observance of an initiation or response during the 30 minute observation

Social Initiations:	Opportunities for Response:
Social Responses:	

Notes:

Frequency recording. Frequency recording, also called *event recording*, involves counting the frequency of a behavior (i.e., how often it occurs) during a specified time interval. For instance, if we used a frequency recording method for hand raising during math class, we would simply make a mark each time the child raised his hand during the class. The frequency of hand raises could then be recorded each month for a three-month period to determine whether the child is exhibiting an increase or decrease in raising his hand.

A key to frequency recording is that the selected intervals remain the same length for the duration of the progress monitoring. For instance, if we recorded hand raising for 20 minutes during math class one month and 40 minutes the next, the results would be inconsistent and not very useful. In cases where the length of the interval is out of the observer's control (for instance, the child spends 20 minutes in the bathroom during the observation in math class), the data may be adjusted accordingly. In the above example, the frequencies of hand raising in the 20-minute observation may be multiplied by 2 to adjust it to a 40-minute observation.

Examples of social behaviors that can be measured via frequency recording include all types of social initiations, all types of social responses, number of inappropriate comments, and verbal expressions of emotion, just to name a few.

Duration recording. Duration recording involves recording the length of time a behavior is performed from beginning to end. For instance, we might record the duration of time a child stays on task, or the amount of time a child spends playing with other children. This recording method is most appropriate for target behaviors that stress duration over frequency. For instance, if the target behavior is social participation with peers (which we would more clearly define if it was indeed the target behavior), frequency recording would tell us how many times the child participated with peers, but not for how long. Length of time participating with peers would be the more appropriate measurement in cases where the child quickly bounces from one social interaction to the next (hit-and-run interactions). If we were using frequency recording, it might appear as though the child was participating a great deal with peers, but in actuality he was not. In contrast, if the child participated with one group of peers for the duration of the observation, the frequency count would only be one, and would not portray an accurate picture of the child's social participation.

The key with duration recording is to clearly delineate the beginning and end points of the behavior and apply this delineation across measurements of the behavior. For instance, duration of conversations may be defined as having a start point of "verbal initiation between child and peer." The end point could be "lack of verbal exchange between child and peer for a period of five seconds." Of course, the definition of "conversation" might vary widely to include a number of different types of conversations (to request assistance, to find out information about another person, to find out information about a topic, etc.). The important thing is that the definition is applied consistently across observations of the target behavior to provide an accurate measure of behavioral change.

All types of social interactions and social participation may be measured via duration recording.

Time sampling procedures. Time sampling provides an alternative method of recording behavioral durations and frequencies. The advantage of time sampling procedures is that they lessen the workload required of the observer, especially for behaviors with high frequencies and long durations – this is especially important when teachers are asked to record social behaviors in the classroom.

Time sampling procedures require observers to record behaviors at specific points in time, or intervals. That is, they do not have to continuously watch for behaviors to occur during the length of the observation period (as is the case with frequency recording), nor do they have to watch for specific beginning points and end points of a behavior (as is the case with duration recording). Using time sampling procedures, observation periods are divided into intervals. For instance, a 30-minute observation can be divided into 30, one-minute intervals, or perhaps 15, two-minute intervals. There are three types of time sampling procedures: whole interval, partial interval, and momentary time sampling.

- **Whole interval recording.** A behavior is considered to have occurred only if it is performed throughout the entire interval. That is, from beginning to end. This recording method is best suited for high-frequency behaviors and behaviors that occur without interruption, such as time on task.

- **Partial interval recording.** Behaviors are considered to have occurred if they are performed at any time during the interval. The behavior does not have to occur for the entire interval. In addition, only one behavioral occurrence per interval is recorded. That is, if the child initiates three interactions in one interval, only one initiation is recorded. This sampling technique is best suited for low-frequency behaviors and behaviors of very short durations, such as eye contact, emotional expressions, or certain inappropriate behaviors.

- **Momentary time sampling.** This is the most time efficient of the three time sampling procedures as observers do not need to watch behavior for the entire interval. Observers record whether a behavior is occurring at a single moment in time, usually at the end of the interval. For instance, if the interval is 15 minutes in duration, then every 5 minutes the observer records whether the behavior is occurring at that moment in time. If the behavior occurred at other points during the interval, but not at that precise moment, the behavior is not recorded as having occurred. Therefore, this method is not recommended for low-frequency behaviors. It is best suited for high-frequency behaviors and behaviors where duration is a primary concern, such as time-on-task, and social participation.

Latency recording. Sometimes referred to as response latency, this refers to the amount of time elapsed between a stimulus and a response. That is, the amount of time between a behavioral directive and the child following through with the directive. For instance, if the child does not respond promptly to teacher directives to "line up for gym class," the response latency would be measured from the moment the teacher gave the directive to the time the child finally lines up. The key to latency recording is to clearly delineate the beginning and end points for the behavior.

Latency recording is the ideal recording method for measuring response time. This includes responses to directives, responses to questions, responses to greetings, or any other social behavior that involves a prompt response on the part of the child. In these cases, latency of response is a much more useful measure than frequency of responses as it measures how quickly or promptly the child responds in interactions.

Response ratio. Response ratio refers to a recording method that I use to measure frequency of social responses. A response ratio is calculated by dividing the total number of responses by the number of opportunities that the child has to respond (i.e., number of times another person initiated an interaction with the child). For instance, if the child has 10 opportunities to respond to the initiations of others, but only responds 5 times, the response ratio would be .5, or 5/10. A perfect response ratio would be 1.0.

Response ratio provides a more relevant measure of social responses than frequency recording as it measures responses in relation to the number of opportunities a child has to respond. Social responses are dependent upon others initiating interactions with the child, thereby giving the child an opportunity to respond. For instance, a child might have zero social responses during an observational period, but this may not reflect his ability to respond to the initiations of others. Instead, it may simply reflect the fact that the child has no opportunities to respond, and is socially isolated.

In contrast, consider a scenario where we record five social responses for a child during our first observational period. At the end of the month, we observe again and record four social responses. This might tell us on the surface that the child's responses have remained relatively stable during the month. However, if we recorded response ratios, we might find that for the first observation the child had 10 opportunities to respond to the initiations of others (response ratio of 5/10), and for the second observation the child had only five opportunities to respond (response ratio of 4/5). This would allow us to conclude that the child is responding more consistently to the responses of others compared to the first observation.

Interviews

Interviews with parents and teachers can also be conducted to provide a measure of social performance. Though interview data do not represent the most systematic and valid measure of change, as they are highly subjective, they do present a good measure of the various stakeholders' perception of change. This perception is important as it is directly linked to the social validity and treatment fidelity of the intervention (see page 249).

Besides gathering information on perceptions of change and progress, interviews with parents and teachers provide information on whether the treatment objectives are still appropriate or whether they need to be modified. The interviews also provide a forum to discuss the direction of the social skills program, specifically, the goals and focus for the next three months. In addition, if parents and teachers will be required to continue to implement strategies and collect data, the interview provides an opportunity to conduct further training and elicit additional feedback on their involvement. The goal is to make sure that everyone involved in the child's social skills program is working towards the same goal, and doing so consistently.

Rating Scales

The behavior rating scales administered to parents, teachers, and the child herself during the initial social skills assessment (see Chapter 5) also provide a measure of progress monitoring. First, the results of the initial assessment provide a baseline measure to compare with subsequent administrations of the instrument in terms of functioning across behavioral, social, and emotional domains. Rating scales should be administered at the end of each quarter to regularly monitor progress.

Standardized measures are recommended for monitoring intervention progress as most standardized measures have established test-retest reliability. Test-retest reliability refers to the stability and consistency of the assessment tool across time. For instance, if we measured the child's present level of social performance one day and measured it again one week later, we would expect the results of the tests to be relatively similar. An assessment tool with poor test-retest reliability is similar to a bathroom scale that provides inconsistent measurements of weight. If you stepped on the scale today and your weight read "174," and tomorrow you stepped on the scale and your weight read "154," and the next day it read "164," you would have a scale with poor test-retest reliability. As such, the scale would be unreliable and, thus, useless.

The same is true for behavior, emotional, and social rating scales with poor test-retest reliability, or those that have no established test-retest reliability. For this reason, non-standardized rating scales should be used with extreme caution as progress monitoring tools.

However, many standardized rating scales of social performance should also be used with caution. Many measure social performance in relationship to the general population, and not in relation to other children with ASD. Therefore, they may not be sensitive enough to detect the social progress (at least initially) of children with ASD. That is, even though the child with ASD is indeed learning skills and making progress, his skills may still be considerably lower than those of his nondisabled peers (thus, his standard score will remain very low).

Although we will want to regularly measure the social functioning of the child with ASD in relation to nondisabled peers, it is also imperative that we monitor his social progress in relation to himself. That is, we need to compare his social functioning today in relation to *his* social performance three months ago to determine whether or not he is making progress. This is precisely the reason why I developed the Autism Social Skills Profile (see pages 73-77): to provide a reliable progress monitoring tool that was sensitive enough to detect changes in the social functioning of children with ASD.

Social Validity and Treatment Fidelity

Social skills programming involves a team effort, consisting of parents, teachers, therapists, and the child himself. It does not matter whether the child is receiving social skills instruction from a private practitioner, a school therapist in a resource room, or as part of a classwide curriculum, each member of the team serves a role that is critical to the success of the social skills program.

Each team member must take ownership and responsibility for the program. Therefore, they must be given ample opportunities to provide input and feedback on a regular basis.

Involvement of team members is critical to both social validity and treatment fidelity, both of which are critical to the success of the social skills program.

Social Validity

It many ways, social validity is similar to what is commonly known as *consumer satisfaction*. In the case of social skills programs, consumers are parents, teachers, and the child. Specifically, social validity refers to the social significance of the treatment objectives, the social significance of the intervention strategies, and the social importance of the intervention results (Gresham & Lambros, 1998). Thus, it involves ensuring that the consumers believe that the selected treatment objectives are indeed important for the child to achieve. If consumers do not believe that the objectives are important, they will be less likely to exert the effort necessary to achieve those objectives. This aspect of social validity is established during the initial social skills assessment, specifically, during the interview process.

Social acceptability of intervention strategies is also critical to the success of the program. If consumers do not think that an intervention strategy will be effective, or if they think it may be harmful to the child, they will be less likely to implement it. In this case, it is imperative to provide information on the efficacy of the proposed strategies and present a rationale to consumers for why the strategy has been selected.

Note:

The social importance of intervention results represents the consumer's perceptions of the intervention results. Measuring behavioral change via standardized rating scales and systematic observations is extremely important, but if the consumer does not believe that the intervention resulted in positive and meaningful change for the child, then the intervention is doomed for failure. A consumer who does not perceive that meaningful results will ensue is likely to disengage, or discontinue, the social skills program completely.

The social importance of intervention results and social acceptability of the intervention strategies can be measured via social validity rating forms such as the one on page 252.

Treatment fidelity refers to the degree to which the intervention strategies were implemented as intended. The social validity of the intervention is directly related to treatment fidelity. Poor treatment fidelity significantly diminishes the results of the social skills program, and diminishes our ability to make decisions regarding the effects of individual strategies.

Treatment fidelity is particularly important in situations where the therapist expects parents and teachers to implement strategies outside the primary therapeutic setting. For instance, suppose the teacher is asked to read a Social Story™ to the child prior to recess about joining in activities peers. If at the end of the month our systematic observations indicate that the child's joining-in behaviors have not changed, we might conclude that the Social Stories intervention was ineffectual. However, this would be a false conclusion if, in reality, the teacher had failed to read the Social Story to the child as instructed. Intervention failure in this case would not be attributed to an ineffectual strategy, but to poor treatment fidelity.

Treatment fidelity may also be affected by incorrectly implemented strategies. Therefore, proper training of consumers (parents and teachers) is a key component of treatment fidelity. It can be measured by directly observing whether the strategy was implemented properly on a given day. Treatment fidelity can also be measured through interviews and self-report forms that ask the parent or teacher to indicate whether they were able to implement the strategy on a particular day, or whether they encountered problems with implementation of the strategy.

Treatment Fidelity

Factors Affecting Treatment Fidelity

Sample Social Validity and Treatment Fidelity Form

Note: This sample form was designed specifically for a video self-modeling intervention, but can be used with other interventions by making just a few modifications.

Teacher Name: _____

Student's Name: _____

Date: _____

Please check the box below to indicate whether the student viewed the video on the designated day. If the child was absent, write "absent" in the box. If school was not in session that day, write "no school." If only a portion of the video was shown that day, write "PS" for partial showing. Finally, if you were not able to show the student the video because of equipment failure, please write "EF" in the box for that day.

Monday	Tuesday	Wednesday	Thursday	Friday

Please indicate how you think the intervention is going this week. Please circle the response that best describes this week of the intervention.

SD = Strongly Disagree   D = Disagree   A = Agree   SA = Strongly Agree

The intervention has interfered with normal classroom activity.
SD   D   A   SA

The intervention is distracting to the other students in the classroom.
SD   D   A   SA

The student enjoys watching the video.
SD   D   A   SA

The intervention is easy to implement.
SD   D   A   SA

I believe the intervention is beneficial to the student.
SD   D   A   SA

I enjoy being part of this intervention.
SD   D   A   SA

Additional Comments:

Accurate data collection is essential for evaluating the effectiveness of an intervention by allowing us to determine whether the child is benefiting from the instruction. If the child is not making progress, the evaluation will tell you so. Not all intervention strategies are effective for all children, and sometimes it is excruciatingly difficult to find the correct strategy for a child. However, thorough and frequent evaluations of social performance provide important information on how to modify the program to best meet the child's needs.

◎ *Progress monitoring involves collecting data on social functioning via observations, interviews, and rating scales.*

◎ *Common types of observation recording systems include frequency recording, duration recording, time sampling, latency recording, and response ratios.*

◎ *Interviews of parents and teachers reflect parent and teacher perceptions of progress. These interviews provide information on the appropriateness of the objectives and the strategies currently being implemented. This information also measures both the social validity and treatment fidelity of the intervention.*

◎ *Rating scales are used to provide a pre- and post-test measure of social performance. It is important to use standardized instruments with established test-retest reliability. It is also important to consider the "norm" or comparison group that was used in the standardization of the rating scale. The scores of many rating scales are based on the social performance of children without ASD. Therefore, they may not be sensitive enough to detect changes in social performance of children with ASD.*

◎ *Social validity and treatment fidelity are critical to the success of a social skills program. Social validity refers to the social significance of the treatment objectives, the social significance of the intervention strategies, and the social importance of the results. Treatment fidelity refers to the degree to which the intervention was implemented as intended.*

Final Words on Teaching Social Interaction Skills to Children and Adolescents With ASD

Social skill programming is an often overlooked aspect of a child's educational and treatment plan. The social skills program presented in this book is meant to guide social skill programming for children with ASD. Social skill deficits are a central feature of ASD and lead to numerous negative behavioral, social, and emotional outcomes. Perhaps most critical, social skill deficits preclude children from developing meaningful social relationships – relationships that many children with ASD so desperately want to establish.

There are many social skill strategies available to parents and practitioners working with children with ASD. However, few, if any, models help parents and practitioners make sense of these strategies and use them effectively. As a result, social skill programming is often disjointed and ineffectual. I have attempted to provide a conceptual framework to help organize and synthesize the various social skills strategies currently available to parents and practitioners. The social skills program presented in this book is not meant to replace these strategies; it is meant to help the reader to better use them.

Teaching social skills is a blend of science and art. The model presented in this book is a reflection of that belief. It provides a systematic approach to structuring and conceptualizing a social skills program, but it also provides enough flexibility to allow the program to adjust or bend to the changing needs of the child. It allows therapists from a wide range of theoretical orientations to utilize a large collection of therapeutic interventions.

To successfully teach social skills to children with ASD, we must broaden our conceptual lens. Instead of selecting intervention strategies simply because they match our theoretical orientation, we should select intervention strategies that meet the unique needs of our clients. Use strategies and intervention modalities that have been empirically validated and supported through research, but do not limit your creativity and ingenuity to only methods you read about in scholarly journals. Emulate great teachers from other disciplines and fields. Whether it is a science teacher, basketball coach, music teacher, master carpenter, or ballet teacher, great teachers embody the principles and techniques that transform the ordinary to the extraordinary.

Although the 5-step model attempts to simplify the process of teaching social skills to children with ASD, teaching social skills to children with ASD is not easy! It is a craft honed through training and experience – training and experience you cannot get simply by reading a book. For instance, buying a book on how to rebuild a carburetor won't make you a skilled mechanic. To become one, you would need to get your hands dirty a few times.

Teaching social skills is no different – except that you are not dealing with a static machine, you are dealing with a dynamic, changing entity, which we refer to as a child. This book provides sufficient information to build declarative and procedural knowledge; however, you will not be a skilled interventionist until you DO it! Sound familiar? Be flexible, and be prepared to make mistakes! The key is to identify mistakes early, and correct them. The social skills program in this book allows you to do that. It will enable you to practice with purpose and evaluate the efficacy of your social skills interventions.

Continually monitor and modify the intervention. Some children with ASD take small baby steps of improvement, while others make dramatic improvements in their social performance. All children with ASD deserve an opportunity to learn social skills and to develop social relationships. It can be done. From a therapist's viewpoint, teaching social skills to children with ASD can be the most difficult, time-consuming, stressful, heart-wrenching, and REWARDING experience of your professional career.

I have one last word of advice for parents of children with ASD. These words come straight from the heart of one of the many wonderful parents whom I have had the good fortune to work with.

Happy Endings

One day as we began our session, I asked the mother of one of my client's (Erin) the typical opening question, "What's new, is there anything that happened over the last week that I need to know about?" Her eyes immediately welled up with tears – I feared the worst. She began softly, "This past weekend the doorbell rang. When I opened the door, I saw a little girl standing on our doorstep. I thought she was selling Girl Scout cookies or something, but before I could say anything, the girl asked to play with Erin!"

This was big news! This was the first time in Erin's life that a child had come to her house and asked to play with her. An occurrence that most children experience on a daily basis was happening to Erin for the first time in her 10 years on earth (the gravity of that fact overwhelmed me like a flash flood).

Though she was quite taken aback by the surprise visitor, Erin's mother immediately invited the girl in and quickly ran to Erin to inform her of her visitor. Erin, obviously thrilled to see the girl, promptly asked her if she would like to play in her room. Erin acted with the composure of a seasoned pro! Mom, on the hand, was reportedly a nervous wreck.

As we sat in my office weeping, Erin's mother turned tears to laughter as she shared one final note regarding the play date experience, "Do you know what the worst part about it was?" I shook my head, not quite expecting that there would be a "worst part." "The worst part," she continued, "was that when I ran into the kitchen to get the girls some juice and cookies (obviously trying to make a good impression on the visitor!), I realized that I had nothing to offer them except milk and crackers!"

In just that one moment, I observed a parent experiencing all the joy, pride – and parental regret – that makes parenting so extraordinarily rewarding. As a mother of a child with ASD once told me, children with ASD may never be the life of the party or "social butterflies," but through effective social skills programming, children with ASD can develop social interaction skills, and most important, can establish meaningful social relationships. So parents, heed the lesson of Erin's mother's faux pas. Stock up on juice and cookies, you never know who will be showing up at your doorstep.

REFERENCES

American Psychiatric Association. (2000). *Diagnostic and statistical manual of mental disorders* (4th ed.). Washington, DC: Author.

Alberto, P., & Troutman, A. (2003). *Applied behavior analysis for teachers* (7th ed.). Columbus, OH: Pearson Merrill Prentice-Hall Publishing.

Anderson, J. R. (1982). Acquisition of cognitive skill. *Psychological Review, 89*, 369-406.

Attwood, T. (1998). *Asperger's Syndrome: A guide for parents and professionals.* Philadelphia: Jessica Kingsley Publishing.

Attwood, T. (2004). *Exploring feelings: Cognitive behavior therapy to manage anxiety.* Arlington, TX: Future Horizons.

Azrin, N. H., & Nunn, R. G. (1973). Habit reversal: A method of eliminating nervous habits and tics. *Behaviour Research and Therapy, 11,* 619-628.

Baker, J. E. (2003). *Social skills training for children and adolescents with Asperger syndrome and social-communication problems.* Shawnee Mission, KS: Autism Asperger Publishing.

Bandura, A. (1977). *Social learning theory.* Englewood Cliffs, NJ: Prentice-Hall.

Bandura, A. (1994). Self-efficacy. In V. S. Ramachaudran (Ed.), *Encyclopedia of human behavior* (Vol. 4, pp. 71-81). New York: Academic Press. (Reprinted in H. Friedman [Ed.], *Encyclopedia of mental health.* San Diego: Academic Press, 1998).

Bandura, A. (1997). *Self-efficacy: The exercise of control.* New York: Freeman.

Baron-Cohen, S. (2004). *Mind reading: An interactive guide to emotions.* London: Jessica Kingsley Publishing.

Baron-Cohen, S. (1989). The autistic child's theory of mind: A case of specific developmental delay. *Journal of Child Psychology and Psychiatry, 30,* 285-297.

Bargh, J. A., Chen, M., & Burrows, L. (1996). The automaticity of social behaviour: Direct effects of trait concept and stereotype activation on action. *Journal of Personality and Social Psychology, 71,* 230-244.

Bellini, S. (2004). Social skill deficits and anxiety in high functioning adolescents with autism spectrum disorders. *Focus on Autism and Other Developmental Disabilities, 19*(2), 78-86.

Bellini, S. (2006). The development of social anxiety in high functioning adolescents with autism spectrum Disorders. *Focus on Autism and Other Related Disorders, 21.*

Bellini, S. (in press). *The Autism Social Skills Profile.* Shawnee Mission, KS: Autism Asperger Publishing.

Bellini, S., & Akullian, J. (2006). *A meta-analysis of video modeling and video self-modeling interventions for children and adolescents with autism spectrum disorders.* Manuscript submitted for publication.

Bernard-Opitz, V., Sriram, N., & Nakhoda-Sapuan, S. (2001). Enhancing social problem solving in children with autism and normal children through computer-assisted instruction. *Journal of Autism and Developmental Disorders, 31*, 377-384.

Biederman, J., Rosenbaum, J. F., Chaloff, J., & Kagan, J. (1995). Behavioral inhibition as a risk factor for anxiety disorders. In J. S. March (Ed.), *Anxiety in children and adolescents* (pp. 61-81). New York: Guilford Press.

Bledsoe, R., Myles, B. S., & Simpson, R. L. (2003). Use of a social story intervention to improve mealtime skills of an adolescent with Asperger Syndrome. *Autism: An International Journal of Research and Practice, 7*, 289-295.

Buron, K. D. (2006). *When my worries get too big!* Shawnee Mission, KS: Autism Asperger Publishing.

Buron, K. D., & Curtis, M. (2003). *The incredible 5-point scale.* Shawnee Mission, KS: Autism Asperger Publishing.

Bracken, B. A. (1992). *Multidimensional Self-Concept Scale.* Austin, TX: Pro-Ed.

Carr, J., Austin, J., Britton, L., Kellum, K., & Bailey, J. (1999). An assessment of social validity trends in applied behavior analysis. *Behavioral Intervention, 14*, 223-231.

Carter, J. F. (1993). Self-management. Education's ultimate goal. *Teaching Exceptional Children, 25*(3), 28-33.

Cautela, J., & Groden, J. (1978). *Relaxation: A comprehensive manual for adults, children, and children with special needs.* Champaign, IL: Research Press.

Charlop-Christy, M. H., & Daneshvar, S. (2003). Using video modeling to teach perspective taking to children with autism. *Journal of Positive Behavior Interventions, 5*(1), 12-21.

Charlop-Christy, M. H., Le, L., & Freedman, K. A. (2000). A comparison of video modeling with in vivo modeling for teaching children with autism. *Journal of Autism and Developmental Disorders, 30*(6), 537-552.

Cohen, S. (2004). Social relationships and health. *American Psychologist, 59*, 676-684.

Coyle, C., & Cole, P. (2004). A videotaped self-modeling and self-monitoring treatment program to decrease off-task behaviour in children with autism. *Journal of Intellectual & Developmental Disabilities, 29*(1), 3-15.

Csoti, M. (2001). *Social awareness skills for children.* Philadelphia: Jessica Kingsley Publishing.

Davis, K. (2005). The challenge of combining competing input in the classroom. *IRCA Reporter, 10*, 12-14.

Davis, K., & Dubie, M. (2004). Sensory integration: Tips to consider. *IRCA Reporter, 9*, 3-8.

Deci, E. L., Koestner, R., & Ryan, R. M. (1999). A meta-analytic review of experiments examining the effects of extrinsic rewards on intrinsic motivation. *Psychological Bulletin, 125*, 627-668.

Donnellan, A. D., & Leary, M. R. (1995). *Movement differences and diversity in autism/mental retardation.* Madison, WI: DRI Press.

Dowrick, P. (1999). A review of self-modeling and related interventions. *Applied and Preventive Psychology, 8,* 23-39.

Elias, M. J., Butler, L. B., Bruno, E. M., Papke, M. R., & Shapiro, T. F. (2005). *Social decision making/social problem solving: A curriculum for academic, social, and emotional learning.* Champaign, IL: Research Press.

Elliot, S., & Gresham, F. (1991). *Social skills intervention guide.* Circle Pines, MN: American Guidance.

Elliott, S. N., Racine, C. N., & Busse, R. T. (1995). Best practices in preschool social skills training. In A. Thomas & J. Grimes (Eds.), *Best practices in school psychology* (3rd ed., pp. 1009-1020). Washington, DC: NASP.

Fitts, P. M. (1964). Perceptual-motor skill learning. In A. W. Melton (Ed.), *Categories of human learning* (pp. 243-85). New York: Academic.

Flavell, J. H., Miller, P. H., & Miller, S. A. (1993). *Cognitive development* (3rd ed.). Englewood Cliffs, NJ: Prentice Hall.

Friedberg, R. D., & McClure, J. M. (2002). *Clinical practice of cognitive therapy with children and adolescents.* Guilford: New York.

Frith, U. (Ed.). (1991). *Autism and Asperger syndrome.* Cambridge, UK: Cambridge University Press.

Ghaziuddin, M., Butler, E., Tsai, L., & Ghaziuddin, N. (1994). Is clumsiness a marker for Asperger syndrome? *Journal of Intellectual Disability Research, 38,* 519-527.

Gillott, A., Furniss, F., & Walter, A. (2001). Anxiety in high-functioning children with autism. *Autism, 5,* 277-286.

Gray, C. A. (1995). Teaching children with autism to read social situations. In K. A. Quill (Ed.), *Teaching children with autism: Strategies to enhance communication and socialization* (pp. 219-242). New York: Delmar.

Gray. C. (2000). *The new social story book: Illustrated edition.* Arlington, TX: Future Horizons.

Green, J., Gilchrist, A., Burton, D., & Cox, A. (2000). Social and psychiatric functioning in adolescents with Asperger syndrome compared with conduct disorder. *Journal of Autism and Developmental Disorders, 30,* 279-293.

Gresham, F. M. (2002). Best practices in social skills training. In A. Thomas & J. Grimes (Eds.), *Best practices in school psychology* (4th ed., pp. 1029-1040). Bethesda, MD: NASP.

Gresham, F. M., & Elliot, S. N. (1990). *Social Skills Rating System Manual.* Circle Pines, MN: American Guidance Service.

Greshman. F. M., & Lambros, K. M. (1998). Behavioral and functional assessment. In T. S. Watson & F. M. Gresham (Eds.), *Handbook of child behavior therapy* (pp. 3-22). New York: Plenum Press.

Gresham, F. M., Sugai, G., & Horner, R. H. (2001). Interpreting outcomes of social skills Training for students with high-incidence disabilities. *Teaching Exceptional Children, 67,* 331-344.

Groden, J., Cautela, J., Prince, S., & Berryman, J. (1994). The impact of stress and anxiety on individuals with autism and developmental disabilities. In E. Schopler & G. B. Mesibov (Eds.), *Behavioral issues in autism* (pp. 177-194). New York: Plenum.

Happe, F. G. (1991). The autobiographical writings of three Asperger syndrome adults: Problems of interpretation and implications for theory. In U. Frith (Ed.), *Autism and Asperger syndrome* (pp. 207-242). Cambridge, UK: Cambridge University Press.

Harrison, P. L., & Oakland, T. (2003). *Adaptive Behavior Assessment System–Second Edition*. San Antonio, TX: The Psychological Corporation.

Howlin, P., Baron-Cohen, S., & Hadwin, J. (1999). *Teaching children with autism to mind-read: A practical guide*. New York: Wiley Publishing.

Hume, K., Bellini, S., & Pratt, C. (2005). The usage and perceived outcomes of early intervention and early childhood programs for young children with autism spectrum disorder. *Topics in Early Childhood Special Education, 25(4),* 195-207.

Jaffee, A., & Gardner, L. (2006). *My book full of feelings*. Shawnee Mission, KS. Autism Asperger Publishing.

Kagan, J., Reznick, J. S., & Snidman, N. (1987). The physiology and psychology of behavioral inhibition in children. *Child Development, 58,* 1459-1473.

Kim, J. A., Szatmari, P., Bryson, S. E., Streiner, D. L., & Wilson, F. J. (2000). The prevalence of anxiety and mood problems among children with autism and Asperger syndrome. *Autism, 4,* 117-132.

Knapczyk, D., & Rodes, P. (2001). *Teaching social competence: Social skills and academic success*. Verona, WI: IEP Resources.

Koegel, L. K., Koegel, R. L., Frea, W., & Green-Hopkins, I. (2003). Priming as a method of coordinating educational services for students with autism. *Language Speech, and Hearing Services in Schools, 34,* 228-235.

Koning, C., & Magill-Evans, J. (2001). Social and language skills in adolescent boys with Asperger syndrome. *Autism, 5,* 23-36.

Klin, A., Volkmar, F. R., Sparrow, S. S., Cicchetti, D. V., & Rourke, B. P. (1995). Validity and neuropsychological characterization of Asperger syndrome: Convergence with nonverbal learning disabilities syndrome. *Journal of Child Psychology and Psychiatry, 36,* 1127-1140.

Ladd, G. W., & Mize, J. (1983). A cognitive-social learning model of social skill training. *Psychological Review, 90,* 127-157.

La Greca, A. M. (1999). *Social Anxiety Scales for Children and Adolescents manual*. Miami, FL: University of Miami.

La Greca, A. M., & Lopez, N. (1998). Social anxiety among adolescents: Linkages with peer relations and friendships. *Journal of Clinical Child Psychology, 26,* 83-94.

Laushey, K. M., & Heflin, L. J. (2000). Enhancing social skills of kindergarten children with autism through the training of multiple peers as tutors. *Journal of Autism and Developmental Disorders, 30,* 183-193.

Manjiviona, J., & Prior, M. (1995). Comparison of Asperger syndrome and high-functioning autistic children on a test of motor impairment. *Journal of Autism and Developmental Disorders, 25,* 23-39.

March, J. S. (1999). *Multidimensional Anxiety Scale for Children manual.* North Tonawanda, NY: Multi-Health Systems, Inc.

Moreno, S. J., & Pratt, C. (1994). *Advice for peer tutors.* Bloomington: Indiana Resource Center for Autism Training.

Myles, B. S., Trautman, M. L., & Schelvan, R. L. (2004). *The hidden curriculum: Practical solutions for understanding unstated rules in social situations.* Shawnee Mission, KS: Autism Asperger Publishing Company.

Nelson, K., Plesa, D., & Hensler, S. (1998). Children's theory of mind: An experiential interpretation. *Human Development, 41,* 7-29.

Neves, D. M., & Anderson, J. R. (1981). Knowledge compilation: Mechanisms for the automatization of cognitive skills. In J. R. Anderson (Ed.), *Cognitive skills and their acquisition* (pp. 57-84). Hillsdale, NJ: Erlbaum.

Odom, S. L., McConnell, S. R., & McEvoy, M. A. (1992). *Social competence of young children with disabilities: Issues and strategies for intervention.* Baltimore: Paul H. Brookes.

Odom, S., & McConnell, S. (Eds.). (1993). *Vanderbilt/Minnesota social interaction project play time/social time: Organizing your classroom to build interaction skills.* Tucson, AZ: Communication Skill Builders.

Ozonoff, S., & Miller, J. N. (1995). Teaching theory of mind. A new approach to social skills training for individuals with autism. *Journal of Autism and Developmental Disorders, 25,* 415-433.

Polsgrove, L. (1979). Self-control: Methods for child training. *Behavioral Disorders, 4,* 116-127.

Pratt, C. (2000). *Peer support programs.* Bloomington: Indiana Resource Center for Autism Training.

Premack, D., & Woodruff, G. (1978). Does the chimpanzee have a theory of mind? *Behavioral and Brain Sciences, 1,* 515-526.

Pressley, M., & McCormick, C. (1995). *Cognition, teaching and assessment.* New York: Harper Collins College Publishers.

Quill, K. (2000). *DO-WATCH-LISTEN-SAY: Social and communication intervention for children with autism.* Baltimore: Brookes Publishing.

Quinn, M. M., Kavale, K. A., Mathur, S. R., Rutherford Jr., R. B., & Forness, S. R. (1999). A meta-analysis of social skills interventions for students with emotional and behavioral disorders. *Journal of Emotional and Behavioral Disorders, 7,* 54-64.

Resnick, L. B., Levine, J. M., & Teasley, S. D. (1991). *Perspectives on socially shared cognition.* Washington, DC: American Psychological Association.

Reynolds, C. R., & Kamphaus, R. W. (1992). *Behavioral Assessment Scale for Children manual.* Circle Pines, MN: American Guidance Service.

Rogers, M. F., & Myles, B. S. (2001). Using social stories and comic strip conversations to interpret social situations for an adolescent with Asperger Syndrome. *Intervention in School and Clinic, 36*(5), 310-313.

Sasso, G. M., Mundschenk, N. A., Melloy, K. J., & Casey, S. D. (1998). A comparison of the effects of organismic and setting variables on the social interaction behavior of children with developmental disabilities and autism. *Focus on Autism and Other Developmental Disabilities, 13*(1), 2-16.

Schreibman, L., Whalen, C., & Stahmer, A. (2000). The use of video priming to reduce disruptive transition behavior in children with autism. *Journal of Positive Behavior Intervention, 2,* 3-12.

Shearer, D. D., Kohler, F. W., Buchan, K. A., & McCullough, K. M. (1996). Promoting independent interactions between preschoolers with autism and their nondisabled peers: An analysis of self-monitoring. *Early Education & Development, 7,* 205–220.

Sherer, M., Pierce, K. L., Paredes, S., Kisacky, K. L., Ingersoll, B., & Schreibman, L. (2001). Enhancing conversation skills in children with autism via video technology: Which is better, "self" or "other" as a model? *Behavioral Modifications, 25*(1), 140-158.

Stafford, N. (2000). Can *emotions* be taught to a low functioning autistic child. *Early Child Development and Care, 164,* 105-126.

Stein, M. B., Torgrud, L. J., & Walker, J. R. (2000). Social phobia symptoms, subtypes, and Severity: Findings from a community sample. *Archives of General Psychiatry, 5,* 1046-1052.

Strain, P. S., & Odom, S. L. (1986). Peer social initiations: An effective intervention for social skill deficits of preschool handicapped children. *Exceptional Children, 52,* 543-552.

Tantam, D. (2000). Psychological disorder in adolescents and adults with Asperger Syndrome. *Autism, 4,* 47-62.

Trepagnier, C. (1996). A possible origin for the social and communicative deficits of autism. *Focus on Autism and Other Developmental Disabilities, 11,* 170-182.

Wellman, H. M., Baron-Cohen, S., Caswell, R. C., Gomez, J. C. Swettenham, J, Toye, E., & Lagattuta, K. (2002). Thought-bubbles help children with autism acquire an alternative to a theory of mind. *Autism, 6,* 343-363.

Wert, B. Y., & Neisworth, J. T. (2003). Effects of video self-modeling on spontaneous requesting in children with autism. *Journal of Positive Behavior Interventions, 5,* 30-34.

Woolf, H. B. (Ed.). (1976). *Webster's new collegiate dictionary* (p. 373). Springfield, MA: Merriam-Webster.

Yack, E., Sutton, S., & Aquilla, P. (2002). *Building bridges through sensory integration* (2nd ed.). Las Vegas, NV: Sensory Resources.

Zanolli, K, Daggett, J., & Adams, T. (1996). Teaching preschool age autistic children to make spontaneous initiations to peers using priming. *Journal of Autism and Developmental Disorders, 2,* 407-422.

Index

A
accommodation, 122-124
adult training, 225-226
anxiety, 5, 13, 25, 26-27, 48-49, 110, 112,
    145, 169, 183, 193, 199, 200
    developmental pathways model of,
        26-27, 200
assimilation, 122-124
attention, 109, 110-111, 145, 193
    overly selective, 36
Autism Social Skills Profile (ASSP), 73-77, 249
automaticity, 20-21, 18, 29, 104, 105, 106

B
behavior contract, 188-190
behavioral rehearsal. *See* Role-playing
biofeedback, 172
body language. *See* Nonverbal communication
brainstorming, 157
bullying, 203, 214

C
"Can't Do" vs. "Won't Do," 107
central nervous system (CNS), 28-29
coaching, 162-163, 197
concentration. *See* Attention
contingency
    systems, 187-190
    See also Reinforcement
Conversation Game, 135, 136, 137
Conversation Map, 179-181. *See also* Social
    initiation

D
data collection, 228-229
depression, 5, 13, 25, 112
development, role of, 34-35, 93
disability awareness, 123, 200-205
doing, 16, 20, 28-30, 134
duration recording, 244-245

E
emotions, reading. *See* Thoughts, feelings and
    interests activities
emotions, regulation of, 18, 113, 169-174
empathy, 21

E (continued)
environment, modifications of, 117, 193-194
    See also Sensory sensitivities
executive function. *See* Doing
eye contact, 36-37, 161-162

F
feeling, 25-27, 134
Five-Step Model, 1, 8-9, 51-52, 256
fluency, 20, 44-45, 104, 116-117
free play, 223, 228-229, 242
frequency recording, 244
friendships, 213
Freud, Sigmund, 138
functional behavior assessment, 102

G
games, 191-192
generalization, 163, 164, 195
    behavioral perspective, 235-236
    cognitive perspective, 236-237
goals and objectives, 88-96, 223-224
    distinction between, 88-90
    establishing criteria, 90-91
    selecting, 93-95
group training, 227-229

H
hidden curriculum. *See* Social rules (unwritten)

I
if-then statements, 130, 131
improvisational activities, 137-138
impulsivity. *See* Attention
Individualized Education Program (IEP), 71, 88,
    89, 90, 91, 96, 176, 240
instructional plan, 94-95
interaction/conversation planning, 178-182
interest inventory, 131, 179
intervention, implementing
    age ranges, 214-215, 222, 229
    format considerations, 213-215, 215-217
    group training, 227-229
    individual sessions, 229-234
    planning, 212-221
    selecting children, 212-213
    structuring, 222-226

Social Skills Instructional Plan

Child's Name: _____

Child's Age: _____

Date of Services: _____ to _____

Type of Programming (individual, group, and/or classwide): _____

Social Objective 1: _____

_____

Skills needed to successfully reach objective (Skills to be taught):

_____

_____

_____

_____

_____

_____

_____

(*Note:* These skills will vary based on the needs/skills of the target child)

Social Objective 2: _____

_____

_____

_____